common fire

common fire

Lives of Commitment in a Complex World

Laurent A. Parks Daloz

Cheryl H. Keen

James P. Keen

Sharon Daloz Parks

Beacon Press

Boston

Beacon Press
25 Beacon Street
Boston, Massachusetts 02108-2892

Beacon Press books are published under the auspices of
the Unitarian Universalist Association of Congregations.

oo 99 98 97 96   8 7 6 5 4 3 2 1

Text design by Janis Owens
Book composition by Willow Graphics, Woodstown, New Jersey
Printed on acid-free, recycled paper
Library of Congress Cataloging-in-Publication Data can be found on page 274.

To our great-grandparents and grandparents,
and to our parents,

L. Albert and Lois Daloz
Harry and Trudy Hollmann
Enid and Robert Keen
Emmett and Eloys Parks,

and to our children,

Kate Daloz
Todd Daloz
Justin Hollmann Keen,

the legacy and the promise of commitment

contents

acknowledgments

The creation and publication of this book reflect the interdependent character of life to which committed lives bear witness. Directly and indirectly, a host of people have informed and sustained this work.

We owe our deepest gratitude to each of the people we interviewed. We promised them anonymity but our appreciation must be public. They were generous with their time, candor, and willingness to reflect with us on that edge between current knowledge and emergent awareness that we call learning.

This study has been graced by the intelligence and commitment of Karen Thorkilsen, our steady and dedicated research associate. Not only did she painstakingly process mountains of interview material with a discerning eye and deft computer wizardry, but she allowed the material to work in her own imagination in a way that contributed significantly to our understanding. As an artist and poet in her own right, and as a fifth reader with editorial skills, she brought a finely tuned aesthetic to the work, keeping us faithful to the data. We are privileged to be accompanied by such an outstanding colleague.

We are deeply grateful also to Craig Dykstra, Jim Wind and other colleagues at The Lilly Endowment. They have steadfastly shared the vision of what this kind of work can bring to our common life, and the Endowment's material and collegial support has played an essential role in making this resource-intensive work possible. Most recently the grant has been ably administered by Annette Wofford at the National Society for Experiential Education. We are grateful that the Keens were supported also by the Millicent Fenwick Research Professorship at Monmouth University. Larry and Sharon are grateful for supportive and challenging colleagues at Lesley College, Harvard University, and The Whidbey Institute.

For their strategic presence in the early phase of the project, we thank Patricia McKernon, Jim Botkin, and Roswitha Botkin. Since then, we have drawn on the insight of several consultants, and a number of colleagues have read all or portions of the manuscript. These include Art Levine, Doug Huneke, Joe Maxwell, Mary Watkins, Mary Belenky, Martha Carmichael, John DeCuevas, Patricia Evans, Nancy Frommelt, Brita Gill-Austern, Charles Halpern, Carol Leland, Almeda McKee, C.G. Newsome, Marcia Sharp, and colleagues at the Clinical Developmental Institute, particularly Ann Fleck Henderson, Gina O'Connell Higgins, Robert Kegan, and Laura Rogers.

We appreciate also others who provided perspectives useful in developing particular aspects of the text. These include Fred Abbott, Arthur Applebaum, Ray Bowen, Elizabeth Christopherson, Sharon Coates, Sally Finestone, Jim Fowler, Zee Gamson, Herb Green, Bill Hanson, Anita Landa, Larry Leverett, Marty Linsky, George Lodge, Jack McCullough, Martha McKenna, Scott McVay, David Mallery, Martha Minow, Mark Murphy, Tom Ogletree, Linda Powell, George Rupp, Mary Sue Sweeney-Price, Sandra Schneiders, Michael Seltzer, Ted Sizer, Willa Spicer, and John Sullivan. In addition, many people in seminars and courses who were early respondents to the work offered invaluable and challenging confirmation.

This type of project requires competent clerical support, and we acknowledge with gratitude the skill and personal commitment of Kate Marrone, Jackie Rutberg, and Sharon Eastwick, who transcribed the interviews, and Gwen Swift, Eugenie Moriconi, Kelly Johnson, and Greg Low, who provided additional forms of assistance.

Because the team lives in two different geographic areas, we are grateful to people who extended hospitality at the halfway point, specifically Stephen Knoblauch, Ingrid Roze, Betsy McGregor, Charles Terry, Irene Seeland, and the wider community of the International Center for Integrative Studies, who also encouraged us with a small grant in the earliest days of the project.

We want to tip our hats also to the technology that enabled a long project to move as smoothly as it did. Along with cars and airplanes, computers, faxes, phones, and e-mail made communication and writing by a long distance team possible. These conveniences did not, however, keep us from using an enormous amount of paper, which we will acknowledge by planting several new trees in the commons of Evansburg.

Like many in the book, we as individuals have been blessed by the presence of mentors. Among them, we count four "senior mentors" to whom we would like to pay special tribute: Adam Curle, Karl Deutsch, Richard R. Niebuhr, and William G. Perry, Jr. Further, mentors occasionally serve as matchmakers, and the study owes a special kind of gratitude to Donald Oliver whose work first brought Jim and Cheryl together, and to James W. Fowler, who introduced Larry and Sharon.

We are grateful to be associated with Beacon Press and the commitments that it represents. We thank our editor Susan Worst and others at the Press for their commitment and skill in bringing this book to publication.

Many others also have believed in this work and have played central roles in sustaining it: students, colleagues, friends, and family.

Finally we are grateful to you, our readers. However this book finally settles in the imagination of mind and soul, with gratitude we count you among those who share the hope that as a human community we will learn how to kindle the fire of commitment to the common good that constitutes the strength we need to become citizens in the new commons.

connection and complexity

The Challenge of the New Commons

A small group of people is gathered in a friend's home. Margo Daiken, a thoughtful professional woman in mid-career, married for the second time, a mother and stepmom, and the head of a small state agency, is describing her growing feeling of uneasiness. Television newscasts and other media make her keenly aware of human suffering on a global scale: a drought and famine in Africa complicated by political instability; a terrorist bomb that kills dozens of children; a multinational corporation that abandons Illinois for Malaysia, eliminating thousands of American jobs; a war of "ethnic cleansing" in Europe, echoed the following week in a story about racial cross-fire in Los Angeles.

"I feel that somehow I ought to respond," she says. "But I guess all I know how to do is what I was taught in Girl Scouts. So I try to be good and fair to the people immediately around me—my family and my co-workers. Yet that doesn't really seem to be enough." She pauses a long time. Then she adds, "I think it is harder to be human than it used to be."

Now consider a class of seventy talented young M.B.A. candidates in a prestigious business school. They are working over a case study about where to site a new plant. As they debate the merits of three possible locations, one student, Raphael, suggests that if the good of the surrounding community and the natural environment is taken into account, the second site is preferable in the long term, "though the intangibles and externalities are hard to translate into bottom-line numbers now." From the top row, a hand shoots up. An articulate young man named Alex calls out, "Save the whales on the weekends!" His dismissive tone conveys that while he may believe in service to the community, it should be kept in a compartment separate from "the real world." As the discussion moves on, Alex seems to have prevailed. Raphael is silent, unconvinced that it is all that simple, yet stuck and uncertain about what to do.

The New Commons

Margo, Raphael, and Alex are not alone. Like all of us, they dwell in a new landscape. The achievements of science and technology, politics and psychology, have stretched our consciousness of space and place, creating a new "mindscape."[1]

Many Americans in an earlier time, and some even today, participated in some kind of a commons—a shared, public space of the sort that anchored the American vision of democracy. One form was the classic New England green ringed by the town hall, grange, courthouse, general store, post office, church, and a flock of households. Other forms of the commons were the square at the county seat in the South, the bodega in the Latino community, Main Street in middle America, a ballpark, school, temple or cathedral in the city, or the fishing wharf on the coast.

Whatever its form, the commons marked the center of a shared world. Despite sometimes sharp differences, the good of the commons—the good of all—could be worked at, figured out and figured out again. By happenstance and intention, people met and talked together with some sense of a shared stake, something in common. To be sure, the memory may be more finely burnished than the reality: for some in this society a sense of participation in the commons only emerged slowly over time, and for others it was never possible at all. For a great many, however, there was—and for a few there remains—a conception of "the commons" as a place where the diverse parts of a community could come together and hold a conversation within a shared sense of participation and responsibility.

Increasingly, this sense of the commons is being eroded.[2] For some, vestiges of it remain in the home where the extended family still gathers around the dinner table, or at the locally owned grocery store, in a religious or therapy group, or at the gym. But for most, our common gathering places are increasingly restaurants, where our association is primarily one of anonymity; the video arcade, where the young are mesmerized into single-syllable conversation by neon violence; the mall, where consumer thirst and adolescent drift are the primary agenda; the high-rise office building, where we meet briefly in elevators; the TV screen, where we feel both engaged and removed; and, for some, the Internet, where we meet fleetingly—and often anonymously—in cyberspace.[3]

As earlier forms of the commons fade and shadowy substitutes take their place, we find ourselves ambivalent inhabitants of a new global commons. We are connected to others and affected by others in new ways. This commons has been created by the technologies of travel and international communication and is illuminated by the growing recognition of our interdependence as a planetary community. The new commons is global in scope, diverse in character, and dauntingly complex. A radically interdependent world economy has dissolved old boundaries, loosed waves of migrant labor, triggered smoldering cultural conflicts, and forced profound social and political reorganization at all levels. We are simultaneously fragmented into loose and shifting associations of individuals, interest groups, and tribes, yet drawn more closely into a larger web of life.[4]

Boundaries are shifting. Old distinctions between work and home, business and government, secular and religious, the social and natural environment, male and female, and between those we call "we" and those we call "they" no longer seem to work as they once did. The Scout virtues of loyalty, obedience, even helpfulness, have lost their clarity.

Many, like Alex, understandably seek to deal with the complexity by sealing it into compartments, saving whales on weekends only—separating profit from environment, work from home, or "reality" from ethics. But others, like Margo and Raphael, are increasingly unable to do that. They cannot so easily disengage the parts from the whole. Something in them refuses to settle for retreating into their own immediate spheres, playing out a circumscribed role with little relation to the larger global reality. As the world shrinks, as the diversity of our species and the magnitude and limitations of the planetary environment upon which we all depend become more evident, they reach out for some new set of connections, some more adequate way to make sense of a world gone boundaryless, a world now paradoxically larger, smaller, and more complex.

Though they may not say so, both Margo and Raphael sense at some level that they are being thrust into a larger sphere of responsibility, one calling for a keener recognition of the diversity, complexity, and ambiguity that have become the warp and woof of the common life we all share. More, they sense that a capacity for connection, for reflective, creative, strategic response to suffering and tough problems lies at the core of what it means to be human. They are recognizing that the reality of the global commons challenges us to broaden and strengthen our understanding of citizenship.

This is a book for people like Margo and Raphael, people who want to make a positive difference in a complex world. And it is for people who are already trying to do that. It is for people who are concerned about our preparedness—and the preparedness of the next generation—to live in ways that will create a sustainable future. This book is also for people like Alex, who are managing to work with a set of assumptions that seem to prevail, yet who may also be open to the questions and perspectives posed by the lives of people committed to the common good in a rapidly changing world.

Studying Lives of Commitment in a Complex World

Like the reader, we, the authors, seek to live and work in ways that take the challenges and opportunities of the new commons seriously, for they affect us directly—both professionally and personally. As educators and researchers, we have been grappling with the implications of the new commons for at least the past two decades.

Larry was reared in New England, served in the Peace Corps in Nepal, returned to further study, taught in West Virginia, Hawaii, and Papua New Guinea, and later developed community-based college programs for adults in Vermont. Cheryl grew up in the Midwest, Jim in Pennsylvania, and together, after studying the formation of social perspectives and political science, respectively, they developed an adult degree program in the Northeast. Subsequently they designed and for over a decade administered the first Governor's School on "Public Issues and the Future" for the State of New Jersey, working with high school students representing the ethnic and geographical diversity of New Jersey. Sharon was reared on the Pacific Coast and has worked with both undergraduate and professional education in small and large, old and new institutions in higher education and religion in both the Western and Eastern United States and also in Hong Kong. As a group, we have had extraordinary opportunities to witness, work with, and learn to understand the power of natural, cultural and intentional educational environments to form, de-form, and transform the way we as human beings perceive our world and our place in it. As scholars and educators, we hold in common a deep respect for the potential at stake in the development of each individual and particularly for the ways in which attention to human development may enhance the will and capacity of people to work and live well together and to face tough, even unprecedented challenges.

We became a research team in our shared and growing concern that as the world becomes more complex, society more diverse, and former certainties more ambiguous, even those who are well educated and trained may become overwhelmed, discouraged, sometimes frightened. We recognized with respect the temptation to make things more manageable by retreating into professional expertise, the politics of control, cynical interpretations, single-issue politics, sound-bite discourse, or numbing entertainment.

In contrast, however, we also knew that human beings have faced critical transitions in the past with the stamina, wit, and moral courage to meet "adaptive challenges"—challenges that require new learning—constructively.[5] Most important, we recognized that throughout our society and in the wider world, there is a wide variety of people who, aware of the new and complex connections among us, are neither simply overwhelmed nor retreating to safe, manageable havens. Rather, wading into the complexity, they are able to work in concrete, particular ways on behalf of our common life. They practice the kind of citizenship that is needed as we enter the twenty-first century. It appeared both important and strategic to undertake a study of such people—people who seem able to live fruitfully in the new commons—in order to achieve a richer understanding of how lives of commitment to the common good are formed and sustained.

Consequently, we designed a study in which we conducted interviews over a period of several years with more than one hundred people who had sustained long-term commitments to work on behalf of the common good, even in the face of global complexity, diversity, and ambiguity. In our interviews we sought to answer four primary questions: "What are such people like?" "How do they become that way?" "What keeps them going in spite of inevitable discouragement?" and "What can be done to encourage this kind of citizenship to meet the challenges of the twenty-first century?"

Our Selection Criteria

We looked for people across a wide range of roles and contexts whose lives seemed to be motivated by some form of the question, "How can we be part of creating a more inclusive 'common' good?" Specifically, our criteria were the following:

Commitment to the common good. We sought people with a certain kind of commitment, widely attainable, but not necessarily present in all who are thought of as "committed." We sought those who held strong convictions yet were not fanatical, who had a clear focus yet were not blind to other perspectives, who held a large and inclusive vision yet were not simply idealists, and who, while working on behalf of particular constituencies, understood themselves to be working on behalf of the whole of life.

Perseverance and resilience. We sought people who had demonstrated perseverance and resilience. Most had sustained more than twenty years of work on behalf of a more just and humane world, but all had demonstrated commitment for at least seven years. We attempted to screen out those who were burning out. In a few cases where people had quit and then returned to the work, we explored what had defeated them earlier and what had enabled them to sustain themselves more effectively the second time.

Ethical congruence between life and work. We interviewed people who worked full time, part time, and as volunteers. But all of their lives reflected a quality of energy and spirit congruent with their work. We sought a certain seamlessness between what they professed and how they lived—both at home and in the practice of their commitments. Although we lay no claim to a foolproof methodology in this respect, we attempted to identify people who, while inevitably imperfect, could be recognized as reasonably decent human beings.

Engagement with diversity and complexity. Given our sense of the global future, it was important that while potential interviewees worked with particular institutions or causes, they also sought to understand the larger, systemic implications of their work and had a critical perspective on their own culture. This criterion in particular distinguishes those we studied from many other community-minded and deeply caring citizens. In his book, *Local Heroes*,[6] Bill Berkowitz has rightly celebrated the vital generosity of such people. But we believe that the emerging demands of twenty-first century citizenship call for an ability not only to care for a particular individual, community, or cause, but also to be able to see the larger implications of one's actions, and to recognize how one's work affects and is affected by the interdependent realities of the new commons. Thus it is the formation of citizens who manifest this kind of strength that we have sought to understand in greater depth.

Demographic Representation

We have attempted to ensure that our sample generally reflects society at large in terms of gender, ethnicity, and social class of origin (see Appendix).

Half are male, half female; of the one hundred people in our core group, ninety were born in the United States (including Puerto Rico). Of those, fifteen are African-American, two are Asian-American, six are Hispanic-American, one is Native American, and sixty-six are of Indo-European descent. We also interviewed ten "internationals" who do not hold U.S. citizenship.[7]

Their roots are working-class, middle-class, and economically elite; thirty-five percent came from working class or poor backgrounds. They range in age from thirty-two to over eighty, with an average age of fifty-three. Roughly one third are Protestant, one tenth are Roman Catholic, and the remainder are Baha'i, Buddhist, Hindu, Jewish, Moslem, Quaker, or Zoroastrian. Just under one fifth describe themselves as having no particular religious affiliation. They are Democrats, Republicans, and Independents. Some grew up with two parents, some with one; some were healthy and loved, some suffered illness, abuse, or neglect.

Many, though not all, are professionals involved in a broad range of sectors, roles, and concerns—often difficult to categorize. The largest group is engaged in some form of education, broadly construed. This category includes lawyers, administrators, youth counselors, homemakers, entrepreneurs, scientists, engineers, writers, and physicians (though not in equal numbers). They work in prominent organizations and small agencies. Some are concerned with economic, social, or political policy, corporate development, environmental issues, religious formation, service learning, or the arts. Others address urban affairs, institutional renewal, ethical business practices, international relations, and issues of human dignity.

Describing Committed Lives: A Different Public Mirror

As the following chapters unveil what we learned in these interviews, we note that it has been observed that, like the distorting mirrors in a fun house, our public mirrors—the media—too often portray people in our society as living "terrible and little lives."[8] This book is not written simply to make us feel good before that dreary perception. Our purpose is to contribute to the creation of another mirror, one that reflects the lives of the many people who live and work in committed and sustained ways amidst the complexity of the new commons on behalf of the common good. They are not "special" or "exceptional," though they are perhaps distinctive, for they manifest qualities and forms of competence that are more in tune with the realities of the emergent world than with some of the assumptions of the past. Unlike many who give their allegiance to only a part of the commons, these people seek to align themselves with the life of the whole and to work on its behalf. Most important, they reflect the potential in all of us to find the strength and quality of commitment needed for the practice of citizenship in the twenty-first century.

This is not, therefore, only a book of stories. It is a book about the patterns we found across the lives of the people we studied as we analyzed the interviews; the patterns are, however, illustrated by the stories and perspectives of our respondents. Together, the patterns and stories help us to understand how these committed people think about themselves and the world, and what led them to live the way they do. They inform our ways of thinking about the ongoing formation of our common life. At the beginning of each chapter we tell a portion of the story of a particular life in a way that reveals the patterns to which the chapter is devoted and gives a glimpse of the kinds of things the people we studied do.

Because we promised anonymity to the people in the sample, all names, places, and many identifying characteristics have been changed. Without that assurance, it would have been more difficult for us to portray them as full human beings complete with shortcomings and human limitations. In a few instances where actual names appear, we are quoting from published biographical material. We did not interview these people, but recognize them as committed to the common good.[9]

We have mentioned the ethnicity of individuals only when that information was important to the dynamic we are describing. The examples used in the text reflect the ethnic profile of the sample. Because we have chosen not to label every speaker, however, this may not be evident in the reading. Thus, in the absence of any identifying information, the reader should not presume the gender or ethnicity of the speaker.

Reader's Choice

Some readers at this point may wish to turn to chapter 2 and enter directly into the stories and patterns that we have found. Others will want to continue through the remainder of this chapter as we describe critical features of the present cultural milieu within which the lives we studied are significant. We will also discuss further what we mean by commitment, additional aspects of the study, and the progression of the book.

Citizenship in a New Context

Recall Margo's growing sense that it seems "harder to be human" these days. Like many others, we too observe and feel a widening gap between the generosity of which the American people are capable and the increasingly fortressed, self-preoccupied, sloganesque, and single-issue orientation that has come to characterize much of public life.

During the period of our study, public concern grew about what has been called the "coarsening of society": mounting violence on both street and screen, widespread anxiety about the changing patterns of family life and employment, increasing numbers of depressed adults and emotionally troubled children, the spread of AIDS, tuberculosis, and other infectious diseases, increased concern about the adequacy of health care. We have seen growing economic disparity divide the Global North from the Global South, while at the same time cutting through the heart of our cities and carving up the rural landscape, tearing at long-standing racial wounds. Indeed, as we stand on new ethical frontiers, asking new questions about governance on earth, exploration in space, and the harnessing of technology for the long-term benefit of the whole earth community, we also recognize that our major institutions—government, the news and entertainment media, corporations, the family, schools, and religion—often seem unable to address fundamental problems in positive and effective ways.[10] These developments have catalyzed renewed attention to "leadership" and "ethics"—words laden with hungers, hopes, and apprehension.

Concern deepens when we turn toward the next generation. Our nation's infant mortality rate has slipped to twenty-fourth among industrialized nations, and almost a quarter of our children now grow up beneath the poverty line.[11] At the extreme but increasingly visible edge, our youth are shooting themselves up with needles, and down with guns. We try to teach our young people to be careful, but many also learn to be fearful. We cannot give them a safe society, so we seek to protect them as individuals. Yet even as we try to shelter our children within the home, the protective membrane grows thinner. Increasingly, market-driven television and computer programs threaten to turn some children into passive consumers, pawns on the economic chess board, while others sink into poverty, locked out of the mainstream economy with little hope of ever having the nurture, education, and skills to enable them to prosper in the twenty-first century. Those young adults still in the economic mainstream are encouraged to hone their competitive edge at all costs, to capture their niche in a world prepared to shunt them aside.

Throughout our public discourse—TV pundit roundtables, teachers' lunchrooms, the cocktail party, newspaper columns, the beauty salon, laundromat, parish council, or locker room—comments about "what this world is coming to" and "kids these days..." are expressions of concern, despair, frustration—and a discouraged yet tenacious hope.

The Legacy of Individualism

As we puzzled through this long list of stresses, setting them in dialogue with the lives of commitment we were studying, we began to recognize more vividly both the legacy of the individualism which marks our society and the challenges that this legacy creates in the interdependent reality of the new commons. As a society, we have placed enormous value and trust in the individual. Individual rights, equality before the law, and personal choice—shaped by the best of our religious, political, and economic traditions—are surely among the great achievements of civilization. They are crucial steps in the evolution of human consciousness.

Yet over the past several decades a growing number of voices have begun to call our attention to the limitations of individualism in light of the challenges of a dynamic and interdependent world. In his seminal 1968 article, "The Tragedy of the Commons," Garrett Hardin exposed the myth that the welfare of all will somehow be protected by sole reliance on individual rights. Not long after, Christopher Lasch in *The Culture of Narcissism* and George C. Lodge in *The New American Ideology* called for a re-balancing of individualism with a more communal conviction. Subsequently, Bellah, Madsen, Sullivan, Swidler, and Tipton detailed the costs to civil society of "radical individualism" in *Habits of the Heart: Individualism and Commitment in American Life*. Amitai Etizoni, Robert Putnam and others have elaborated the growing evidence that civic participation is diminishing and that current forms of individualism have a limited utility for society as a whole.[12]

It is becoming increasingly clear even to middle- and upper-class folk—people for whom our society is presumed to work—that their well being depends not only upon their talent, initiative, and ability to work hard, but also upon the quality of our common life. We have pushed the myth of individual freedom, strength, rights, expression, competition, salvation, and specialization to an edge that cannot hold. Yet the imprint of individualism is so pervasive, familiar, and therefore powerful that we understandably still rely on that ideology as the primary motif for our economic, political, psychological, and other cultural arrangements. Thus enchanted by unharnessed individualism and bereft of a sense of participation in a meaningful commons, the temptation to "armor up" is strong, even required. We do so in many forms of thought and action, each of which diminishes and hardens our sense of what it means to be human.

Busyness and Consumerism

For many of us, a daily, persistent form of armoring is simple busyness. A market culture rooted in an ideology of individualism creates a demanding workplace where some work ever harder to purchase things they do not need, while others, working equally hard, cannot secure the basics of food, shelter, and health care. Across both genders and all working groups, we are working more hours in an economy that has a preference for long-hour and multiple part-time jobs above a fraying safety net. Busyness enables many to consume more goods and services and a few to amass material wealth, but "a poverty of time is stressing our social fabric." Health, family nurture, community engagement, and true leisure all suffer.[13]

It takes clear space, contemplative time, and good conversation to engage and understand complex problems. Busyness, consumerism, and their accompanying anxiety can easily become substitutes for meaning and clarity of purpose, numbing our capacity to act responsively. Allowing us to be selectively attentive and to filter out complexity and ambiguity, they foster superficial thinking, short-term perspectives, and inappropriate humility. As long as we are busy, we can feel both overwhelmed and "involved." Swamped by the demands of securing a life for ourselves, we can more easily justify begging off from responsibility for the commons. Thus, along with individual cycles of busyness and consumerism, two primary forms of personal and social fortification emerge: cynicism and tribalism.

Cynicism

Armored thought is particularly evident in the growing cynicism that characterizes both public and private discourse.[14] Cynicism should not be confused with skepticism. Democracy requires healthy skepticism—the ability to stand back, question, and reveal the distance between ideals and practice. Skepticism is open to being informed in the service of shared purpose. Cynicism, in contrast, is the hardened, defensive crust of individualistic resignation, often a veneer over despair.

We tend to think of youth as a time of idealism, hope, potential, and opportunity. But our teenagers are no more adept than adults at escaping the fumes of cynical discourse and practice. Tragically, cynicism is not only on the rise, but its development has been particularly marked among those under thirty years of age.[15] When children learn early to be suspicious of the market manipulation that pervades their lives, when adolescents discover that conventional cynicism passes for sophistication, and when young adults are led to presume that all politicians, professors, managers, and other authorities are committed primarily to expedient self-interest, opportunities for initiation into meaningful aspirations shrivel.

In a time of pervasive complexity, cynicism provides the false comfort of the simple conviction that all human motivation can be reduced to narrow self-interest and conflicting autonomous choices. Thus there is little imagination of a collective will, of shared participation and belonging. In a climate of pervasive cynicism, every gesture in the name of the public good is demeaned and every act of generosity dismissed as merely self-serving. "Enlightened self-interest" becomes the parched and only ground in which hope for the common good must struggle to take root.[16]

Tribalism

Armored, cynical thought in the face of complexity is intimately linked with armored forms of action which foster "tribalism"—fortified social arrangements. Grounded in our fundamental needs for survival and belonging, the hardening of tribal boundaries insulates and defends "me and mine" against what appears to be an overwhelmingly complex and threatening world.

Tribalism, a word we use with care (see Chapter 3), springs from the belief that caring for oneself and perhaps immediate others is all one can reasonably do. The understandable attraction is to make a dignified retreat into fortified enclaves defined by profession, lifestyle, ethnicity or region, age, or class. This then gives rise to single-issue and polarized politics; fundamentalistic, intolerant religion; indiscriminately relativized ethics; and a divided economy. Tribalism can shore up some forms of privilege or alternately defend against assaults upon fundamental dignities, but in either case, it obscures the reality that we all share a stake in the wealth and health of the planetary commons.

Tribalism makes role-based morality appealing—the assumption that if I simply carry out my role as a lawyer or physician, parent or public advocate, business person or government regulator, and everyone else does the same, somehow everything will turn out all right. Like Alex, one does not attempt to consider the interdependent good of society as a whole, how the actions of one sector will affect another, and what is at stake when certain alliances are in place and others are neglected. As Margo and Raphael were beginning to recognize, responsibility to the whole is thus deferred (implicitly or explicitly) to somewhere or someone else when one tries to take refuge in a role and social enclave—seeking a home in the semblance of a "manageable piece." As the practice of citizenship is thereby reduced simply to securing a future for oneself and one's clan, we become increasingly naive about the vital connections among things, and thus, ironically, more vulnerable.

All human beings need identifiable networks of belonging to ground us in a positive sense of place and identity. Indeed, we have found this to be a key element in the formation of lives committed to the common good. But in the interdependent reality of the new commons, hardened social and organizational boundaries that prohibit constructive talk across tribal lines are artificial and dangerous constructs.

In their tribal forms, the traditional conservative and liberal formulations have both become inadequate. The conservative position asserts a narrow view in which a set of deeply held values is imposed upon all in the hope of creating a unified community. Inevitably the full participation of significant elements of the community is precluded. On the other hand, in its effort to include all, the liberal point of view is caught in a practice of relativism in which a minimalist conception of the common good undermines the formation of a shared moral compass, discouraging committed action by failing to acknowledge sufficiently both personal responsibility and the importance of conviction. Conservatives appear to take the "moral high road" by emphasizing personal conduct, but ignore the interdependence of the new commons. Liberals recognize systemic diversity, complexity, and ambiguity, but tend to lack the gumption to seek new and more adequate moral ground in the midst of legitimate cultural diversity. If we are to engage the challenges of the twenty-first century, neither stance is adequate. We must kindle a common fire and forge a new synthesis of practical wisdom.[17]

Heroes, Altruists, Activists, and Volunteers

In a culture of individualism, the human capacity to be in relation, to feel compassion and to care for those outside one's own tribe is likely to be cast in the forms of heroism, altruism, activism, and volunteering. When disaster strikes, for example, genuine heroes do emerge. Hurricanes, floods, earthquakes, or war create a breach in our usual fortified arrangements, enabling many people to set aside narrow self-interest and connect across tribal borders—sometimes at the cost of heroic personal sacrifice. These occasional acts under unusual conditions tell us something important about what we are capable of and who we are as a society, but "disasters" and "heroes" are always cast as special in ways that set them apart from our everyday lives.

In our individualistic culture, behavior which serves the welfare of others—whether episodic or routine—is typically described by theorists of human nature as "altruistic." But as the ethicist Alasdair MacIntyre has observed, the notion of "altruism" developed only in the eighteenth century in the wake of the ascent and triumph of the "ego-centric self." Since "human nature" was declared to be, at bottom, selfish, altruism became at once both necessary and impossible.[18] Thus, "altruistic" behavior came to be seen as exceptional or even aberrant behavior.

In a similar vein, those who work steadfastly in the public arena—particularly if they are committed to fundamental change or a single pressing issue—may be labeled "activists." This description is often reserved for people who appear to have stepped beyond conventional political tribes and norms and are perceived as dedicating themselves to a cause outside of the mainstream of society. Whether their objectives are worthy or dubious, "activists" also tend to be regarded as aberrant—exceptions to the rest of us.

Volunteerism—giving one's time without remuneration—is a hallmark of American society and should in every way be encouraged. It is also a complex element in a culture of individualism. Volunteerism arises from the recognition of the bonds upon which all life depends, and many of those we studied began or still work as volunteers. But often "volunteerism" is perceived as different from "real work" which is defined as monetarily rewarding, typically in the service of one's own livelihood. Moreover, while volunteering to care for others can often be a positive first step into a wider understanding and commitment, in a culture of individualism, volunteerism may serve primarily to comfort one's own uneasy conscience. We reassure ourselves that though most of our energies are spent in shoring up our own immediate security, this can be balanced by giving sincere, if occasional, personal and material comfort to the less competitive, less fortified, and less successful others. Though we may volunteer as individuals to give an hour of such vital personal help as food, counsel, or child care, if we treat only the symptons and fail to recognize the sources of the problems—poor housing, inadequate schools, chronic unemployment, or inappropriate monetary policies—then our capacity to imagine a way of helping that might illumine and heal the problems fades out like dying embers, and the commons becomes a cold and angry place.[19]

Commitment to the Common Good

Although the people we studied often represented, even combined, some of the elements of heroism, altruism, activism, or volunteerism, they are best understood as citizens—ordinary people in most respects who simply practice commitment as a way of life. But commitment can take many forms. What, exactly, do we mean by *commitment*?

One form takes on a hard edge, serving as armor in the face of threat. Indeed, one might see the great tragedies of the twentieth century as commitment gone wrong, for it was the threatening complexity of modernity that led to the ideological totalitarianism that engulfed Europe in war and genocide—giving rise to events which still shape and distort our lives. The commitment of totalitarianism is characterized by a low tolerance of ambiguity and high levels of authoritarianism and conformity. It takes one's own ethnic group, political ideology, or religious conviction to be the sole possible basis for the good of the whole. H. Richard Niebuhr calls this "henotheism," a commitment to some part—often to the state or to an exclusive religious view—in the name of the whole.[20] Such commitment clearly fails the demands of the new commons and is the antithesis of the commitment of the people we studied.

Further, we were not studying commitment in the abstract as a purely psychological phenomenon. What one is committed to matters; the content and focus of commitment matters. After all, one may be committed to one's child, Marxism, health care reform, or the Red Sox. We were interested in a particular kind of commitment—commitment to the common good.

Thus our conviction of the need for a new stance in the new commons led us to seek out people who, while working in very concrete settings, saw their commitments to particular people, groups, and concerns as finally a part of the survival and prosperity of the whole earth community. That is, we sought people who could hold together the "micro" and the "macro," who were able to connect their everyday work with the larger concerns of the new global commons. The people we studied cannot ignore the interdependent, systemic reach of their own actions—the ripple effect of words, decisions, and behavior.

This does not mean that they were necessarily working toward some universally shared vision of "the common good," a kind of Utopia to be imposed on all. What constitutes "the common good" is, of course, always open to interpretation and dispute. We live in an age in which many barely reconcilable views of the common good bump up against each other, often with disastrous results. Nevertheless, we believe that viable views of the common good would include such core elements as a global scope, a recognition of diversity, and a vision of society as composed of individuals whose own well-being is inextricably bound up with the good of the whole. Increasingly and necessarily, "the common good" refers to the well-being of the whole earth community—its safety, the integrity of basic institutions and practices, and the sustaining of the living systems of our planet home. The common good also suggests broadly shared goals toward which the members of the community strive—human flourishing, prosperity, and moral development. A recognition of the common good thus casts light on the significance of openness to new learning, critical and systemic thought, and the search for "right naming"—images, metaphors, language—that convey the deepest truths of our common life.[21]

The Comparison Group

Ours was not a study of the sort in which a "control group" is appropriate. But in the course of our analysis, we did identify twenty interviewees who serve as a comparison group. In this group there was less evidence of systemic awareness and a critical perspective. Some were on the edge of burnout; their loyalty was limited to their immediate constituency; they were locked into a single answer for complex problems; or they simply felt too overwhelmed to grapple with larger issues. By comparing this group with the one hundred "core interviews," we were able to cast some patterns in sharper relief (see Appendix).

Underlying Perspectives and Assumptions

When we started this inquiry, we did, of course, bring our prior experiences, analytical lenses, and disciplinary constructs to the work, and our interpretations reflect those perspectives. Our backgrounds include political science, social and educational psychology, constructive-developmental psychology, theology, and international development. In the course of the study we have been informed by other literatures and disciplines as well.

Because we were aware of the power of the natural and social environment in the formation of personality, we expected that home life would be significant, that intensive group experiences were formative for adolescents, that mentors were important during young adulthood, and that committed people were likely to be sustained by networks of people who shared their concerns. But we could not be certain that this would be the case or what additional influences would emerge as salient.

Indeed, there were surprises. We expected, for instance, to hear more about the importance of didactic moral lessons, the elaborated content of religious belief, and events creating dramatic shifts in a life's direction. This was not the case. Moreover, the most powerful pattern to emerge across all of the lives we studied was quite unanticipated (see Chapter 3).

As we have discussed this study in a variety of public forums, people often ask for the single most crucial thing they can do to raise socially aware and responsible children. We do have a response for them, but it is important to say at the outset that there is no "Gandhi pill." No single event can ensure that a person will or will not live a life of commitment to the common good. It is a mix of key ingredients that matters.

Taken in isolation, many of the important experiences that we describe here—a loving home, for example—are desirable components of any healthy life. Clearly, there is no certainty that a child from a loving home will grow into a life of commitment, but add a parent who works actively for the public good and the possibility increases. Then add opportunities for service during adolescence, cross-cultural experiences, and a good mentoring experience in young adulthood, and the likelihood grows still stronger. In general, we have become persuaded that the greater the number and depth of certain key experiences one has, the greater the probability of living a committed life, and although there are no guarantees, this work can significantly inform the effort to foster commitment to the common good.

The Organization of the Book

The chapter titles are chosen to underscore our conviction that an awareness of the connections among things—of interrelatedness, broadly construed—is a key sensibility among those whose lives are committed to the common good.

Thus all but one of our chapter titles share the prefixes "con" or "com," derived from the Latin "with." The exception is "courage," rooted in the French "coeur," meaning "heart." We have studied people with "heart"—people imperfect, to be sure—who demonstrate informed, practical and compassionate wisdom, a seasoned and strategic strength fitting to the challenges of the twenty-first century.

The chapters unfold so as to reveal a constellation of interdependent patterns by which committed lives are formed. In this chapter, we have begun with a look at the intensification of "Connection and Complexity" in the new commons. Chapter 2, "Community," suggests that while many homes and neighborhoods have become tribal fortresses, in contrast, most of the people we interviewed grew up in hospitable spaces—neighborhoods, schools, and mentoring environments—peopled by important threshold figures such as "public parents," teachers, and mentors. These environments successively fostered trustworthy belonging and the confidence that it was possible to make a difference, to become at home in the world.

Chapter 3, "Compassion," recognizes the tap root of the moral imagination, the capacity to "feel with" those who are "other." In a world in which cultures are colliding, we see in committed lives the signal importance of constructive engagement with those who are significantly different from oneself.

Chapter 4, "Conviction," discusses how committed people have cultivated powerful and effective "habits of mind." In a society which too often has reduced education to training or even entertainment and where busyness eclipses time for reflection, these ways of thinking enable committed people to engage the challenges of the new commons.

In a society struggling to assess the effect of contemporary media on imagination, faith, and human behavior, such forms of language as images, stories, and symbols are critical to the encouragement and sustenance of the consciousness of committed people. Chapter 5, "Courage," describes how that happens.

Chapter 6, "Confession," grapples with the costs of commitment, the role of "taboo motivations" that are a part of every life, the deep wounding that some have experienced, and the role of each in the formation and sustaining of commitment. In a world in which cynical interpretations of human motivation abound, these people understand much about the complexity and ambiguity within as well as outside the self.

In Chapter 7, "Commitment," we discuss the paradoxical nature of commitment itself—how time is both more immediate and remote, how one may be committed to a particular place, yet at home in many places, and how the very act of commitment is at once a matter of holding on and letting go.

At two points in the text the reader will encounter extended narratives that we have designated "Interludes." We have chosen to present these stories intact and without commentary because of our core conviction, confirmed by the study, that all human lives are interdependent with others, and that too often we tell stories of individuals in isolation, obscuring this reality. "For the Hundreds of Years that Come After" and "Evansburg" illustrate two different kinds of connection—one across time and generations and one within a single community. They tangibly illustrate the ways in which lives of commitment are not isolated, but are best understood as patterns of strength woven into the fabric of the commons.

The Epilogue, "Compass Points," invites reflection on some of the implications of the patterns we have found for twelve sectors in our society. We draw attention to the power of each sector in the commons, suggesting some directions in which they might move in cultivating a common strength for the common good.

We hope that the reader will recognize the common fire of spirit, compassion, imagination, realism, and the hope that animates committed lives. Such people have learned to trust appropriately and act with courage, to live within and beyond tribe in affinity with those who are other, to practice critical habits of mind and a responsible imagination, to manage their own mixed emotions and motives, and to live with a recognition of the interdependence of all life—manifest in a paradoxical sense of time and space. They help us imagine ways of building a more promising future.

We turn now to Chapter 2. In the story of Bill Wallace we see how the environments in which we live affect our capacity to become more trusting and more confident—increasingly at home in the complex and widening world of the twenty-first century.

community

Becoming at Home in the World

Finding the Sweet Spot

We meet Bill Wallace at the headquarters of Enviro-Tech Resources, on the fifth floor of a graciously renovated old brick waterworks building in a suburb outside of Philadelphia. He takes us into a conference room dominated by an elegant piece of textile art and two large windows through which we can see his employees moving about with comfortable efficiency.

"We're environmental engineers and contractors," he tells us. "We have 17 branches and 350 employees. We basically work on hazardous waste sites across the country, addressing problems of organics and metals—heavy diesels, coal tars, things like that. We work almost exclusively for the utilities, transportation, the process industries such as petroleum and steel."

"One of our difficulties—which is being played out on Capitol Hill—is that the country literally does not have the money to clean up the sites that have been identified in a manner that meets the most stringent interpretation of the requirements, which I would call the edible dirt standards. We're trying to fig-ure out a paradigm shift right now in this marketplace."

We ask how he feels about the current regulation climate. He smiles at the obvious. "If the regulations are taken away, people won't do anything. Now, you may ask, 'Where's the moral fiber of these folks?' but it's 'the tragedy of the commons.' If just one good-hearted person running a foundry on the west end of town says, 'I don't like the fact that we're putting out iron oxide emissions, and we're going to clean this down to the lowest imaginable level,' and the guy on the east end of town decides, 'To hell with it, I don't care,' then, frankly, the second guy's costs are going to be a lot lower. The first guy can't keep his business competitive if he's the only one who cleans up his act. There have to be regulations that everyone has to meet or nothing is done. And then the question is, What's the level of those regulations, and how safe are they in terms of sustaining the environment? What are their implications with respect to the economics and the market?

"Most people," he goes on, "don't understand that although we have environmental standards, they're difficult to interpret. So we do a lot of interpreting to industry about what the regulatory conditions are, and how you meet them. A big piece of our game is understanding the technologies that might be used to restore sites. We've been pioneers in what's called bioremediation, using indigenous microorganisms to clean up in a natural way, as opposed to putting a lot of iron on the site and burning everything to a crisp. So we try to be relatively innovative and understand what companies might do in a cost-effective manner, and at the same time meet the regulatory requirements, or go beyond them if we can."

He pauses. We ask how he manages to hold it all together, and he smiles again. "Well," he says, "it isn't easy. It's one thing to understand in the laboratory what to do, and it's quite another to make it happen on these sites."

The year Bill Wallace turned nine he spent the entire summer playing baseball in a field across from his home in their working-class Dayton suburb. There was something deeply satisfying about the game for him. "The crack of the bat against the ball," he tells us. "What baseball players call that 'sweet spot.' You connect with the ball and everything comes together. You know, you feel it inside. It's who you are. That's where I first understood who I was, in my gut, playing sports."

Back in his home it was harder to know who he was. He felt his parents loved him, but his father was on the road much of the time, selling industrial fencing, and when he came home, there was constant tension: "My dad had a huge anger." Though his parents found some partnership in his dad's business, "the emotional life in our house always was a little bit fragile," and he often felt trapped between his father's "rabid interest" in state and national politics and his mother's deep religious interest. "Those two driving passions in each of their lives were fairly dominating. So family life was very stultifying. Sports were the place where I could be myself."

Fortunately, he was athletic and excelled in track, basketball, and football. Moreover, he was smart. He won the school Latin award, but his real interest was in math and science, and he fondly remembers Mr. Waring, a sixth grade teacher who "really loved science." That year, he won the American Legion Award for all-around excellence in academics, athletics, and good citizenship. "I was a very dutiful kid. Duty, honor, country. I had to be an all-American in everything I did."

His father worked actively on the Taft election campaign, and Bill, who kept a scrapbook of clippings, was "crestfallen" when Taft lost. His father, who quietly hoped his son would become either president or a major league pitcher, must have been pleased to watch his political interest. But Bill wasn't so sure. "I was interested in politics certainly, but I also knew that Dad's brand of politics was probably not mine."

He regards the enormous vitality he inherited from his father as a gift, but he also absorbed some of his mother's deep interiority. "I've always understood that even though I had this abundant outgoing energy, there is an internal life that's really important." Though from early on he resisted his mother's answers to religious questions, he regularly attended church, and "poetry and scripture were just burned into my mind over time," creating a love for language and symbol which "has always been very important to me." And the questions stuck. "I'm one of those people who asks the ontological questions—you know, Who am I, What does it mean to be?"

He looks back on life in Dayton as a secure equilibrium, a kind of "blessed innocence—a nice protected environment." But when he was sixteen, the family moved to Lansing. There, the friendships, the successes, the neighborhood buffers that had held him were gone. "It was traumatic. I had been a good student and a good athlete. I felt I had to claw my way back, and that was really hard."

Once again sports were central to his feeling of self-worth, and eventually he became captain of the football team. This time, however, his teammates were different. "In Dayton, I played ball against a lot of black kids; in Lansing I played ball *with* a lot of black kids." He also met Emily, captain of the cheerleaders. It was "a fifties romance," and they were married a few years later. Her father, John Geraghty, "a quintessential automotive engineer," became a role model.

An English teacher, Miss Farren, also helped. She loved language, and he can still recite with enormous pleasure the opening stanzas of T.S. Eliot's

"Prufrock." But she pushed him hard. "You think you're so good," she once told him. "Well, just you wait until college. You're going to find a whole lot of people much better than you, so you'd better start to work."

"Of course," he notes ironically, "that fed into the insecure side of me, so there were good and bad points about it."

Bill's first day at the university was "ecstatic." Away from the confining tensions in his family, "At last I could do it my own way." He did. His second year he discovered Professor Towle, "a real good advisor," who said, 'Let's take a look at what you're doing; here's a way you can do what you want; and we'll give you a degree for it." Later, he designed his own Master's, combining mechanics and materials.

But it was another professor, one Josh Davis, who was pivotal in his life. It bothered Bill when professors seemed to take more interest in their research than teaching, and he used to enjoy sitting at the back of his classes challenging under-prepared profs. One day in thermodynamics, he did this with Davis, and rather than snap back, Davis welcomed the questions. That night, Bill learned later, Davis told his wife, "I found a live one!"

Davis became his dissertation advisor, and when Davis moved to California to take a position in materials research, he invited Bill to join him and finish his thesis there. The defense work at Pacific Tech was "exciting, groundbreaking work" and "on the cutting edge."

A few years later, Bill and Davis went to Case Western as a "package deal." During that time, a citizen's group raised public concern about air pollution. Bill was proud of his profession, and it disturbed him that engineers, who could solve the problem, might be contributing to it. But it turned out that it was not just a technical fix. When he joined the county advisory committee, "It changed my life. I found out, to my horror, that my profession hadn't prepared me for the kind of questions that were asked, nor was I prepared to deal with the messy world of public policy." On the one hand, he thought they were making things too simple—"lots of emotion, but not much fact." On the other hand, it was clear that "the only thing industry could smell was money."

He took what he learned there and spent the next several years creating an undergraduate double major in "Technology and Society" that he proudly notes became a national model. But after ten years, he made the move to industry, first as a consultant, then as an executive. Under Reagan's environmental policies, however, the business went into a tailspin. "When we tried to merge with another company, we went through three rounds of venture capital and got our heads handed to us. Failed miserably."

Meanwhile, their children had become teenagers, and Emily, his partner of seventeen years, "the dearest person in the world to me," announced one Saturday morning, "You're leaving," and packed his bags. He had missed the warning signals. When he checked with their friends, they all told him he'd better go. That failure smashed through his armor right where the crest read "Success."

Nevertheless, he stayed home that night, put on his earphones, listened to Beethoven, and read Paul Tillich. "It was a long dark night of the soul. I sat up that entire night wrestling with my pride and the enormous humiliation and pain of being told to leave by this woman I dearly loved. It was one of the best nights in my life, but it was hard. About five in the morning, truly distraught, with Beethoven crashing around in the background, I found this great piece by Tillich called 'You are Accepted.' And I said to myself, 'It will be hard, it will be humiliating, but I'm going to stick if I can.'"

He and Emily found "a great counselor, a real hero," and old wounds began to heal. "I've gotten better at understanding my own failure and my own inadequacies," he tells us. "I think when you do that, you can see it in other people more compassionately. So it puts things in better balance. Before, I was into individual excellence, but—even though it had to be clubbed into me—I discovered the power of doing things as an organization. I'm a person of power, that's what I enjoy, and I have to watch myself all the time. But it's such a better deal to interest other people in the ideas and set them working."

When we ask what elements in his environment help him do that, he replies, "In this business we have a really great set of people. Emily and I really are a pretty good pair. And I still have a lot of interests, and people I love still in Cleveland and all over the country." But it isn't easy. "These businesses are hard to run because industry right now is downsizing and working with thin organizations and not much backup. You live by your wits, and the market whipsaws you. But there's always an element of excitement, and I need risk—I'd get bored without it." He seems to flourish on that edge. "That's where chaos is, but it's also where contributions are."

"It sounds like the 'crack of the bat' kind of thing for you," we observe.

He grins in recognition and replies, "The great plus in doing environmental work is that despite enormous controversy in whatever you do, you have the feeling, if you do the work honestly and with your own standards, that you're doing something for the good of people. And, sure, there's a whole set of people out there who say you're helping industry get away easier than it should. But I don't mind that. It's in that kind of discourse, even if it's angry, that you get to the real truth of the matter.

"See, the sweet spot for me is in organizations. Martin Buber said that 'all life is meeting.' Well, in this world you meet in these messy commercial organizations. That's where the sweet spot is for me. And I was fortunate enough to understand that in some sort of inchoate way and move in that direction."

"And what's toughest?" we ask.

"Fratricidal wars between people," he replies immediately. "Two very good people—both of whom are important in the organization—who hate each other." He pauses, then, "Strange as it may sound, I want this place to be a caring community, in the larger sense. David Maister wrote a book about professional service firms. I use a phrase of his all the time: 'Your clients don't care how much you know until they know how much you care.' We've got all kinds of different people, but we have to treat each other with trust and respect and we have to care for each other. So I say to our people, "Don't tell me you can do it out there, if you can't do it in here." So we have to have a standard of trust and respect and care and decency here that we can take out, and if we can, we'll be damn successful."

Bill's story is important because it gives us glimpses, not only of an individual, but of his life world—the social and natural environments that enabled him to become at home in the new commons.

It is a story of "interbeing." "'Interbeing' is a word that is not in the dictionary yet," acknowledges the Buddhist monk Thich Nhat Hanh, but "'to be' is to inter-be. We cannot just be by ourselves alone. We have to inter-be with every other thing."[1] One of the people we interviewed spoke of interbeing this way:

> As a metaphor, I think of how the skin is a permeable membrane. There's air flow between your skin and your inside all the time. I think that's how our relationship is with the world. There's this fluidity between the inner life and the external, a constant give and take so things that are happening on the outside do really come in to affect your own personal development and vice versa.

Indeed, as our consciousness begins to absorb the daily experience of living in a more complex social world, the dynamic, relational, and interdependent character of all of life[2] becomes increasingly evident, and the ancient debate between nature and nurture reforms itself yet again.

[25]

Clearly, both nature and nurture have a hand in who we become.³ But as educators seeking to foster generous and responsible citizenship in the twenty-first century, we are concerned primarily with the questions, "What are the elements in people's primary environments—homes, neighborhoods, schools, workplaces, and other institutions—that nurture the capacity to act on behalf of the common good?" "How do people like Bill Wallace become citizens who are at home on the new commons?" Answers to these questions can inform important choices and policies that are before us as individuals, organizations, and a society.

At Home in the World: A Sense of Trust and Agency

To be "at home" means many things. But for most, a positive sense of being at home arises from experiences of interbeing that enable us to know we are connected in trustworthy ways and have some confidence that we can make a difference. Erik Erikson taught that the first great question of a human life is how to establish a sense of basic trust. His second and third great questions asked how we learn to stand on our own two feet with confidence, and how we learn to act with purpose. As we saw in Wallace's story, no one escapes some measure of mistrust, shame, and doubt,⁴ but when these prevail, we may become defensive or passive. What is needed to undergird the qualities of citizenship required in the twenty-first century is a significant measure of trust and agency. We flourish best when grounding trust and agency are learned in the home from the beginning.

At Home during the Early Years

At the Heart's Core

"I was loved, therefore I am," writes Sam Keen.⁵ "The first element of moral education is to learn what it means to be cared for and to care," writes ethicist Nel Noddings.⁶ Commitment to the common good rests in a healthy sense of trust and agency, which in turn grows from the experience of being loved and the opportunity to care. This conviction is reflected in the lives of many of those we studied. When we asked Susan Jay, an ethicist-scholar, when and how she had learned that she could make a difference, she responded: "Constantly. I was bathed in that from the beginning. My parents thought it was hot stuff that I could walk, you know? So I knew I made a difference in their lives because I brought them so much joy."

Thus, central to our understanding of human development is that it matters who our partners are in the dance of life. Through the interplay between the potential we are all born with and the conditions that the world hands us, through the constant interaction of self and other, we create meaning—we learn who we are and how life is. As the self dances with the beautiful and terrible rough-and-tumble of the world, patterns are composed that we come to perceive as the character and quality of the motion of life itself.

This meaning-making activity lies at the core of every human life.[7] How it occurs and what it teaches is critical, because while we may or may not act in a manner consistent with what we say we believe, we will act in a manner congruent with how we ultimately make meaning—with what we finally can and cannot trust, with what we feel we can and cannot do.[8]

At its most basic and best, a loving home provides shelter, safety, nourishment, and a place to learn that the world is dependable, at least in some significant measure. In this first "holding environment,"[9] the kind of meaning we compose is largely dependent upon the quality of the interaction between parent and child.

The Early Home Environment

The primary mediators of reality during our early years are our parents, or for some, grandparents, step or foster parents, or older siblings. They teach us how things are: whom to trust, whom to shun, what is safe and what is dangerous, how to love, and how to hate. In the mini-commons of the home, we learn in a preverbal, bone-deep way, fundamental dispositions toward generosity or meanness, respect or scorn, equality or domination.[10] Through the give and take of these early relationships, the child composes core patterns of life with others.

In a classic study, Mary Ainsworth closely observed mother-child pairs over a period of months, finding that the most effective parenting was that which allowed the child appropriate attachment while still sponsoring independent exploration.[11] Watch a father and his infant daughter "conversing" in gestures. As the father is holding the child, first he moves his hand toward her, then her hand moves to meet it. As they touch, he smiles; then she smiles, and so on. The two carry on a wonderful interaction as each responds to an earlier response.[12] When the dance succeeds, the adult's actions are sympathetically tuned to the child's, and the infant begins to learn that indeed, the world will work for her. The child thus develops a rudimentary sense of both trust and agency—a sense of being held and heard and the ability to act with confidence.

As Bill Wallace's story suggests (and as we will discuss in Chapter 6), not all of the people we interviewed were well loved, supported, or recognized in this way. In about one third of the families a parent had died, was absent, disabled, or otherwise dysfunctional. And yet almost all described at least one "good enough"[13] parent or other adult in their early years who enabled them to compose some sense of trust and confidence.[14]

Paulo Garcia, now an attorney who works particularly with workplace issues, told us: "My mother passed when I was two. And so my brothers and sisters and I were raised mostly by my father and relatives. He was caring and very giving to us and to others. He always felt that if you could do something for yourself that you could also do something for others."

Garcia's grandmother also played a vital role in his life. Living in northern New Mexico, he felt the sting of discrimination early. He remembers even as a very young boy realizing that there was no recognition of Hispanic ethnicity — just "O" for other, which he and others interpreted as "zero." Yet his grandmother, a strong woman widely known as a healer, taught him that for six generations his family had been important keepers of the culture and Catholic faith in their region, and encouraged him to continue the tradition. This gave him the strength to challenge schoolmates and teachers who made racist assumptions. "When you are abused emotionally, you can become a bitter person," he says. "That's why I thank God for my grandmother who was the first to help me channel the negative experiences I had in a positive way."

A Home with Open Doors

Human growth requires a healthy mix of the familiar and the unfamiliar, the reliable and the unexpected. A good home provides the protection of sturdy walls and a sheltering roof, but windows and doors are also essential. Through windows, we glimpse a larger world, and through the doors come neighbors, friends, and strangers with stories, sights, sounds, and smells that nourish a sense of participating in a wider belonging. The childhood homes of the people we studied ranged widely from cramped to spacious, barren to opulent. But common to most was a core of love surrounded by a kind of porous boundary allowing interchange with the wider world, planting seeds for participation in an enlarged sphere.

A Public Parent

A primary way by which this exchange can occur is through the caring activity of a "public parent." Slightly more than half of the people in our study described at least one parent who was publicly active in a manner that conveyed concern and care for the wider community, either through their job or through additional volunteer commitments. These included a school principal who was a mother and a respected leader in the wider community, a businessman who wrestled with city hall to create a playground, a homemaker who helped to start a school for mentally retarded children, a farmer who regularly gave away a portion of his produce, a high school coach who built both teamwork and community, and Bill Wallace's father, whose interest in politics provided access to a wider public commitment.

In a few cases there were two public parents. Laura Henny, now a secretary for a legal aid organization, had a father who was a used car dealer widely known for being unusually fair and trustworthy, and a mother who built a comparable reputation selling real estate. Barbara Fox, a Baptist minister and member of the state board of education, describes her mother as "emotionally strong, spiritually strong, intellectually astute, and determined to know the truth." As the state's director of alcohol education, she brought home stories of the living conditions of migrant workers, stories that helped galvanize her daughter's commitment to the wider world. Fox's father was a minister and a physician who taught poor people how to finance their homes.

Even when the parents' vision was focused only on their own particular community, the child—still seeing local community as world—could grow that germ of community participation into a larger, more embracing commitment. For example, a man committed to international development warmly recalled his father's dedication to local town affairs. What matters, it seems, is to grow up in a family that cares about and participates in a wider public life.[15]

Busy parents today sometimes assume that to have "quality time" with their children they should set aside their outside commitments and focus exclusively on child and family for whatever few minutes are available. Others believe that their children will not understand or be interested in what they are doing. In contrast, many of the people we interviewed described having at least some access to their parents' work and to what it meant, either through direct participation or conversations overheard.

Listening from the Stairway

We were both amused and charmed to find an interesting pattern that we describe as "listening from the stairway" in which children sitting at the top of stairways overheard adult conversations about community affairs that nourished their sense of connection to a larger world. One woman remembers watching through the banister with her sister as debates raged in the living room over two neighbors who had lost their jobs when they refused to take an oath during the McCarthy era. And Stanley Tate, a theologian who has been able to create and sustain dialogue between liberals and conservatives, remembers sitting at the top of the stairs as a child, legs dangling through the slats of the banister, watching his father, who was the Justice of the Peace, carry out his work in the front room of their home. People would come bearing a variety of needs, woes, and disputes. His father not only mediated the law, but did so in a manner that conveyed a kind of thoughtful care for the whole community.

The Practice of Hospitality

The wider world becomes present in the home also through the practice of hospitality. Although he now travels widely as an international development officer coordinating relief efforts, Arthur Schwartz grew up in a secluded religious homestead in Ohio. Yet visits from the outside world played a critical role.

> We had missionaries from all over the world who would spend a night or two with us, and they'd talk about the work of the church in Haiti or in Australia. So I was part of a worldwide endeavor even though I grew up way outside of a small town. We were on a first name basis with people around the world. It was very empowering.

Others remembered hosting exchange students or foreign dignitaries, or simply observing their parents' friendships across obvious tribal lines. When messages of inclusion and hospitality were established in the home early, they seem to have served as a kind of inoculation against the toxic forms of exclusion that the child would later confront elsewhere.[16] But sometimes the world would simply invade. Fathers were called to war, racial injustice or poverty brought personal suffering, and painful national events appeared, unbidden, on the doorstep.

The world arrived in many homes through printed or electronic media—newspapers, books, maps, letters, magazines, radio, or television (see Chapter 5). What gave it significance as a formative influence, however, was the meaning imparted to the news through family discussion. Perhaps because of conversation with adults about the outside world, many recalled the power of particular historical events in their lives: the deaths of Sacco and Vanzetti, Joseph Stalin, President Kennedy, or Martin Luther King. In some important sense, these youngsters learned that they were a part of history rather than simply observers, or victims, of it.

Transforming the Meaning of "Home"

To become at home in the world of the new commons, we do not so much "leave home," as undergo transformations in the meaning of "home." Lifespan psychology, the study of how we change and evolve throughout our lives, has now permeated much of conventional culture. We have learned that people move through a series of passages—infancy, childhood, adolescence, young adulthood, mid-life, maturity, and old age. Each era presents new tasks and the potential to recognize and manage the relationship between oneself and the world more adequately. There is no shortage of literature about the stages of life's journey, from Shakespeare's "seven ages" to Levinson's four eras.[17] As the story is usually told, people move into, through, and out of each period in a sequence, taking on new characteristics and leaving the old behind as they advance through the seasons or ascend the steps of a ladder. The prevailing metaphor is that of an individual pilgrim on a "developmental journey."

The metaphor of journey is both powerful and limited. True, life may be seen as a sequence of departures and arrivals; sometimes we do leave important places and relationships behind. But more often they undergo transformation. It is closer to the truth to say that over time some parts of us remain constant and some change. Patterns woven into our sense of self in one environment often remain a part of the tapestry of our inner life even as we change. We never leave home entirely behind. We grow and become both by letting go and holding on, leaving and staying, journeying and abiding. A good life is a balance of home and pilgrimage.[18]

In this way of seeing, though we may indeed move from one geographical location to another, the growth of the self may be understood less as a journey and more as a series of transformations in the meaning of home. With each transformation, the boundary shifts outward to embrace the neighborhood, the community, the society, and perhaps ultimately the world. Thus, when human development happens well, both initially and throughout our lives, we experience home as a familiar center of belonging and identity, surrounded by a permeable membrane which makes it possible to sustain and enlarge our sense of self while admitting elements of the widening world. Through successive transformations of the ways we make meaning of ourselves and our world, our sphere of trust and agency is continually enlarged.

Commitment to the common good rests, in part, in an anchored sense of "home" within the wider life of the commons. How, then, do our personal and institutional environments foster the grounded belonging we need, while simultaneously enlarging our ability to recognize the whole planetary commons as "home," and ourselves as citizens within it? To begin with, we learn that our family home is a part of a neighborhood.

At Home in the Neighborhood

For the people we interviewed, the steps out of the family home and into the larger world were most successful when encouragement from inside the home was followed by recognition from important others in a safe and welcoming environment outside. "Home" came to mean not only the familial household but also a larger geographic and relational world. Whatever sense of trust and agency had been cultivated in the earliest years was now cast into a larger realm we call "neighborhood."

Catherine McCarty works in the Roman Catholic Church at the national level, developing programs and policies for family and youth. "The neighborhood was there my whole time growing up," she told us.

> We lived in a neighborhood that was kind of an Irish Catholic neighborhood. But then right next door was the Italian neighborhood, and down the street was the Jewish neighborhood. My overriding sense was that all these people were reliable people. The neighborhood was kind of an extended family. My father knew all of these people because he was an engineering inspector for the city. During World War II we always got our meat from the kosher butcher—the triplets, Hirsh, Mirsch, and Yessl. My mother would get certain things only from the Italian neighborhood, and I often went to get these things for her and got to know all of these people. If I were to say what's really sort of outstanding, it is the sense of communal participation that was there.
>
> Summers were wonderful. All the families in the neighborhood would be out together on their front porches and stoops, and we would block off the street and put on

plays together. But all the parents were out there with us. In my own home there was also the neighborhood flow, people in and people out.

New places, more people

When children begin going to school, for most—their world of places and people—significantly enlarges. This venture coincides with a turning point in how children think. A new ability to take another person's perspective opens a fresh passion for fairness, and the growing facility for placing things in an ordered sequence enables children to see some actions as "better" or "worse," and hence to form the beginning of a conscience.[19] These developments shed light on the significance of the partnership between the family home and neighborhood.

Although for many children nowadays the neighborhood is less cohesive, less geographically concentrated, and more dangerous than in Catherine's day, it can still fascinate youngsters. Many people told stories of exploring and defining their neighborhoods. One man recalls his father taking him on walks around New York every weekend when he was young. On his rides to Grandmother's house across town, an eight-year-old city boy was amazed to discover how big the world was, and a small-town girl could name fifteen nationalities among her neighbors. Thus, as they moved through their elementary school years, the people we studied were developing a tangible neighborhood map that created an expanded sense of who "we" are, a sense defined, in part, by a broader ecology of institutions.

School dominates the lives of most children from the age of five until puberty. In school, most of our interviewees clearly acquired important knowledge, learned essential social, cognitive, and practical skills, and strengthened their sense of competence. Perhaps because schools are so integral to childhood, we heard relatively little about them *per se*, except as a background hum of daily life and occasionally as a setting of frustration or hurt. Interestingly, however, the schools that did stand out as memorable were those that intentionally created a pervasive ethos of mutual respect, caring, and productive learning, which set them apart from a wider social environment less attentive to the practices needed for positive human becoming.[20]

We did, however, hear a great deal about coaches or particular teachers like Wallace's Miss Farren. Schoolteachers who took a personal interest, who offered positive and productive learning experiences, have lingered for decades in the memory of the people we interviewed.[21] Most recalled such teachers by name.

While school provides an important opportunity for membership in a larger community, religious institutions can provide a sense of distinctiveness within an enlarging world. People we interviewed sighted a wider world when they saw maps of distant holy lands, learned stories of their people in Africa or Israel, listened to missionaries speak, or heard that people of all races were equally valued in God's eyes. Some met children of different ethnicities at church camp or when they visited people of their religious faith in another town. For those in our sample who describe themselves as having been positively influenced by religious institutions, their experience seems to have given them a secure sense of belonging to a particular people who were also a part of a yet wider world.

Other places and institutions were also important. To a degree that surprised us, places such as the ballfield, public library, museum, or zoo were described as memorable and decisive in people's lives. An environmentalist traces his passion for natural history to Saturday mornings in the neighborhood museum. For some the park was a kind of "commons" where kids came together across class boundaries. One woman recalls regularly dressing up to go to the local library with her grandmother as though they were going to church (in part, because they were African-American and in a climate of racism felt that they had to take extra care to be recognized as "respectable"). These were typically publicly supported institutions whose resources were available without charge. Had they charged a fee, many in our sample would have been unable to benefit from them.

People Who Recognize You
A sense of growing self-esteem is vital to the formation of the conviction that one can make a positive difference. In many stories, we heard about important and helpful neighborhood adults as well as parents. There were teachers who taught productive work habits, celebrated successes, and "watched out for you even after school;" coaches who took time, ministers who "took an interest in the kids and were like friends of the family;" a friend's mother who "really tuned in to each person" who visited; and a young couple "who were always attentive to me and my siblings." Clearly, parents were not alone in raising their children.

Catherine McCarty recalls how she started piano lessons.

A neighbor across the street said to my mother (I must have been five), "That child should be taking piano lessons because I've watched her skip rope" [laughs]. My mother listened to her. Now that was another important person in my life, my piano teacher. I studied with the same person until I was eighteen years of age—from age six to age eighteen—that's a long time. And I never realized until I went back to piano lessons as an adult what a special relationship that is. That's an hour a week when someone is concentrating on you alone, and she was very supportive of me.

Several of our interviewees, bedridden for significant periods as children, spoke of meaningful conversations with caring medical practitioners and other adults during their convalescence. The combination of direct attention, real talk, and just the respite from some of the pressures of being a kid seems to have had a special power in preparing the young mind for a future of confident and constructive engagement in the world.[22]

Can Do

Many of the people we studied learned an important sense of "can do" during these neighborhood years. Developing agency and creativity took the forms of making things to give or to sell, playing games and instruments, and becoming proficient at schoolwork. Tracy Flanagan, who now addresses state policy on affordable housing, was the oldest kid in the neighborhood.

All the kids would come calling at our house, and my job would be to create a new kind of game. I created a town one summer, the summer I was 6. We had a mayor's office. I was a florist and the mayor. Everybody got to pick what they wanted to be, and they picked their own section of a backyard, and we played Petersville for an entire summer.

Later she remarked, "I developed a sense of what I could do and that I could have an impact. And that's a real sense of power: 'I can do things that really pull people together. I can do things that bring people joy. I can do things that clean up the neighborhood.'"

Justin Jordan now heads a staff of several hundred people in six different countries to promote economic development. As a boy, with his older brother and a friend, he started an organization in a closet in the basement of his home.

At first it was a secret because we didn't really know what it was. It was like your classic clubhouse. We called it X2 because it was like a spy club. And another friend started X1. Over a period of three years or more it evolved and began to get some goals. Then we were discovered, and we went public and it turned into a kind of club that had various clubs in it—like stamp collecting, coins. Also we had a pollution club called Environment and Ecology, and we had a Helping People club which was, you know, what could you do to help an old person in the neighborhood do their shopping? There was an apartment building down the street where there were a couple of old ladies, and I used to run and get milk for them. That fit into that club. Eventually we had the whole cellar kind of like an organization. My brother was vice president and I was president.

Recognizing Justice and Injustice

When we asked Justin if he remembered feeling strongly about anything as a child, he replied, "I remember feeling strongly about unfairness in the world. That it isn't fair that some people have things and others don't, and if there's so much in the world, how could it possibly be that people are poor or treated badly?" Then he added, "I remember my mother being very clear that she didn't want us to live in an all-white neighborhood and go to all-white schools, and my parents thought about that a lot when they were thinking about neighborhoods to live in." Justin's comments reveal how children's early sense of compassion and justice often corresponds with a parental or family sense of values.

Several echoed Justin's awareness of gaps and contradictions: Why did some people—often neighbors—live in conditions that were so obviously less desirable than their own? Why were some children treated unfairly just because they spoke another language? For some it had simply been bewildering; others had spoken up and discovered that they could make a difference. Said one woman:

I have never been able to think I was better, worked harder, any of that. None of those filters that other people protect themselves from the pain of humanity with have ever been available to me. So even in kindergarten, I was going home saying, "Agnes doesn't look like she's got a warm enough coat." And my parents would respond, particularly my dad.

Some discovered the contradictions by being on the receiving end of injustice, though at this age several appear to have been protected in some measure from the full sting of the prejudice. Cecil Baldwin, who later became Dean of a major professional school, told us:

My parents were skillful in shielding us against the harsher aspects of discrimination. I remember I used to walk past a big white school where fellows I played with went, on my way to a little two-room school heated by a coal stove, using the books that my friends had discarded. And I asked Mother, "Why do I have to go to Washington

Grammar School and I can't go to the Third Street School?" And my mother said, "Well, you know, sometimes people are afraid of what they don't understand or of what is different." And she said, "We're different and white people don't understand that, and therefore they're afraid." Well, what my mother was saying to me was, "It isn't something that's wrong with you."

The continuing formation of trust and agency, so crucial to citizenship in the twenty-first century, is significantly shaped by the degree to which one can be at home in the neighborhood. Yet there comes a time when the neighborhood may become too small.

Home in a Community

As children grow into the adolescent years, self and home expand in forms that incorporate, yet transcend the orbit of direct parental or neighborhood influence. The dance of inter-being is transformed once again as one sees and is seen in new ways, and trust and agency are again recomposed.

Physical-emotional changes, obvious and familiar, are accompanied by an equally far-reaching cognitive transformation. A new vulnerability and a new strength are born of the achievement of a more mature form of perspective-taking: the ability to hold another person's point of view at the same time as one's own. It now becomes possible to see oneself through the eyes of others and thus to become self-conscious. This new awareness opens the adolescent to the tyranny of the "they." "They" now matter in a whole new way, and the desire to belong becomes at once more fragile and fierce. The question, "Who am I?", so important in the adolescent years, is permeated by the question, "With whom do I belong and who are *we?*"

As generations of traditional cultures have recognized through rites of passage, adolescence signals the threshhold of adulthood, the time when we join our community on new terms. We use the word "community" because it suggests that people are bound up with one another, sharing, despite differences, a common identity.[23] When this transition happens well, it marks an emancipation from the literal and concrete world of the child-in-the-neighborhood into the strength of a growing and more reflective person-in-community. Whether or not adulthood will include commitment to the common good depends, in part, upon the quality and mix of home and pilgrimage.

Home and Pilgrimage

With the onset of puberty, the metaphors of home and pilgrimage—and the vital relationship between them—take on new meaning. In the lives of the people we studied, home and neighborhood generally remained familiar anchors, but travel across town, across the state, across the world emerged with new power. Sometimes there were trips with friends—with athletic teams, the school band, or one's own family—and sometimes one traveled alone to an international exchange program or youth conference. Whatever the form, these experiences were particularly significant for the formation of commitment to the common good when they opened up a sense of trustworthy belonging to a wider world and included constructive encounters with others different from oneself and one's own people. Seventy-two percent of the people we interviewed had had significant travel experience by the end of their young adulthood. This is particularly interesting in the light of Howard Gardner's observation in his study of the formation of leaders that "future tyrants" generally elect "not to venture far from their homelands."[24]

When Laura Bingham was a high school senior, she participated in the "Wrigley Forum," a program that brought together thirty-six students from all over the world. They travelled together across the country for three months, forming tight friendships with one another.

> For me, the most exciting thing was that I learned about human beings. That had more power than boundaries or countries. The young woman from the United Arab Republic made friends with the woman from Israel. And then we learned that when they went back to their countries they would never even be allowed to write to each other.

In contrast to a journey, which could be unending, a pilgrimage requires both venturing and returning. A good pilgrimage leads to discovery and transformation, but it isn't complete until you have returned home and told your story. "Home" is where someone hears and cares about that story, helps you sort out what you have seen, heard, and done—whether it be a triumph, a defeat, a high adventure, or a wash. "Home base" for this re-composing of self and world might be some combination of the family home, school, religious community, scouts, the Y, a friend's home, or the hangout.

Peers and Additional Adults

According to conventional wisdom, the single greatest influence on adolescents is other adolescents. As a consequence, adults make much of the demons of peer pressure, while too often abdicating their own continuing influence. The problem, in fact, is not the peer pressure itself but where the pressure leads. The yearning to belong may steer one adolescent to an armed gang, and another to help friends rehab a home. Thus, the content of belonging—the nature of the social glue—is crucial. In a healthy community, adults have much to say about the content and norms of adolescent belonging.

When home base functions well in the teenager's life, there is a good mix of both peers and adults. As adolescents develop the capacity to reflect, they may begin to wonder about the adequacy of parental voices and test those voices in a wider circle of other admired adults. Parents remain important, but in new ways.

Sometimes the widening circle of adults is essential to survival. When Paul Chen was in the seventh grade, beatings at the hands of his drunken father grew so bad that he would stay away from home for days at a time. The owner of a neighborhood candy store gave him shelter, advice, and occasional work; a youth worker encouraged him to join the local Boy's Club; and a math teacher helped him piece his life back together after he finally had a nervous breakdown.

But for most, both adults and peers matter in the formation of commitment to the common good. A viable peer group is as significant for an adolescent as a primary caregiver is for an infant. The emerging teenager yearns for recognition from others who appear to be "just like me," in whose eyes she can see herself. Sometimes the cords of connection and identity are woven in profound and nourishing ways; sometimes they are superficial or even dangerous. This is precisely why it is so critical for adults to mediate the norms of belonging and purpose as teenagers are forming groups of identification.

When we first began exploring the formation of commitment to the common good, we invited people in various audiences to reflect on their own experience of the commons. As they did so, we repeatedly heard comments such as, "In the commons I grew up in, there were more people who cared about you." One man reflected that in his teenage years, before organized baseball leagues for kids, the ballpark had been a place where people of all generations played and gathered and worked out the concerns of the community. A man sitting next to him responded with quiet pride, "When I was growing up, it was becoming dangerous. The adults didn't know it, so we kids created a safe playground. We could all get there safely—and the blacks wouldn't dare come there." We then recognized together that the second playground had not fostered a sense of the commons—a sense that "everyone counts"—but rather a "democracy with exceptions." In the absence of aware and committed adults, the potential of important connections with others in an enlarging world had been precluded.

In contrast, Tracy Flanagan traced her work as a mediator in energy development disputes to her early teens when several socially concerned priests used to visit her home. One of them, Mike Latrobe, was disturbed by the growing unrest in the two small black neighborhoods in the town.

> Mike came over one day, very concerned about this racial problem, and announced to my parents that he wanted to create a meeting where white kids would go as representatives. He wanted it to be kids talking to kids. He also asked Kevin Reilly, who was this very good-looking guy, three years older than me and president of the CYO, and then asked me, a geeky, nerdy freshman in high school.
>
> Mike wanted me to go to the house of one of the black families, the home of a woman who also was concerned and very active in defusing the situation. As it turned out, we were kind of the lightning rod for the anger of a lot of these kids. And yet because he asked me to do it, I felt like, "Well, yeah, I guess I can do this." And it was, you know, pretty nervewracking, but also it was not something where I felt that I was in over my head. It was just scary. And I think that's one of the things about assuming responsibility at a very young age and doing it successfully. You learn that almost everything can be scary, but if you kind of have a sense of who you are and what the situation is, you can deal with it.

Tracy's account reveals the power of adults to create safe space and facilitate encounters that can help young people meet one another with the strength of their frustration, rage, openness, and generosity in a world that is growing ever more complex, multicultural, and often frightening. Adolescents may well need to form groups of belonging based on ethnic identity or other forms of common experience. Adults who represent committed citizenship in the new commons can affirm that need, yet also encourage them to "keep the door open," so that others can be welcomed across the threshold, and people within the group can also develop relationships outside. Committed adults can encourage (sometimes with the gift of good humor) the formation of communities in which the terms of belonging invite inclusion, fairness, honesty, and other values by which the moral courage of future generations can be nourished.[25]

It is significant also that Tracy believed she could do something that seemed frightening because Mike thought she could. Her story reveals the power of adults to create a safe space for the development of trust and the ability to take action.

A Task to Do

"The young do not need to be preached at; they need to be given a task," writes Harold Loukes, a Quaker educator.[26] In adolescence, all the precursors of a sense of agency are brought to the test of finding tasks with real meaning in the adult world. We have just seen how Mike conveyed this to Tracy, and how she remembers it still. Similarly, Maria Velasquez, now developing leadership among urban youth by creating an innovative high school, was befriended by a Costa Rican woman who became a second mother to her, challenging her to move out into the world, locating financial resources for her projects, and "always saying, 'Do.'" The people we interviewed particularly prized memories of adults who talked and worked with them in ways that conveyed that they had something to offer in the adult world.

Yet one might develop a sense of efficacy and not necessarily place it in the service of a larger public good. To do that, it seems necessary to learn in some way that one has a place in the wider world and to develop a sense of "on-behalf-ness." In a world that seems increasingly to view teens as burdensome, untrustworthy, and potential trouble, how did the people in our sample learn this?[27]

Working with Others for Others

The kind of task that enables adolescents to learn that their contribution can be vital need not necessarily be sustained for a long period of time, nor need it be the kind of "charity work" that often comes to mind. The power comes from working with other people to make a positive difference.

Will Johnson, who has advanced the economic development of immigrant populations, told us:

> The social crucible of my development was the segregated South of the early forties, and it was very painful. We couldn't walk on the same side of the street as a white person. We couldn't try on clothes in department stores. Schools were segregated. I became aware of the wrongness of this through the influence of my Sunday School teacher and my older sister. My older sister was involved in the college chapter of NAACP. In 1953, she went to the National Convention in Dallas, and came back with the slogan, "Free by '63." I became intrigued. When I was fourteen, I organized the local Youth Council for NAACP. Many of my friends were apprehensive about what they considered radical views, and although I did have a lot of involvement with band, choir, and leadership in student government, I spent most of those years involved in church, and NAACP, and worked with Medgar Evers in voter registration.

Jack Hiebert, a minister who has created innovative learning environments and challenges people to re-examine faith in the context of the new commons was asked, "When do you think you began to become aware of a larger world?" He responded, "One part of that is probably spending every summer out of doors, later going to camp, counseling in camps." Looking back on counseling at Y camp when he was fourteen, fifteen, and sixteen, he says, "I came naturally to work with people, to create learning environments for people, to take people places—up mountains or out in boats—to have a lot of fun with people and create ways for them to have a good—even transforming—experience."

Leadership

As these accounts reveal, the formation of leadership emerges in an explicit way during these years. "Leadership" can mean many things, but surely it includes the ability to mobilize others in positive ways. Many of the people we interviewed had opportunities to practice some form of leadership in adolescence.

In another example, Rubin Gutterman, who owns a profitable software company and seeks to help clients create an exemplary work environment, told us:

> At my synagogue, there was a woman who was a fantastic teacher who had a pretty profound influence. We would be Hebrew school teachers for the younger kids in a leadership development program. So they were taking thirteen to seventeen year old kids, and in the midst of your adolescent problems, teaching you how to be leaders. Literally, like the concept of active listening. That was taught to me when I was fourteen. I think it taught us all to be more empathetic and more discerning.

Conversation

As Rubin's account suggests, undergirding this readiness for leadership is a new capacity for serious conversation. In contrast to mere swagger, conforming silence, or pent-up outbursts, conversation can provide crucial pathways to finding one's place in the life of the wider commons. People speak of how important it was to be able to talk about things that "really mattered." Susan Jay recalls her church youth group:

> We had youth camp every summer and then would meet once or twice each semester for a weekend retreat. It was a group that was about something important: serious discussions about life issues—sex and politics and pressing theological issues. It mattered to me so much that in those groups there was an affirmation of honesty and integrity and pushing you beyond the bounds of what you used to think.

Then she adds: "The youth leaders were incredibly important in affirming a sense of a wider purpose, affirming my concerns, and giving me responsibility for beginning to act them out."[28]

This kind of conversation doesn't always take the form of direct face-to-face talk. In addition to the proverbial telephone phenomenon of the adolescent years, there is also the activity of sharing poetry, writing letters, creating music, sharing a science or art project, and notable among those we studied, engaging in a project on behalf of the community.

Conversations that matter arise from the teen's deepening sense of what life is about, a flock of new questions, and hunger for confirmation that others understand and wonder too. The opportunity to share the delight and angst of these mysteries welcomes adolescents into the more complex, luminous, and shadowy world they are now entering. These kinds of conversations help them find a place of trustworthy belonging. When they can explore concerns that "really matter" to themselves and the life of the wider community, their commitment to the common good grows richer.

A Community to Grow Up In

To foster commitment to the common good, a community must strengthen trust by providing a fundamental level of physical and emotional safety along with respect for the individuality of each member.[29] But to function well for adolescents, it must strengthen agency by also offering participation in the decisions that govern community life. With some exceptions, we did not see this quality of community as typical of what our society offers youth. A few remembered feeling that there was space for them to express themselves regularly and comfortably, and some remembered schools where questions were welcomed and insights affirmed, but many recalled only oases in otherwise numbing rhythms of superficial activities and discourse. Some remembered how good it was to be able to ride the subway all over the city, but most recalled a growing constraint on where you could and couldn't feel free to go. It seems clear that the conditions that formed our interviewees generally exist only in partial, temporary, or diluted forms today. Yet the quality of community available to our youth as they become young adults in the wider society has far-reaching significance for the formation of responsible citizenship.

Becoming at Home in Society

Young adulthood begins with the completion of the tasks of adolescence—gaining a consciousness of one's identity and capacity to contribute within a wider community. But this new sense of self and agency must now find a home. Two central questions loom: "What is my work?" and "Who will be my partners?" In adulthood, the great questions of love and work present the challenges of trust and agency in yet another frame.

By "work" we do not mean simply a job or career but rather a sense of one's calling—born from some reflection on life's purpose. Whether or not one is college bound, the task of young adulthood is to find and be found by a viable life "dream"—and to go to work on it.[30] In that quest, the twenty-something years are particularly tender and strategic. So much is possible; participation in the life of the commons can gather strength, moving toward more effective articulation. But along with the promise of their strength, young adults are also inevitably vulnerable to the quality of the environments within which they seek a place in a diverse, complex, and enlarging world. Mentors are guides in this process.

Mentors

At least three quarters of the people we studied were significantly influenced by mentors or mentoring environments.[31] Mentors challenge, support, and inspire. Although they have been around since well before Homer gave the name "Mentor" to the incarnation of Athena as caretaker of Odysseus's son, the term has only appeared in the social science literature of human development within the last two decades.

The term "mentor" has been widely used in recent years to mean anyone from a children's counselor to a teacher of adults. We restrict the term to mean a somewhat more experienced person of either gender who enables young adults to make the transition from the adolescent's dependence upon (and resistance to) authority, to the adult's ability to include him or herself in the arena of authority and responsibility. The timing of this transition is not necessarily determined by age. While it typically begins in the late teens and concludes in the late twenties or early thirties, for some this journey does not really commence until one is much older.[32]

Mentors appear in many forms, including senior managers, professors, inspiring speakers and writers, master artists, job supervisors, coaches, public leaders, college chaplains. They function as compelling women and men who recognize and support the emerging competence of the young adult, challenge limited notions of possibility, and offer themselves as beacons toward significant purpose. Often mentors know their protégés over an extended period of time; sometimes they serve only briefly in "mentoring moments"; and some—authors, for example—exercise influence only from afar.

When they influence the formation of commitment, mentors usually embody that commitment themselves, often modeling ways of seeing problems and offering helpful analyses. While passionately invested, they have a long-term perspective that draws the protege into the larger, systemic awareness crucial to the ability to see oneself not only in relation to work and profession, but to the society and the global commons as a whole. As the following Interlude portrays, mentors recognize the promise of young adult lives and give clues to finding practical pathways into adult commitments.

People tend to be drawn to mentors who know or have experienced something that they sense they need to learn. In times of rapid and discontinuous change, however, the wisdom young adults need has often not yet been sufficiently cultivated by the older generation. Young people seeking work in the new commons may require, for example, new multicultural awareness and new technical skills along with the ability to cross the boundaries of discrete departments, disciplines, organizations, and sectors. It is often difficult to find mentors who can accompany them, much less serve as beacons of possibility. Nevertheless, they may be well served by adults who are willing to mentor by working shoulder to shoulder, providing good and wise company into territory unfamiliar to both.

Mentoring Environments

If one is to enter the world of adult work as it *now is,* a mentor who can "teach you the ropes" and "help you climb the corporate ladder" may be enough. We have come to believe, however, that if young adults are to form and act on a vision of society *as it could become,* they may well require more than a mentor alone. In a complex age of cultural transition, a *mentoring environment* may be even more significant. For young adults need to know that if they choose the road less travelled, they will not be alone. There must be the promise of a new sociality. The questions of love and work, partners and purpose are intimately linked.

In a mentoring environment a number of strategic influences are accessible to young adults. These include *mentors* with complementary strengths and perspectives who gather around great questions and important tasks; *a diverse group of friends and colleagues* who share *common challenges and hopes*; and *resources* such as time, critical learning experiences, texts, and, when necessary, equipment, technical skills, and other knowledge. A mentoring environment that serves the formation of commitment extends the influence of the mentor and creates expectations not simply of "my career" but rather "our common work on behalf of the larger good."

Though the lives of some who are committed to the common good appear lonely or even heroic, more often than not during their young adult years they were part of a mentoring community, sometimes several. This experience seems to have anchored a confidence that, though they may not have remained in direct contact, many others share the dream and the work.

College and the Cultivation of Commitment

The dynamics of home and pilgrimage continue into the young adult years, but now the task is to begin a pilgrimage that will return to a new home—a place in the adult world. Higher education is not the only route to adult commitment, and a college education was not a selection criterion for our study. Yet all but two of our one hundred core interviewees turned out to be college educated, though not all had completed their degrees at traditional ages. Many have had further education. We believe that another study of committed lives could yield a larger percentage of people who have not completed college,[33] but, at least in principle, a college or university represents the elements of a good mentoring environment, helping people to cultivate the thinking, social, and technical skills needed in the new commons, and can be a primary catalyst in galvanizing adult commitment to the common good.[34] An effective college education includes experiences that challenge unexamined assumptions, sustain more complex understandings of oneself and others, and enable students to form commitments in a relativized world.[35]

Good mentoring environments often exhibit this cultural sophistication and yet are small enough to allow for individual attention. Tracy Flanagan found that her chosen school, small and near a major city, provided this and more.

In sophomore year, I was ready to leave school—just didn't know what I was doing. Some of the people were extremely bright, but here we were in college being handed Nietzsche, and questioning: "What does it all mean?" But I had wonderful, mind-opening teachers. I met Dorothy Day and Rollo May. It was in college that I first had the sense of myself as a whole person.

Barbara Fox was also initiated into the wider life of the commons during the college years.

I had my most important interracial, international experience of my life when I was a senior in college. The Hollingsworth Fellowship sponsored young people from all over the world, and our theme was: "World peace can be brought about only by world understanding." You can't understand people unless you live with them. The experience came at the time in life when it's needed most, when you're developing your philosophy for life.

Combined with great teachers, such experiences can be profound. Erik Norris, a career diplomat and ambassador, recalled a political science teacher and his spouse who invited students to their home, awakening Erik's awareness of politics, and a "very demanding but inspiring" French professor who "made me focus on values."

And recall Bill Wallace. When he went to California with Davis, he became "totally discouraged" with his dissertation. The theoretical part went easily, but the exacting electrical experiments were impossible. "I just couldn't do it, and I finally gave up in total frustration." For the first time in his life he had failed, and "it was devastating." His mentor just encouraged him to continue the defense work instead and then casually added, "If you're going to quit your dissertation, why don't you give me your notebooks and stuff? I might want to look at this again."

Bill handed over the notebooks and went to work full time, helping to design what he believed was a defensive system for nuclear weapons, missile shields using carbon materials to protect the nosecone from a radar signature. "It was very exciting work," he told us, "if you didn't have to think about what you were doing." But some "internal part" of him inconveniently "bubbled up." He did have to think about it. It did not take him long to realize that the work was not defensive but rather "offensive as hell." After six months he went to Davis and said, "I can't work on this."

Handing back the notebooks, Davis said, "Bill, I saved your thesis stuff, why don't you just take a look at it again—we should at least write an article about it so it doesn't get lost." Bill completed the dissertation within a month. "If it weren't for Davis," he chuckles, "I'd have thrown that thing away."

The Critical Years: Finding Work in the World
As Bill Wallace's story dramatizes, young adults need mentors and mentoring

environments to usher them into the world of adult work.[36] College may be an initial mentoring environment, but graduation can be a critical juncture. A job? Graduate or professional school? Travel? The choices are life-determining.

Keenly attuned to the manifold "mentoring voices" of their culture, young adults may turn to the voices of "realism" if their aspirations are met with indifference, cynicism, or even ridicule. "Work that really matters" may be replaced by "compensation that I can count on," as the young adult steps into the untried terrain of adult life.[37]

In contrast, R. Lowell Rankin, a foundation officer who negotiates complex financial arrangements for inner city renewal, remembers:

> In my senior year I had that funny feeling that everyone knew exactly what they were going to do with the rest of their lives, and I wasn't quite sure why I didn't, and I wasn't fully willing to admit to myself or anyone else that I didn't. And law school sounded pretty good to me, although I took both business and law school tests. My roommate and best friend was going to law school, and it seemed like a reasonable thing to do, though I guess as I look back, I must have been ill at ease with that decision.
>
> That Spring, about seven or eight of us signed up for a wonderful guy, a historian, who offered an elective course on Nigeria that met at a coffee house. Then I remember hearing about the Peace Corps. I told myself, "I'll take the Peace Corps test because it seems to be a national political development." I persuaded myself I was taking it just out of intellectual curiosity.
>
> Later my father called and said, "You have a telegram here from Sargent Shriver, and it says you've been accepted to go into the Peace Corps in Guinea." I had never heard of it. I went home and my father said, "Why don't you call the law school and see what they say?" I think he thought I'd be talked out of it. I called them and they basically said, "Go. You've got a place here when you come back." So once the law school had said you'll be even more interesting to us then, I decided I'd do it.
>
> The Peace Corps was a wonderful time to see what I could do on my own. It was two of the most educational and intense years of my life. I taught secondary school, was thrilled about the kids I was working with and their potential. It was an opportunity to do anything and everything. I worked on developing a library. I was very much caught up in the Peace Corps ethic that we were there to do good, and yet a lot of reality set in. We may have done some good, but what Africa did for us has created a lifetime debt.

Very few of our interviewees completed young adulthood still floundering. Peace Corps, travel, some graduate and professional programs, the feminist and civil rights movements, and some early jobs all provided mentoring environments for the formation of young adult commitments to the larger good. For some it was earlier and for others later, but by an average age of twenty-six, most had chosen a path through which they could serve the common good, though not all were engaged in the specific work that eventually became their life work. And, generally, the evolution of their commitment was gradual.[38] Thus, one person served as a Navy nurse for several years before developing a multi-service health center in a small coastal city; another cared for her family before becoming a teacher and later an educational reformer; another was drawn from the formal study of economics into community finance and development.

Deepening Commitment

While most had found their vocation by the end of their twenties or early thirties, some experienced later periods of significant deepening or reorientation. A future philosopher and environmentalist suffered severe depression in his late twenties, haunted by bottomless questions: "Why is there such destructiveness? What does a person do?" It was not until his mid-thirties that further study enabled him to build the kind of insight and response that has made him an important cultural leader and a great mentor. And only when Anita Cohen had children of her own did she develop the conviction that "the stories on television could be a lot better" and build an organization to address those issues. Cecil Baldwin, who had been shielded from the worst stings of racial prejudice said,

> It wasn't until I was in my forties, at the time of the Supreme Court Decision desegregating schools, that I suddenly grasped the enormous disservice placed upon black people, and the critical leadership of black churches—the lone institution that black people own, control, program, finance, and direct.

Mid-life Reordering

Mid-life often brings a press for a reordering of priorities and a still further deepening of the trust and agency that ground commitment. As with Bill Wallace, mid-life can be a time when one's wounds and one's power may be transformed yet again, now into a more mature wisdom and a new quality of contribution. As an awareness of mortality catches up with us and the future is no longer infinitely revisable, some recognize that the young adult dream was too partial, inadequate, or unmet, and lost years must be grieved. Unrealized potential, unfinished business, and unmet longings may well up—or be called to one's attention—and burst through the assumptions and armor plates of the years.

Yet there is the possibility of learning how to live in more life-bearing ways with whatever has been one's suffering and defeat—the things that will always hurt. Disappointments can clarify and reheal in the open air of full adult strength, releasing new energy to make good on the promise of life. If we attend to this inner work well, the essence of the young adult dream can resurface with potentially more mature power in the mid-life and later adult years.[39]

In the mid-life years, a few of those we studied changed the area of their commitment, taking up new agendas or searching out positions that would strengthen their influence. A number took time off to do the kind of reordering work just described. For most, the middle years brought with them an intensification of commitment. Said one person:

> In my twenties and thirties things were so complex I felt pretty overwhelmed. In my late forties, time is shorter, and I feel more at one with what I am doing. I feel more confidence in saying, "Yes, it's complex, I don't know how it's going to come out, but this is what I must do....Yes there's ambiguity, yes, there's paradox, yes, it's muddy. But we must do this."

Several women postponed this reordering until their fifties, then took on new commitments. They are still going strong in their seventies.[40] Marie Warner discovered that the university where her husband was a renowned scholar would not accept her for studies because she was forty-eight. She was so furious and vocal that the chancellor appointed her and several faculty members to a committee that started a continuing education center for women. Later, developing interests that both she and her husband could share, she became a docent at the city museum, then head of the program, then a trustee. Her minister, who was working to develop lay leadership, asked her to take major responsibility for adult education. This unexpectedly led her to develop a program for the homeless, eventually coordinating fifteen agencies. Some of the homeless have since become real friends. Now in her late seventies, she reflects:

> These people are my home. I grew up with all the superficial accoutrements of a privileged person—to be able to handle any social situation, especially as a woman and in the society I was in. Now the great joy is sloughing off all those layers, like an onion, to find that there's a me that is particularly able to relate and is lovable.

Virtually all of our older interviewees express a deepening confirmation of life. When we asked Ben Greystone, a pioneer in urban renewal still teaching public health at sixty-eight, what would be at stake if he quit his work, he responded:

When they offered me early retirement, I turned it down. There aren't many people in this school who teach this kind of stuff, and the students would lose. I'm not so egotistical as to think the world is going to stop because of me, but I have stirred up a hell of a lot and involved a lot of people in the process. But I think most of them can go on without me. I mean, it's hitting lately. You suddenly realize you've affected vast numbers of people. I came up with what we now call the "Vital Cities" program three decades ago. I see the state health officer and she says it's going to be the model for the state. I don't have to tell her what to do; she'll go on because of her values. There are a lot of people like this.

The Formative Power of Context

Most of the people we interviewed seem to recognize in their adult years that, just as they have been influenced by their own settings, in order to influence people they in turn must look to the shaping power of the contexts in which people live. Thus, a United Nations worker observed that for programs to be successful "you have to create an environment in which people are going to have more say in their lives." And an attorney told us, "Most people most of the time are not going to be heroes, so we need to create the conditions in which they can be their best; we need to structure certain kinds of rules that make us decent to each other."

Who Are My Partners?

No one has a vocation alone.[41] One of our strongest findings is that whether single or married, virtually everyone spoke of the importance of partners—kindred spirits—who share and help sustain the work. They may be family members, friends, former schoolmates, professional colleagues, or members of the same religious community. Often geographically dispersed, they are linked by mail, telephone, fax, meetings, common projects, e-mail—but most of all by a connection of heart and mind. As one person put it, "They are the people you call (or sometimes just think about) when you are down, when you are up, when you are just trying to muddle through." They provide perspective, comfort, advice, challenge, and most of all, the confirmation that one is not alone in the sometimes bone-aching, heart-weary commitment to the new commons.

Single, Married, Partnered

Twenty-four percent of the core group had never married or were divorced; sixty-seven percent were married, some for the second time; four had taken religious vows of celibacy and chastity; and three were partnered. Single, unpartnered people tended to be clear that the choice to be single was a good one for them. Being single enabled them, they said, to give more of themselves to the work—though some felt a certain stigma in a coupled world. Those who were married to spouses who shared their commitments likewise believed that their choice strengthened the quality of their work. We did hear, however, a complex, ambiguous kind of pain voiced by some whose spouses did not share their commitments.

Most of the divorced women had found their work hard to sustain within their marriages and had either found it difficult or chosen not to remarry. In most cases, divorced men remarried partners who shared their commitments. Most of the long-married women described partnerships in which they had shared collaborative work with their spouses from the start.[42]

Among those partnered in some form, most spoke of "a rich give and take," emotional support, and challenging conversations.[43] In several cases, the partners help keep them honest. "She tells me I am not Jesus," said one man dryly. Another felt her husband's recognition and support were crucial to her commitment, though they do not directly share the same work.

Those who were parents often conveyed that their children (and grandchildren) helped to ground their commitment. Surely not all lives need to be lived out in families, traditionally understood. But our study strongly suggests that some form of responsibility to particular others, or work that corresponds to the challenges and joys that marriage and children can bring fosters the development of the self-knowledge, perspective, and passion that nourishes committed citizenship.

Threshold People and Hospitable Space

Reflecting on the experiences and conditions that shaped the lives of our interviewees, it is clear that no single event or influence will ensure a committed life. Moreover, no one life includes all the contributing factors we identified. Some lives might have had only a few powerful formative experiences; others might have been shaped by many less intense ones. Taken in combination, however, it does appear that certain experiences increase the likelihood of forming the citizens we need in the twenty-first century.

We see two master patterns: trustworthy and transformational relationships with *threshold people*, and *hospitable spaces* within which those relationships may develop and new forms of agency be practiced. Together these serve as powerful antidotes to negative forms of individualism and tribalism, enabling committed people to act positively and dwell with confidence in the midst of all of life's confounding richness.

Threshold people include:
- loving parents who care for the wider world;
- welcoming and diverse neighbors, teachers, and other children;
- peers and additional adults who nourish loyalty and positive purpose in the adolescent years;
- mentors who challenge, support, and inspire young adults;
- spouses, partners, and other family members who share common commitments;
- children and grandchildren who embody the promise and responsibilities of the future;
- professional colleagues and other kindred spirits who provide good company and invigorate vision.

Hospitable and safe spaces include:
- A home where trust and agency are nourished, hospitality is practiced, and the wider world is present;
- A neighborhood where it is safe to explore and discover different places and people;
- A community both within and beyond the neighborhood where physical, emotional, and intellectual safety is protected, and meaningful participation occurs;
- Intensive learning environments where group interaction is cultivated, responsibility is learned from shared tasks, and everyday experience can be brought into dialogue with larger meanings;
- Institutional environments (for example, day care centers, schools, youth groups, religious organizations, museums, libraries, recreational programs, and work places) that sponsor positive forms of belonging and learning, cultivate an awareness of living on the global commons, and teach that it is possible to contribute to the larger public good;
- Places that provide for reflection and renewal in adult life and thus enhance the deepening of commitment.

A Key Element

While no single experience can ensure a committed life, we found one common thread in the life experience of everyone we studied. We devote the next chapter to elaborating what we call *a constructive engagement with otherness*. In the story of Jo Chapman, we see a person who has made a choice to go "through the Trap" and build bridges between people who are in some respects very different, yet who inevitably share the new commons. We have learned that a constructive encounter with others who are significantly different from oneself is key to the development of a capacity for trustworthy belonging and confident agency in a diverse and complex world, a capacity that transcends the traps of individualism and tribalism and enables people to become at home in the new commons.

compassion

Living Within and Beyond Tribe

Through the Trap

Rising some twenty-five feet, the north wall parallels the Interstate for a quarter of a mile. Daily, thousands of commuters speed past it on their way into and back from the city. At either end, a guard tower marks the corner. From there the wall cuts south, finally enclosing some ten acres and twelve hundred men convicted of everything from burglary and fraud to rape, extortion, and murder. Several times a month now for eleven years, Joanna Chapman has driven the mile and a half from her gracious colonial home in suburban Quincy to the Barton Penitentiary parking lot at the base of the wall. The guards at the reception office know her well and no longer demand identification papers. But otherwise the procedure of going through "the Trap" into the compound remains the same time after time. Tonight she is bringing Professor Michael Carlyle, a sociologist, to speak to the inmates. She has invited us to join them.

The benches bolted to the tile floor of the large waiting room are nearly empty. We cross to the far side and greet Jo and the Professor standing by a glass wall. On the other side of the wall, guards move easily, laughing soundlessly at some private joke. At the window, a man slides an aluminum clipboard under the rim. We sign our names under a list of a dozen or so others. Then, pointing to a phone beside us, he picks up his phone and asks for our driver's licenses. We hold them up against the glass. Squinting to make out a resemblance between the pictures and their owners, he recoils in mock horror. We laugh, relieved, and he waves us on.

Jo shows us to a wall of lockers. "You have to empty your pockets," she says. "Everything?" we ask. "Everything," she replies. Change, keys, pocketknife. Handkerchief? Handkerchief. "You have to be able to pull out your pockets."

Eventually we are ushered to a huge, red steel door by a young man with "Rec Staff" on his blue sweatshirt. He introduces himself as Brad. "Ever been through the Trap before?" he asks. "No," we reply. "Hmmm," he smiles enigmatically and turns away. "It's a good thing you didn't wear jeans," Jo remarks. "The prisoners wear jeans, so visitors can't wear them."

We wait for several minutes for the timed door to open. When it finally does, we enter a small room the size of a garage with a high ceiling. The far wall is a sliding portcullis of gray bars between huge plates of glass. Stencilled in large letters on the glass are the words, "Keep hands off."

Overhead, rows of dark windows look down on us. We remove our belts and shoes and step through a metal-detecting arch like those at airports. A sudden electronic snarl goes through us like a shock. "You wearing a watch?" asks the attendant. She takes it, examines it closely, then hands it back on the other side of the arch. We slip into our shoes and replace our belts. After another short wait, the bars rumble aside, and we move down the corridor, through another set of bars, through another steel door, into a maze of yellow concrete hallways, and finally to an armored door opening into the icy February night. Above us on either side, concrete walls slope steeply upwards to a guard tower. We have come through the wall into the compound itself.

"We got off easy," Jo whispers as we walk swiftly past a row of low brick buildings. "Usually they would have made you leave the watch there." We turn into one of the buildings, wind our way through more corridors, more bars, and emerge finally into what feels like a small gymnasium, though a loose assortment of books on steel shelves suggests a library. Forty or fifty folding steel chairs are set in rows facing a podium. Above the podium hangs a large painted mural of a scene in Vietnam: surrounded by ominous jungle, an infantryman in fatigues carrying an automatic weapon looks warily about for VC.

Professor Carlyle goes up to check out the podium, and slowly the chairs fill with men dressed in denim, some still wearing their standard issue blue wool navy caps. They slouch in the chairs easily. Several come over to speak to Jo. "Thank you for bringing the professor, Mrs. Chapman," says one man with exquisite politeness. "We remember him from last year." A guard sits nearby on the other side of a counter, indifferently reading a tool catalogue. Periodically, his radio squawks something loud and indecipherable. Nobody seems to notice. Jo moves about the room efficiently, checking with Carlyle, conversing with Brad, and chatting softly with the inmates as they arrive. We watch the prisoners, who, because of tonight's topic, are all African-American men, most between twenty-five and thirty-five years old. Some look like executives, some reveal long wasted years—each, we realize, represents a tragedy. At 7:45, about two-thirds of the chairs are filled; Jo asks for attention and introduces the evening speaker.

"We have a real treat tonight. You remember Professor Carlyle from Harvard who spoke last year? You were so enthusiastic about his talk that we invited him to come again. I'm sure you will enjoy him as much this time. Professor Carlyle?"

Michael Carlyle rises with a smile, looks over his audience, and begins. "The topic of our discussion is 'Malcolm and Martin—What Have They to Say to Us Today?'"

Above him, to one side of the mural a black MIA flag sways softly. Above that, a row of windows looks down on us. It appears that they do not open to the outside. The radio continues to snarl periodically.

"A lot of people feel that Martin did the most for black people." He scans the room for nods, but the men are impassive. "And then, a lot feel that Malcolm was more important." A few of the men glance at one another. "But, you see, I don't think either one of these men was important by himself. You have to see them both together." He shakes his clasped hands in front of his chest as he says this. "Together."

The men are listening now. He goes on to speak of the particular contribution that each made to the larger community. From time to time we hear "All right," "Yessir," even "Amen." Carlyle's father was a Baptist preacher and the style was not lost on him. As he moves into his talk it almost seems that his Georgia accent thickens. Several of the men lean on the chairs ahead of them, alert now.

Carlyle keeps the talk short and never talks down. He closes with his final point. "Malcolm was always trying to change individuals; Martin was trying to change society. You have to do both if you want real progress. It's important to change an individual who thinks there's no hope, and it's important to change the system that destroys hope. You have to do both."

After his presentation, there are questions. Almost all begin with a brief note of respect and thanks to Carlyle for coming. An older man, missing several teeth, rises, removing his cap as he speaks. "You've talked about how these men worked to help others, but you have to help yourself or it won't do no good, right?" And Carlyle replies, "Sure, but you also have to ask for help. You can't do it alone!" And to make sure the point gets across, he repeats it, adding "You can only help people with people," clapping each syllable home as he speaks.

A younger man with a scar across his eye challenges: "Why didn't Martin and Malcolm get together in the sixties and work for all the people?"

"Well, what do you think?" Carlyle replies, parrying. Several men look eager; one raises his hand. "I read Malcolm's autobiography and they were both religious in their own ways. They needed each other, but they didn't know it." Carlyle nods and says that there were a lot of political pressures at the time pulling them apart. Another man comments that economic pressures also tear people apart. Others nod.

Then one of the men who remembered Carlyle from the year before, a clean-cut man in his early forties stands up. "A lot of people get hung up on whose holocaust is biggest. But what about the children? I was in Vietnam for two years, and I saw a lot of pretty terrible things, but I haven't seen anything as bad as it is with the kids in the streets right here. We've got to get our morals back. If we can't do that, all the money in the world won't make no difference. How can we be part of the solution instead of part of the problem?" He says this last with a conscious rhetorical flourish and garners a smattering of applause. Another man then stands up: "We hear so much about problems in our communities, especially with the younger brothers—drugs, rapes, kids getting killed. As a black man, what are your solutions?"

Carlyle strokes his chin and says, "Among other things, I think you've got to organize the churches. One of the saddest things is that the African-American community has walked away from religion—its greatest asset. Why don't you invite some black ministers to come here and talk with you about what is needed out there?" They discuss this idea for a few moments, then he glances at his watch and at the guard no longer absorbed in his catalogue. "Well, I think it's about that time."

He thanks them for inviting him, and there is a warm round of applause, genuine smiles from the men. This was a good evening, that's clear.

Jo walks confidently to the front of the room, all poise. But her eyes are moist. She thanks Carlyle again, then, "Before we break, I want to announce another opportunity we have coming up. Have you guys heard about the *Alternatives to Violence* program?" There are a few nods, but most faces are blank.

"It's a weekend course. . . ." Then she corrects herself. "Well, not really a course; it's an experience. It includes people from outside, and the idea is to develop other ways of acting instead of violence. It's not just talk. So if you want to sign up, you must be ready to share. What you put in, you'll get out. The program is used all over the country and everybody says it is the best experience you'll ever have. Without doubt, it was one of the best I've had, myself." Her advocacy is genuine; she has told us earlier that the experience is at least as transformative for participants from the Quincy community as for the inmates. "Sign up over here. And thanks for coming!"

The men rise and mill about. Most move slowly out of the library. A small knot surrounds Carlyle, and the clean-cut man talks with Jo about a college course he wants to take when he gets out shortly. "They're taking me back at my old job," he tells her, "and this time I'm going to do it right."

Outside, we make our way through the sharp cold, talking about Carlyle's idea for bringing the ministers in. Swiftly reaching the wall, we wait impatiently until we are ushered back through the Trap. This time, it seems to go more quickly, and in no time we are bidding farewell as we head for our cars. Overhead, the stars snap crisply.

In a different age, Quincy's Main Street would be swept every day. Trimmed curbs, generous sidewalks, crusty maples and elegant, preserved elms speak of an attention to tradition that self-consciously reflects the town's patrician roots. Just down the street from the birthplace of John Adams is the Chapman house, one of the antiques on the street. Brick with white wood trim, it carries a modest "1832" above the handsome Georgian door. A few days after our evening at the prison, we open the low, iron gate and walk up the brick path.

Jo greets us warmly at the door. An attractive woman in her late forties, wearing casual slacks and a hand-knit sweater, she mirrors the simple elegance of the neighborhood. Taking our coat, she ushers us into the living room where we are welcomed by her grandmother's silver tea set and a plateful of almond cookies.

"Can you tell us more about your work and how you came to it?" we ask.

"The work I value most is working in the prison," she begins. "Expanding opportunities for inmates, doing educational programs. My work is to connect people from the community with the educational programs in the prison. We now have over 150 volunteers who offer programs for hundreds of inmates: tutoring in literacy, GED, English as a Second Language, Health Issues, Job Search, Anger Management, Calligraphy . . . you name it." She pauses for a moment. "But you know, that's only half of it. It's a dual goal, really—educating the people on the inside, but also enabling people on the outside to see the humanity of the people in the prison. It's really about making connections across the walls, about feeling the self-worth of everybody and of caring and supporting each other."

"That must be interesting in a community like this," we observe, pointedly glancing across at the large oil painting over the carved oak mantlepiece. Her quick laugh melts into a canny smile.

"Oh yes. People look at me and see the wife of a successful physician. I like that. They are usually a bit startled when I start talking about the prison. But they do respond. At first, they come in wearing their social service hats and their angel halos and are all set to do good for the inmates. One of the greatest thrills that I have is seeing them receive instead of just giving."

"What kinds of things do they receive?" we ask.

"Just the basic surprises," she replies. "You know, when you are from a privileged background and you first come into a roomful of prison inmates, you see only a group of men dressed in dark denim pants and jackets with white shirts. Every face seems the same, and you don't even distinguish individuality of build. But in reality they're all different—black, Hispanic, white. Some come from well-off families, others never had a chance. Everyone has his own private and painful story.

"Most people enter expecting them to be tough or stupid or mysterious. Everything conspires to have you see what you expect to see, and by the time you have gone through the Trap, you feel that everyone is suspicious of everyone else. But as you begin to actually look at the prisoners and make eye contact, in most, you see a softness around their eyes. There is hurt and real pain. Not ugly or intimidating—not meanness, but softness." She stops for a moment in thought, then adds, "It is not so much that each man has a secret he is fiercely withholding, as a question he is silently and warily asking. 'Why are you here, and how do you see me?'"

Then she observes that if the class being offered to the prisoners is about something like money management, or drawing, or something else that is primarily technical in nature, it takes time to get past the awkwardness, the notknowing, the sense of distance. On the other hand, if the class is about something like managing emotions, or parenting, "You get through the discomfort in about two minutes." The feelings come through raw and poignant, and a human bond is formed between teacher and student, volunteer and inmate.

"These prisoners are human beings who are anxious to move on. Many are ill-educated, most struggle with addiction, but they also have goals and aspirations that are just as real as our own." She holds us with her eyes as she says this. She means it.

Jo is particularly gratified by the success of the "Alternatives to Violence" program in which Quincy residents spend sixteen hours with a group of inmates over a weekend. "It's very intense. We talk about the roots of anger, how to deal with it, and the transforming power that can come from anger. People from this community very quickly realize that they could have been in prison too, because their own anger has been just as powerful, and they have as many problems in dealing with it. So there's a lot of commonality that they begin to share and feel."

"So how does someone like you get involved in a prison?" we ask.

"Well, I guess I've had this philosophy all my life about giving back to society in some form or another. I was trained as a schoolteacher, taught first grade, and stopped when my daughters needed me at home. When we moved to Quincy, we went to the Unitarian Church. The girls were in school by then, so I looked over the committees and saw 'Social Action Committee.'

"I went to the meeting and I'll never forget it because it just blew my mind. I expected to be part of a group to plan activities. But the chair of the committee just said, 'This committee operates a little differently than most committees—each one of us dreams up our own project and does it.' So instead of becoming part of a group I was out there by myself trying to figure out what to do."

"You didn't just turn off and never come back?" we ask.

"No. I thought, 'Well, okay, what am I going to do as a project?' We lived not too far from the prison, and I was curious about it. So I went over and met the superintendent and told him that I was to do a project for my church and did he have anything for volunteers to do?

"Looking back on it," she laughs, "it must have been hysterical. Here's Miss Goody-Goody Two Shoes coming in, and he had no idea what to do with me. But he said they could use some curtains in the infirmary. So I said, fine. And I didn't even know how to sew!"

Jo went back home, pulled together a group of women, and they sewed a barrage of sunny, yellow curtains. Later, they hung Christmas decorations in the dining hall. Before long, they had involved several other churches. They did a show of the men's art, wrote a weekly newspaper column, established links with the library, lobbied at the State House. Ultimately, her network became the established funnel for local funds; they developed courses inside the walls, and perhaps most importantly, helped to educate people outside the walls by bringing them through the Trap.

Jo's movement over the years from gathering curtains to gathering energy, time, and money from the community was not without its struggles and doubts. "Prison administrations change," she tells us, "and sometimes the doors are closed to volunteers. Like right now, the superintendent is great, but he has to work in a system where budgets are being cut and at the same time stretched to fill gaps of tragic proportions. The public mood is that prisoners should just bust rocks. They've just taken TV away and cut back on our courses. It's hard when you see people who have had their first positive learning experience suddenly abandoned. Sometimes the waste is overwhelming. And it's sad to see how the stresses on the guards have some of the same consequences—alcoholism, broken homes, limited hopes—all of which play out on the prisoners. The whole system costs far more than the budget can ever show. We have to keep asking ourselves who we can really help." She pauses and looks down for a moment.

"Yet sometimes I'm my own challenge. I've always had a lot of insecurity. I've always thought of myself as reticent about speaking out . . . I find I'm always telling myself that I can be better, that I'm never quite good enough. But it's also one of the things that propels me to keep going. That and seeing the ones who make it—and the people in the community who change.

"People have come to work in the prison who you'd never think would set foot in one. The backgrounds and expertise they have are really amazing. And some become transformed people. Several have redirected their careers because of their experience at the prison, and most come to understand issues of crime very differently than they did before."

"So you are a kind of bridge?"

"That's my greatest joy. And you can see a kind of ripple effect. I have people coming up to me all the time saying, 'I know the kind of things you're doing at the prison and some day I'll get involved.' It astounds me. At least, they know it's there."

According to the brochure, the purpose of Barton Penitentiary Outreach is to provide educational programs for the inmates. But the larger truth is captured by a logo of clasped hands linking "programs in the prison" with "programs in the community." Thus, Jo's story is an important moral tale, not because it is a story of noblesse oblige, which it is, but because it is a story of people encountering each other across conventional social boundaries and learning to see one another in more truthful and responsible ways.

"Morality begins precisely when my egoism has been called into question, and I learn to take the other into account," says Thomas Ogletree.[1] According to Jo, almost without exception, the people from her community who have moved through the Trap say that what they have learned is how human the inmates are. They have learned how to "take the other into account." Conversely, prisoners have learned that townspeople are also more human than their stereotypes have allowed. Jo and her colleagues have found a way to bring together people of very different backgrounds to discover a shared humanity. This discovery of shared bonds lies at the heart of commitment to the common good.

A Constructive, Enlarging Engagement Beyond Tribe

The single most important pattern we have found in the lives of people committed to the common good is what we have come to call *a constructive, enlarging engagement with the other*. It is the primary dynamic that drives the evolution described in the previous chapter, and it appeared at some point during the formation of the commitment of everyone in our sample. We had not anticipated this finding, but early in the study as people told us their stories, we began to hear about important encounters with others significantly different from themselves. On the surface, the forms of difference were variable. But when we examined this pattern more closely, the differences that were significant in the formation of commitment to the common good were differences defined by "tribe."

The Importance of Tribe

A sense of tribe is deeply embedded in the human soul. All of us are appropriately dependent upon and interdependent with networks of belonging.[2] Grounded in the quest for survival and security, millennia of human existence in bands and tribes have fundamentally shaped our attitudes and behaviors as a species. Yet, as one church executive told us,

In a technological society "tribe" becomes a dirty word, suggesting something wild, uncivilized, unlearned. But using it as a negative word is a problem. Our folklore, our power, our history, our legacy, our community connections all come from life in tribes. Tribes may be the only source of power that we have. The problem is that whites don't seem to know that they are a tribe too. Whites too often think, "We are normal individuals, you are a tribe."

So we use the word "tribe" with caution, as a metaphor to acknowledge an aspect of human evolution at the core of our social identity. Our prosperity as social beings is woven by patterns of kinship, mutual assistance, and affection. Despite individualism's triumph, the industrial revolution, the power of nation states and international corporations, nothing has finally erased the human need to belong, to share an identity with others whom we recognize as "like me" and "one of us."[3]

In an increasingly complex society, many people today belong to several tribes. Our sense of connection may be based on family of origin, ethnicity, geographical region, nationality, religion, or language. But tribal bonds can also be grounded in profession, lifestyle, economic class, education, sports, or participation in a particular institution such as a corporation, place of worship, firm, labor union, university, or club. Within these broad tribal loyalties, we may further tribalize into factions such as sales or production, Crips or Lords, faculty or administration, liberal or conservative, old or young, jock or nerd, Cowboys or Forty-niners.

The Trap of Tribalism

A sense of belonging and participating in a meaningful tribe is how we first begin to identify ourselves as a part of a larger social whole. But every network of belonging has its limits—boundaries that you may not cross if you still want to belong.

Invariably there are tensions between loyalty to our own tribal networks and faithfulness to larger, more inclusive commitments. But the power of tribe need not be antithetical to the need for a wider commitment to the new commons—the common good that reaches beyond tribe. Indeed, we believe that those who best practice a commitment to an inclusive common good are paradoxically those who can simultaneously reach across tribes and remain firmly rooted in the particularities of their own. It is not a question of relinquishing our tribal identities. Rather, the work is to recognize when the virtue of tribe becomes the trap of "tribal*ism*." As we are concerned with it here, tribalism exists whenever the rules for "them" are different than they are for "us." When we would tolerate "them" being treated in a manner we would not condone for "our own," we are living within firm tribalist bonds. Tribalism becomes particularly toxic when those we regard as different and outside are subordinated, stigmatized, and perceived as either threatening or of no account. As Ronald Marstin has suggested, justice is a matter of who is included and who is excluded; justice is a matter of who and what we can tolerate neglecting.[4]

The capacity of the people we studied to live both within and beyond tribe appears to have been significantly shaped by their engagement across differences that were sometimes dramatic, sometimes subtle. But always the storytellers would describe some event or experience of "otherness" that jolted their idea of who they were and where they stood in the world, challenging their previously held assumptions about who was "one of us" and who was not. This kind of constructive, enlarging experience with the other counters the tribal fear of the outsider and tills the ground in which a seed of commitment—not just to me and mine, but to a larger, more inclusive *common* good—can be planted.

Encounter with "Otherness"

The encounters with otherness described by those we studied took many forms. An artist who has established a nationally recognized program enabling the elderly rural poor to realize their artistic talents spent his childhood in a lively mix of European cultures in Chicago; a housing advocate grew up in Denver but became friends with girls from Mexico during a Scouting Jamboree; a prominent civil rights leader was confined with asthma as a child and read about people from other countries; and a man who has spent over fifty years working for peace was reared in an upper-class WASP community, yet became best buddies with an Italian boy "from across the tracks" and fell in love with an Irish Roman Catholic girl.

But the differences were not only in ethnicity or nationality. Some had family members or friends who were "other" because of a disability or mental illness. A woman, who now works with the homeless, traces her commitment to having been asked by her teacher to care for retarded children in her school. The experience helped her to get over "the initial fear you get of people who are so significantly different." And in a few cases, the "other" was not another human. One person described the importance of learning to care for abused animals, and another spoke movingly of how his encounter with dolphins enlarged his understanding of both communication and intelligence.

How significant the difference was varied with the spoken and unspoken definitions of their own tribe. But whatever its particular form, the encounter challenged some earlier boundary and opened the way to a larger sense of self and world.

Most of the people we studied described encounters that occurred early in their lives, and for some it was a feature of life from the beginning. One in five of our interviewees grew up with parents who differed in ethnic, religious, or political loyalties. But schools were where children most often encountered difference. Sometimes this occurred informally, and sometimes through the curriculum. When teachers managed the engagement with otherness well, when the schools made an explicit attempt to communicate the value of these encounters to the children, and when families were supportive, more profound engagement and learning was possible.

A talented cross-cultural educator was in the middle grades during the civil rights movement.

> In our neighborhood, houses were being bombed because people had sold to black families. My classroom was one of the first classrooms that had a black student come into it, and it was sort of the highlight of the Young Christian Student Movement. They were trying to get us early—at ten and eleven years of age—into relationships with children from other cultures and racial backgrounds. And my parents were always very encouraging and supportive of that, as was my extended family as well.

Sometimes, however, such encounters did not occur until college. In the dorm, classroom, theater, a study abroad program, or on the athletic field,[5] a Presbyterian prep school boy for the first time met a Jew, a middle-class black student learned Spanish in Mexico, a Midwestern farm boy ran up against Eastern elitism. And for a few, it was as adults that they first had a significant encounter with someone "other": on the first job, in the military, in the Peace Corps, in an urban law partnership, or with a prison reform project in graduate school.[6]

When Georgia-born, African-American Shirley Reeves, who later became an equal housing advocate, walked into her first job and found herself plucking chickens next to a white girl, "It was like, 'You're kidding!'" But they became good friends. Later when she joined the Navy, boot camp underlined the lesson.

> Believe me, when you're in boot camp, you're equal. You built relationships because you were away from home, and for some of those girls it was the first time—the homesickness and all. It was just the beginning of people seeing you as you are, that you are a person, that you bleed red just like everybody else. That was a real turning point for me, and it started the transformation of my life.

In another instance, a young Maria Lopez set off for a women's conference in the Midwest prepared to feel culturally alienated among "gringas." Yet after considerable struggle, she returned with a new sense of common cause with other women, both Hispanic and gringa. While remaining loyal to her own tribe, she was able to begin a new dialogue across tribes.[7] Sharing experiences with women who were "other" enabled her to weave a new pattern of identity into her earlier one.

A Felt, Empathic Connection

Of itself, an encounter with otherness is hardly transformative. Many of us daily meet people from differing tribes and remain untouched, for when these encounters mesh well with our usual assumptions, our sense of self and tribe simply stays intact. Or if our experience is negative, we may even build our tribal walls higher. For the encounter to become a constructive engagement that fosters commitment to the common good, something more is needed.

As we sifted through dozens of accounts, it became apparent that what distinguished a simple encounter from a *constructive engagement* was that some threshold had been crossed, and people had come to feel a *connection* with the other. Through what Mary Watkins refers to as "sympathetic identification,"[8] they felt that the "other" experienced some fundamental aspect of life in the same way as they did.[9]

Leroy Meade, a black civil rights leader, recalled an incident when he was an officer with the American occupation forces in Germany after World War II. One of the clerks in his office, Dieter Langer, was a former German army officer. The two men became friends, and before long their families grew close as well. At one point all of their children came down with chicken pox, and Langer confessed that he was afraid his children might have infected Meade's. That moment marked a flash of recognition. "I saw that underneath Dieter Langer was a human being struggling with the same realities as I—he a German and I an American. But it was the same. He wanted for his children the same kind of world that I wanted for my children."

Though the critical element here is feeling—specifically, a feeling of empathic connection with the other—the nature of the particular feelings ranged widely. Sometimes cross-tribal bonds were formed by the shared joy of going through an intense experience together—international summer camp, a youth group project, or playing basketball on the same team. Or sometimes an empathic bond was formed out of sheer respect. Thus, as a teenager, Everett

Fuller, the son of a prominent New England family, worked for a summer picking carrots beside a deaf-mute Polish immigrant who taught him the simple and essential wisdom of personal integrity. Likewise, Rene LeTourneau, raised in an intellectual French Canadian family, shoveled coal for a summer with Sam, "a gorilla of a man," who revealed unexpected depths of insight while making "the most beautiful speeches about education I ever heard." In each of these instances, a former tribalism was challenged and the prior sense of "we" and "they" recomposed. This empathic recomposing of we and they makes possible a commitment to the *common* good, rather than simply to me and mine.

Not So Self-Evident

It may seem obvious that the ability to sense the feelings of others, to respect and respond to their emotional experience, is an important part of a willingness to cast one's lot with another. Indeed, the relationship between the capacity for empathy and caring for others has been well documented.[10] But in an individualistic and sometimes rationalistic society, this is not necessarily self-evident.

When we first began to share the emerging patterns of our study and described the salience of a constructive, enlarging engagement with the other across tribal boundaries, a thoughtful lawyer who had been involved for two decades in legal reform on behalf of disenfranchised groups, was skeptical. He could not recall an engagement with the other of that sort, he told us. Growing up in a homogeneous, upper-middle-class, secular Jewish environment, he had become socially committed, he believed, simply through political and intellectual conviction. After we explained further, he reflected, then asked: "Could it be a feeling?" He went on to say that when he had first become involved in civil rights work in the South as a young man, he had on one occasion found himself in a dangerous position where he recognized that he was as powerless and as vulnerable as a black person in that situation would be. "It was," he told us, "a terrible feeling." His encounter with otherness had not been a face-to-face meeting with a particular "other;" it had been a moment of *feeling* himself to be in the place of a people "other" than himself.

Many people also spoke of how reading expanded their awareness of the inner lives of others. We will revisit this observation in Chapter 5.

Compassion

The character and significance of this shared feeling with the other emerges clearly in Samuel and Pearl Oliner's study of the rescuers of Jewish Holocaust victims. The Oliners compared the empathy scores of rescuers with those of nonrescuers and found no particular differences between the two groups on such measures of shared feeling as affection, anxiety, pleasure, humor, or "a general susceptibility to others' moods." Only on one item did the rescuers stand out: "their tendency to be moved by pain. Sadness and helplessness aroused their empathy."[11]

Empathy is the ability to understand and share another's feelings. Compassion, the Oliners say, adds a "general sense of responsibility and tendency to make commitments." Somewhere in their lives, the rescuers had developed the capacity to connect with and to be moved by another's pain, but they also knew that they had a responsibility to others and the wherewithal to act on that sense of responsibility.

In a similar fashion, the committed citizens we studied could feel compassion, the capacity to "suffer with." What distinguished their encounters with otherness from the sort one might have as a tourist or in more casual encounters was a resonance with the particular suffering of the other and the capacity not only for empathy but for compassion which moves one to action.

Consider, for example, the story of Peteris Zieds, now a scientist working to create an ecologically sound future. Toward the end of World War II, at the age of sixteen, he was taken from his home in German-occupied Latvia, drafted into the retreating German army, and assigned to a hospital ship. The ship was horribly overcrowded. Wounded and dying German boys, most of them his own age, lay stashed in the hold. There were almost no doctors, and Peteris and his companions were pressed into service.

> They were wounded—half a head off, leg busted up, infected, smelling like hell, moaning without help. Nobody would come help. They were on the floors, you know, like fishes. So we were running all over the place trying to help them. You could barely go five minutes. You smell the blood and the decomposition and you pick up the shit and the urine and then go back up on deck and sniff the [fresh] air.

The experience was both disorienting and intense. On the one hand, the Germans were the enemy; on the other, they were just boys his own age—in terrible pain. Something shifted in Peteris.[12] "Somehow it became a human activity. It wasn't because of the war. It was people needing help, and it was very difficult because the atmosphere was very heavy. But somehow it had to be done. It didn't matter whether they were Germans or Turks or whatever."

When the ship docked, he emerged from the dark hull just as one of the dead was received by his grieving family—and he saw the whole scene in a larger light. "They put on his jacket. He was full with decorations, you know? Really a hero for the German army. All kinds of ceremony. Not an officer, just a sergeant going home to his native town. That was an incredible impression. You suddenly feel like everything looks so ridiculous."

For weeks afterward, he struggled to make sense of the contradictions as his unit was moved east, into the maw of the advancing Russian army. He recalls marching toward the front past wounded and dying soldiers streaming west. "It was incomprehensible; it was ridiculous. And this was not my war." So one day, with two days' rations—a slab of salami and a loaf of coarse bread extended with finely ground hay and sawdust—Peteris went AWOL.

A few days later, tired and hungry, he found himself walking through a quiet village, miles from the fighting. A small boy, perhaps five years old, sat near the side of the road, holding a large piece of black rye bread, slavered with butter and garnished with scallions. "And I was looking at the bread and looking at the bread and I thought 'I haven't eaten for years.' Such a nice bread!"

For his part, the boy was fascinated by the sight of a soldier in his village. As he passed, Peteris smiled, and they talked. Then the boy looked up at him, looked at the bread, and asked, "Do you want it?"

> So I took it. And I thanked him. And I went someplace quiet to eat my bread. And it was a kind of hope in that spontaneous sharing. For me he was a giver of bread, giver of life, and a child. He just offered it. And it pierced, you see, the cruelty I had seen and was living, the barbaric ways, and it was like a confirmation that bread, a sacrament.

Fifty years later, recalling that moment, Peteris weeps.

While not all of the encounters that move us to reorder our loyalties are this dramatic, it is important to underscore that the kind of engagement we seek to describe is not achieved simply by mere proximity to the other nor by sharing an enjoyment of the other's folklore, cuisine, or art. These forms of "meeting" may serve as important preludes. But the encounter that enlarges one's sense of connection and responsibility forges a recognition of a shared capacity for the feelings that lie at the core of our essential humanity: fear, joy, yearning, delight, suffering, hope, love.

If not discouraged, this sensibility can be present in the very young. Among those we studied, some were open from an early age to seeing, feeling, and consequently acting in response to another's suffering. For example, Dhan Kumar Basnayat, a social scientist working with the poorest people of Nepal, told us of an incident when, as a boy from a relatively privileged class, he was moved to give one of his only two pairs of shoes to an Untouchable man with a badly cut foot. Another time he dismayed his father by pawning a new watch to buy medicine for a poor woman. "I could never see people in trouble," he told us, "whatever kind of trouble—maybe not enough clothes, maybe in pain, maybe diseased—I could not just walk past and ignore them. I had to do something about it."

While such early encounters do not necessarily involve the complexity and strength of commitment that can occur later in life, they do seem to provide a kind of imprint, a felt sense of possibility. Whenever and however it occurs, a constructive engagement with otherness defuses tribal fear of the outsider, and for many anchors an enduring confidence in a wider belonging.

A Pattern of Engagement with Otherness

It would be misleading to convey the impression that an enlarging, constructive engagement with the other is typically a single event after which everything is dramatically different. For most, the encounters we have described are best understood as crystallized moments of memory in a larger pattern of engagement with otherness. Most typically, successive experiences over time create a way of being in the world which is continually open to rediscovering that "we" and "they" share common bonds.

Kate Hopkins is president of a state college located in one of the poorest counties in Maine. With intelligence and good humor she weathers budget cuts, shifting population patterns, and ongoing curricular development, while creating an environment of uncommon community involvement and global awareness on the part of both students and faculty. She also serves on a national board addressing women's issues in education and is part of an international team of American and Eastern European educators addressing common concerns. Listening to Kate's story, it was clear that multiple encounters beyond tribe have shaped her present commitments.

Kate Hopkins grew up Roman Catholic in what she describes as a homogenous, upper-middle class, essentially white urban community in Canada. But her parents "were very involved in charitable giving—both time and money." She remembers with her father "always going into very different neighborhoods from ours, dropping things off—hams, turkeys, and whatever." Her first and closest friend was a girl across the street. "She wasn't Catholic, so we could never go to school together, and we grew up knowing we couldn't be in each other's weddings." And many of her father's business associates were Jewish. "My parents went to bar mitzvahs and Jewish weddings, and Jews were guests in our home. I remember one man who ran a toy company, and he and his wife and two children would visit us. His wife had been in a concentration camp, and I'll never forget the numbers she had tattooed on her arm."

From the time she was nine, Kate's family spent summers in New Hampshire. There she saw rural poverty. She recalls riding along back roads to church on Sundays, bewildered to see people she had met in town during the week living in homes she could only describe as shacks.

When she was in high school, she followed in her mother's footsteps and became a volunteer at the hospital. Children came there from all over the world. She found it overwhelming that there were that many children in one place who needed hospitalization. "I also learned," she tells us, "about families that were very different than mine, obviously, because there were some very sick children whose parents never came to visit them."

In college, during a cultural exchange program she was introduced to black-white issues in the United States. "It was '66 or '67 and Stokeley Carmichael had just written *Black Power*, and we'd certainly never read any of that." Later after graduation, she went to work in upstate New York in children's welfare services. She looks back on her naivete with amazement, but her innocence cracked open one night during the uprising in the Attica prison. She went to a meeting in the neighborhood where she was working and found herself one of only two whites there. People were desperately trying to learn what was happening to their sons and relatives. Were they being killed? Were they killing? A local minister had gone to Attica to learn more, but he came back empty-handed.

"I was outraged that this could be going on," Kate says "What do you mean they can't find out where their sons are? All sorts of people had died and the whole thing was this unbelievable tragedy. These were people that I knew, people from the community where I was living and working."

Marginality

Sometimes *we* are the other. A number of the people in the sample grew up feeling marginal. Although "marginality" frequently carries a sense of being of lesser value,[13] living at the edge of one's tribe or society appears to contribute to the ability to move between tribes. Especially when parents, teachers, and others help to interpret difference in positive ways, marginality may place one in a position to recognize more easily the stranger next door.

Marginality functions differently, however, for those who have it thrust upon them than for those who choose it. Those who did not choose their marginal status often experience feeling *different* as a painful burden. They may feel trapped in their marginality—at best tolerated but not truly recognized, and at worst, sealed off and scorned. Many physically disabled people have felt this way, as have those who suffer from racial, sexual, class, or other prejudices.

Marginality often has a positive cast, however, when it arises from a valued form of difference. Feeling *special*, they move across boundaries with relative ease. They may feel special in their families or be part of a subgroup holding unique values that distinguish them in generally admirable ways from the rest of the tribe. Quaker young people, for instance, may identify with mainstream culture in many respects, yet know they are a part of a religious community that shares a respected heritage and expects them to practice an uncommon regard for others. We define the first type of marginality as "vulnerability-based marginality," and the second as "value-based marginality."

Vulnerability-Based Marginality

Three fifths of those we studied experienced marginality as a consequence of circumstance rather than choice: racial discrimination, sexual orientation, physical disability, intellectual or educational attainment, illness, family pain, poverty—or wealth. Often the suffering initially occurred when they were young children, and the ache went deep. For some a sense of marginality came from such circumstances as simply feeling too small, too fat, too smart—in some way simply too different. Whatever its source, among those we studied, it appeared that although few would wish it on others, most have been able to transform the pain of their marginality into a deepened capacity for compassion and a strength of identity and purpose. This has also been observed in an important study of women leaders who have promoted social change, suggesting that "early experiences of personal discrimination and acute awareness of social injustice were a source of subsequent commitment."[14]

We heard this form of marginality in our interview with Luisandra Hernandez, a physician who has received national recognition for her leadership in public health. For the first eighteen years of her life, she had to live with a heart condition that she knows would have been corrected in childhood had her family been wealthy. Nevertheless, her mother always expected and encouraged her to fulfill her highest potential. Years later when Luisandra came face to face with the gap in health care between rich and poor, both the sting and strength of her own experience led her to work as a physician for medical justice.

The potential power of vulnerability-based marginality was evident also in the story of Tom Emmons, a chemical engineer and former executive in a Fortune 500 company, who now works to enable the business sector to see its investment in issues of educational reform. When he was growing up, his parents valued education, but "we were considered part of the poor white trash strata, and I certainly would have been considered an 'at risk' student in many respects. In school, there were only two or three kids who were white and poor. Consequently, when I looked for relationships to build, I made friends with kids from other cultures and other religions—people who would accept me and look beyond my social and economic status. Many of them were 'outs' also. So the outs kind of got together and built relationships where you could be an 'in'."

He became valedictorian of his high school class, was admitted to Yale, Harvard, and MIT but received no scholarship money. A local grocer hired him for the summer and said, "Don't bother to go to college; just keep working here and some day you'll be able to manage a department." It made him "mad as hell." He got loans, managed to go to a university nearby, and eventually established a scholarship fund in his hometown. Recently, when he was an executive-in-residence at a small college "I was challenged by a black kid from the ghetto who assumed I was a rich Ivy Leaguer and said 'What can you teach me? I come from the ghetto.' So I told him my story, and we're still friends, because he was able to see the similarity—the analogy of his background and mine."

Vulnerability-based marginality can numb the will and fuel despair; it can also nourish compassionate action and fire an imagination of possibility. We will examine the factors that make the difference in Chapter 6.

Value-Based Marginality

Some believe that people can only become sensitive and respond effectively to the welfare of others when they have been wounded themselves. We have not found this to be the case. Rather, another important kind of value-based marginality, experienced by one third of our sample, also appears to foster the capacity to care for the common good.

Douglas Huneke, author of a gripping case study of Fritz Graebe, a German engineer who rescued hundreds of Jews during the Holocaust, describes what he calls the "religiously-inspired non-conformity" that appears to have spawned a number of rescuers.[15] By this he means membership in a community that holds a set of religious values which place them at odds with the surrounding majority culture, but which instill in them a responsiveness to the needs of others: for example, the Huguenot village of Le Chambon in France where villagers sheltered thousands of Jews during World War II.[16]

Not all of the marginal communities and families in our study, however, are religiously inspired. We also saw the significant influence of small progressive schools or powerful short-term affiliations and experiences such as conferences, intensive learning communities, task forces, or political coalitions which held values at odds with prevailing mores. And for some the family nourished important values distinct from those of the mainstream, though not explicitly religious. We have chosen, therefore, the broader term, "value-based marginality."

Though in one sense a "tribe" themselves, families and communities can play a vital role in the formation of a commitment to the well-being of all, particularly when they extend respect to difference, to the stranger, to the other across tribal boundaries. In this way, they model that simultaneous embrace of both inclusiveness and particularity that we spoke of earlier.

The paradoxical power of such value-based tribes to nurture a commitment to the larger good is exemplified in John Schwarz, whose career has led him from developing marketing co-ops in Angola to coordinating relief efforts in Rwanda. When John was growing up, he and most of his friends were Mennonite, a Christian community with a commitment to peace and to a lifestyle of non-conformity. The community was, in his words, "a closed circle." Yet his house was geographically located at the edge of the village, and he went to school with a mix of kids. Moreover, his father was one of the first to promote mechanized farm equipment among his brethren, and subsequently worked as a missionary in Mississippi and later in Central America. John remembers the excitement of riding with his dad through the Delta country taking seeds and new technology to poor farm families. "So I grew up with that double story. First, being separate from society—that I shouldn't take on America's beliefs—but second that I should also be involved in society. I shouldn't just stay in the small community: 'In the world but not of the world.'"

A value-inspired community gave John a protected space in which he could experience a social vision distinct from that of the majority culture, yet also be connected with it. Our study strongly confirms that many less sharply bounded forms of value-based communities, such as Scouts, mainstream religious communities or service organizations, can influence their members in a similar, if perhaps somewhat less concentrated, fashion.

We have also seen a related effect, particularly in the lives of some women and people of color who grew up in value-based communities that substantially protected them from prejudice in their early years. When they later encountered discrimination, they were able to address it with matter-of-fact, steady confidence—sometimes with a healthy measure of outrage. College president Kate Hopkins, for example, was schooled in all-female institutions until she went to college. In her first year, when a boyfriend let slip his presumption that she could not excel in math because she was a woman, she was astounded—but undaunted. Ever since, she has practiced a special commitment to women who have grown up more vulnerable than she to gender bias.

Although not all still share the particular values of families and communities that earlier set them apart, it appears that participation in these communities gave them a positive, grounded identity that prepared them to stand apart from, yet remain related to, the prevailing culture.

The Gifts of Marginality

Even when it carries a price, marginality can also bear certain gifts: greater self-knowledge, greater awareness of others, and a kind of comfort with life at the edge. The central gift of marginality, however, is its power to promote both empathy with the other and a critical perspective on one's own tribe.

By unveiling the tendency of every tribe to assume that its own campfire burns at the center of the world, marginality can foster a point of view from which to recognize the possibility of our dependence upon a common fire— one that warms but does not destroy. It is not that being marginal enables one to be "objective" in the sense of having a detached or disinterested view.[17] Rather, much as a navigator fixes the ship's position by triangulating several different readings, marginality makes it possible to hold several different perspectives and so gain a more complex and sensitive way of seeing, unavailable to those with only one point of view. Held thus in a network of interconnected perspectives—including how one is seen by others—one can develop a deeper, more critical and informed understanding both of the other and of one's own self and tribe.

Jay LaDuke, an advocate working in state government on behalf of native peoples, knows one reason why he is effective:

> I know how to go down a river with one foot in this canoe and one foot in that canoe and never fall in the middle of the river. Most people can't move back and forth be-

tween two worlds, and I can do that. I can go up and be with Indian people and be totally at home. I can come down here, put on a suit, go down to the State Capital, and deal just as well as any big-time lawyer lobbyist who's been doing this forever.

When one stands at the margins, astride the boundary between tribes, one stands also at the center of a larger and more adequate whole.

The Conviction That Everyone Counts

Forming a sense of one's own particularity, one's own tribe, is an essential human activity. But the kind of citizens we need in the complex social and ecological realities of the twenty-first century are the kind that Cornel West describes in his book, *Race Matters*. West writes of "race-transcending prophets," people who never lose contact with their own particularity, yet refuse to be confined to it.[18] They are able to engage with people of other tribes as full human beings, enlarging rather than relinquishing their networks of belonging. Having practiced compassion across tribal boundaries, sometimes nourished by the circumstances of marginality, they have come to a deeply held conviction that *everyone counts*.

The poet Adrienne Rich has eloquently recognized "resemblance in difference" as a spiritual fact and "the only hope for a humane civil life."[19] Seeing both "resemblance" and "difference" is critical. Commitment to the commons has not been forged when, as often happens, we merely allow "them" to join "us." Seeing resemblance in difference does not mean blurring the distinctions that constitute the integrity of the particular, nor denying differences that are experienced as difficult or repugnant. It means that one has recognized a shared resonance of spirit in our common life which both transcends and permeates one's own and the other's distinctiveness, a spirit that is at the heart of what it means to dwell together on this earth.

When the integrity of one's own difference goes unrecognized, the pain is searing. An African-American, Roy Matthews, whom we will meet shortly, spent his university years in a desegregated, but racist environment, and remembers how "you would get crushed just by the fact that you were so different and so misunderstood." And Mitch Gunderson, who grew up in the mainstream of his working-class community in Minnesota, suddenly felt invisible to the rich international elites with whom he worked when he first came to the

United Nations. "They assumed," he told us, "that because I was male and I was an American that I had also come from a privileged background." It was a cultural shock. "I had to realize that they were just treating me as if I were one of them. I mean, it was an odd experience."

Tim Richardson, who served for many years in political office, recalled that though he had been involved in many community projects, he first really "got" the resemblance in difference when he became the head of a nontraditional community college in a rural area not far from where he had grown up:

> With poor rural people we got to a point of just pure appreciation for the skills and abilities that people had. I remember the names of some of those early students, mostly women, and the incredible capacity they had. And how they had just been sta-tistics in a report, "Headstart Mothers." I got this incredibly personal exposure and af-filiation with people who I had been walking by on the streets or who I'd grown up with. Some of those guys I'd played baseball with and thought of them as friends, but I hadn't seen them then as three-dimensional people.

And R. Lowell Rankin, whom we met in the last chapter, reflecting on his time in the Peace Corps, similarly observes that "wisdom can be found in all kinds of places, and not necessarily—and even often not—among the so-called smart or educated people." He described this transformed way of seeing as

> directly helpful in my current position because it allows me, when I'm considering a project, to simply place a different value than I would have on the input from a grass-roots organization or a committee of residents from low-income communities. The problem is resources; the problem is not a question of their ability as human beings to make a contribution.

In recognizing this resemblance in difference, these people have learned how to see, feel, and know that finally the good of the other cannot be divorced from one's own good because we all participate in the single and interdependent commons of life. Everyone counts.

Even Those You Oppose

Everyone? In the closing paragraphs of his autobiography, *Long Walk to Freedom*, Nelson Mandela writes of his twenty-seven years as a political prisoner.

> It was during those long and lonely years that my hunger for the freedom of my own people became a hunger for the freedom of all people, white and black. I knew as

well as I knew anything that the oppressor must be liberated just as surely as the oppressed. A man who takes away another man's freedom is a prisoner of hatred, locked behind the bars of prejudice and narrow-mindedness. I am not truly free if I am taking away someone else's freedom, just as surely as I am not free when my freedom is taken from me. The oppressed and the oppressor alike are robbed of their humanity.

When I walked out of prison, that was my mission, to liberate the oppressed and the oppressor both....The true test of our devotion to freedom is just beginning.[20]

In our interviews we often asked, "Is there any way in which you work on behalf of even those whom you oppose?" This was not an easy question for most. But Sarah Morgan, an urban minister, was very clear.

If our collective call is not one that leads us to justice and mercy, then there will be no peace. We will continuously be instruments of our own oppression and our complacency will enable the oppression of others. People usually like to separate religion and life. But if my work can do anything of substance, it would be to make real for people the fact that they are inextricably bound—that one *is* the other—and that how we live reflects what it is we claim to believe. That means that if there is anyone in a lower class around, or anyone who is hungry, or enslaved, then that's a reminder that we are in that state with them.

In this chapter, we have suggested that the encounter with difference becomes a constructive engagement when an emotional tie is formed that transcends tribal lines. But forming sustained commitment to the common good entails more than a felt bond, narrowly understood. Just as Jo Chapman has come to understand her world differently after going through the Trap, we also need to make sense of our experience of the other, to think about it in more satisfying and adequate ways. In Chapter 4, the story of Sue Drucker illustrates the "habits of mind" that accompany the formation of commitment to the common good. Chapter 4 is preceded, however, by an Interlude, a story without commentary that illustrates the elements of commitment we have described thus far.

introduction to the first interlude

An interlude is a composition of a somewhat different character inserted between the primary movements of a larger work. This interlude tells a story that confirms the power of mentoring and the engagement with otherness discussed in Chapters 2 and 3, and prepares us for the discussion of systemic thought, a critical habit of mind discussed in Chapter 4.

In the course of our study the interdependent power of committed lives became increasingly evident in two forms. The first of these is the power of mentorship across generations. When we discovered that one interviewee had been the mentor for another, we knew we were on to a special story and became active sleuths. In the end, we interviewed four people, all descended through the bonds of mentoring from the great educator and political advocate, Mary McLeod Bethune. They are Dr. Dorothy Height (whose name, with her permission, we have not attempted to disguise), Rosalyn Williams, Roy Matthews, and Jim Jackson. In composing the story of these five lives into a single piece, we have given an extended account of Roy Matthews' life so the reader can glimpse how mentoring relationships may open critical pathways toward commitment, not only across the generations, but within a single life seen whole. We begin and end with the youngest, Jim, who now stewards both the legacy and the promise.

For The Hundreds of Years that Come After

I leave you love. I leave you hope. I leave you the chal-
lenge of developing confidence in one another. I leave
you a thirst for education. I leave you responsibility for
the use of power. I leave you faith. I leave you racial
dignity. I leave you a desire to live harmoniously with
your fellow man. I leave you a responsibility to our
young people.

MARY MCLEOD BETHUNE
(1875–1955)

The frigid wind slaps our faces as we emerge from the mouth of the subway station into Hartford Park. We walk swiftly through the rows of naked trees, past a clump of newspaper frozen against a park bench, past a brace of businessmen pushing through the cold, and across the hard, gray street to the steel and glass doors of the highest building in the city. The massive stone lintel reads, "First National Insurance Company."

Inside, we survey the lobby, wondering if we will recognize Jim Jackson. It is not difficult. He is the only African American in sight, and he is already moving toward us, his hand extended beneath a welcoming smile. He is half a head taller than anyone else and moves in his brown tailored three-piece suit as though he had been born in it.

"Roy spoke so highly of you," we say as we ride up in the elevator toward the company cafeteria. "Well," he replies, "he's a pretty special person. I wouldn't be here if it weren't for him." And he chuckles at the obvious.

Over coffee, we ask what he does here. "I am an account rep in the international group. We develop benefit programs for multinational companies. It's stimulating work. I get to travel a lot, meet people. And," he adds—eyes apologetic but with determined satisfaction—"the money's good."

Jim first came to First National six years ago as a young intern with "Passages," a placement firm for minority youth headed by Roy Matthews. Since joining the company full time, he has had three promotions in two years.

The odds of that happening, he readily acknowledges, "were not good at all" for the third son of a single mother growing up in the inner city. In that community, fewer than half the young men under eighteen finish high school, and by the age of twenty-one, a quarter are in prison. But he was bright and his mother was a teacher. She would read to him as a child, and he scored well on the metropolitan reading tests in fourth grade. "My mom was determined not to let the streets get us," he tells us, and he was groomed for entrance into the distinguished Hartford Academy.

Every Sunday, she would herd the kids off to church. When Jim was eight years old, a church-sponsored Big Brother arrived on the doorstep. Henry Jackson became an enormously important influence. "He has instructed and taken care of me. He means the world to me." A year later, Jackson became Jim's stepfather.

In the seventh grade, he had surgery for an abscess on his leg and spent four months in bed. Rather than send him to summer school, his parents simply had him repeat the year. Although he felt left behind by his friends, "It was perhaps the best thing that ever happened to me," he said. He became a star student the following year, and eventually became senior class president. That year, the headmaster urged him to apply to prestigious Haverford College. Jim was uncomfortable with the idea. The place seemed too liberal, and besides, he probably wouldn't be admitted. He was wrong on both counts. He loved the place, and graduated with honors in Economics. During his freshman year, looking for summer work, he had heard about a headhunting firm that specialized in placing minority people. With a hefty tuition bill in his mailbox, he thought, "Why not? What do I have to lose?"

When he walked in the door of the firm several weeks later, however, he found himself thinking, "Maybe a lot." The office was tucked in a back room of a Federated Bank branch in a shopping center. Save for a utilitarian desk, a phone, two chairs, and a stack of unhung pictures, there was only the vaguely anxious face of Roy Matthews to greet him. "This does not look good," Jim thought.

Matthews greeted him warmly, however, and "we clicked almost immediately. It almost felt as though we had known each other for years." They talked for an hour. The program was just beginning. He would be one of the first. He left that afternoon, still unsure. Matthews seemed solid, but could he trust the program? No one had ever heard of these people. What was he getting into?

A sturdy, balding man in his mid-forties, Roy Matthews ushers us into his new sixth-floor downtown office. "Passages is a national organization," he explains, "founded in St. Louis in 1972. Now there are twenty-seven affiliates from San Francisco to Boston. We have about thirty-five hundred interns and more than a thousand corporate sponsors involved in trying to get more black and Latino college students into business, industry and engineering. We began here in 1983 with thirty-four young people and eighteen companies, and this past year we had 178 interns working in over sixty corporations. It has been tremendously successful. Here we have twenty to twenty-five graduates every year who are going into the corporate world—young people committed to helping their communities. As they move into positions of authority in the private sector, they'll use those resources to contribute to public life. So this is a public ministry for me in a way, trying to cultivate young leaders with strong links in the corporate world who also want to do things in the community. Part of the success is that I have brought strong spiritual, moral themes to what we're trying to do."

He goes on to explain how the program provides a kind of home for young people like Jim Jackson where they can have some guidance and develop a feeling of responsibility for one another as well as for the larger society. They have training almost every Saturday during the summer. At 9:00 A.M. there is a seminar on what the investment community is all about. At ten, they learn to write a good, succinct memorandum. At eleven, they have a seminar on how to work on team projects, and so on from eight to four on Saturdays. "From eight to nine is my time with them when I try to help support them in what they want to do," Roy says. "It's difficult for these kids. Some of them have to go into the rest room at the end of the regular work day and take their business suits off and put on clothes that they can walk down Morgan Street in. That's tough at eighteen, twenty-one years old. I help them understand why it's important for them to hold that tension for a while and not let go of it. If we are going to have equity in this society, I have to believe that at some point black folks will have to have the kind of power that other communities have for things to really change. But the art is how one gets into those positions of power without being co-opted." That, Roy is clear, "is where the values come in."

"We talk about what is important to hold on to—their connections to their community, the worth of their culture, and the lives of the people they have grown up with; how to be your own person and to choose the people you relate to, yet understand that in the working environment you need to be able to work with everyone." He emphasizes, "We know which values are good for us, and we know which ones aren't good for us, and we've got to be public about the ones that we believe aren't good for us. We need prophetic voices in the system, and this is a place where they can learn to acquire and use power responsibly."

As if hearing himself, he pauses to take a mental breath, then continues. "I've tried to instill in all of these people the idea that power is necessary—using corporate, institutional power. And I think that Jim is beginning to understand how the relationship that I helped put together with the senior people at First National gives him a voice that very few people his age have. Jim will have genuine, institutional power." He pauses again, smiling to himself, then shifts the topic.

"But I should add that all during this I have become more and more involved as senior pastor with the First Baptist Church down in Garfield. So I have two full-time, eighty-hour-a-week jobs in a way," he says ruefully. Then he tells us how crucial this small congregation is to the people of that rapidly expanding, multiethnic working-class city.

"No one prepared Garfield for the great deluge of Southeast Asians, Haitians and Latinos. And now the folks who have been there a long time blame all the problems on the newcomers. And I want to say to them that the future of Garfield depends upon taking advantage of the energy that these new people bring. There's so much fear of brown faces, black faces, languages that they don't understand. Yet that's what we've always been; we've always taken the energy of newcomers and used that to build the country. I think I can articulate that and help people listen to those ideas, and think in those terms. Hopefully my voice will be one of many around the world that will begin to help people better understand what is happening. This is what it means to think more globally, to hold the knowledge that we are all on the planet together and need to see our diversity as a strength rather than a source of conflict."

Where did all this come from, we wonder? How did this man come to hold those values, that vision so deeply? And why has he not burned out after four decades of struggle as a black person in a racist society?

The only son of a black preacher, Roy Matthews, Jr. spent his first years in a small town west of Raleigh surrounded by chickens, hogs, corn fields, and relatives. Everyone knew everyone else in Davistown, and from early on he knew that as the preacher's son, he had a special place in the universe. One Sunday when Roy was six years old, his father suffered a stroke in the midst of a sermon. He vividly recalls his father's funeral. The "mothers of the church" surrounded him in their white dresses and sang the music that has always saturated his soul. "It was as though they were saying, 'You have lost a parent but now you have another set of collective parents.' I knew that my father had died, but I knew that everything was going to be okay." And from that time on, people would bend down and say, "Boy, you're gonna be a preacher!"

The family moved into Raleigh shortly after this, but he remained a part of the same church community, and grew up in a large extended family held together by his mother's parents, sisters, and their families. It was a time of "tremendous love and care."

At the same time, special though he felt, young Roy knew that he was black in a white world, and he was reminded daily that to be black was to be inferior. In one of his most vivid memories, "We were standing at the bus stop, my mom and I—I must have been nine years old or so—and these white guys drove by and hit my mom with what I thought was a snowball, but they had a rock in the middle of it. And I remember she just cried. Man, you talk about bitterness and hatred. I just wanted to kill those guys!"

Why not? What kept that bitterness from eating its way into Matthews's life, driving him to soothe the pain in violence?

"Two things. Hatred was just not an emotion that was acceptable or encouraged or tolerated in my household. We were told that there were these whites out there that felt that way, but that we were to pray for them and that it would be a detriment to us to hate them back. The other thing was that we were told in church that those kind of folks couldn't defeat us, that it really wasn't important to get even with them, that it was more important for us to understand that there were going to be those kinds of attacks and that kind of oppression in life, but that those folks are not going to win in the end. Those little incidents were of no significance because the battle was larger. But I tell you, I had that anger for a long, long time—a very, very long time."

His mother, Emma, was president of the church choir. She had a beautiful voice, and there was a song she used to sing:

> *Like a ship that's tossed and driven,*
> *Battered by an angry sea,*
> *When the storms of life are raging,*
> *And its fury falls on me . . .*
> *The Lord will make a way somehow.*

When the congregation would hear that, Roy recalls, "it was all over." Life was difficult, but moments like these were rich and full of meaning. "I think that crucible that we grew up in prepared us for a lot of things."

But Emma worked as a daynurse for white families. Matthews was intensely jealous of these white children who somehow merited his mother's presence more than he. When they called her "Mom," it would drive him crazy. At the same time, he saw the poverty of their affluent lives, saw their mother drink herself to death, and some part of him knew that they too needed "Mom."

In her absence, his grandmother, part Cherokee and "fiercely independent," cared for the family, imparting pride, integrity, and deep faith. After she died, his mother's sister become a second mother. "She was the one that I knew would be there," he recalls. "She taught us patience, fidelity, and long-suffering." But perhaps her most important gift was music. When he was in seventh grade, she bought him a clarinet that the family could ill afford, and never missed a concert. His years in the school band fed a lifelong love of music. Combined with the sense of community that came with it, music became a central source of connection and renewal.

For the men in Roy's world, life was crushing. Most jobs were demeaning, and alcoholism was pervasive. He felt their pain deeply. Even education promised only a partial escape from the oppressive social conditions of segregated Raleigh. Emma's youngest brother, Howard, had fought in World War II and turned his G.I. Bill into a degree at prestigious Fiske University. It was he who brought the wider world into the Matthews home, watched the news with the children and talked about the larger issues. Yet Uncle Howard worked his entire life as a post office clerk, often supervised by whites with half his education—men, Roy notes with less edge than one might expect, who would not even know the titles of the books that Howard read. And once, when Roy was waiting on tables at a posh party in a white suburb, he was devastated to discover that one of his fellow waiters was his high school principal. "High school principals were like gods. I just could not believe it. Not him! Then it began to hit what this was all about."

At the same time, his maternal grandfather was a mythic figure: "All the values of the family were embodied in him." Despite his race, Emmett A. Beaulieu, a construction engineer, was given his own crew of city workers, and left his initials on fire hydrants all over the city, distinguished for the care with which the concrete was feathered to the sidewalk, the angle exactly right. Artistic, he could draw anything; creative, he ran his own restaurant in spite of restrictive Jim Crow laws; and proud, he refused to eat food left for him on the back porch by whites for whom as a young man he had performed menial labor. Stories like this taught Roy "that's who we were, that's who we were supposed to be—people who did not allow circumstances to define us or get us down. We were to overcome those things."

Good grades at school were always important at home, and Roy lived up to expectations. But when he looked out of his high school window one day to see five thousand college students marching together, the challenge was more than personal and intellectual. "I'd never seen that large a group of black people, so the opportunity to participate was very compelling. My first public consciousness was formed out of that." He learned nonviolent methods and helped to organize his classmates in the civil rights movement. Salutatorian of his class, Roy was selected to be one of the first black students at Duke University.

He was not happy there. As a "social experiment," he was at best condescended to, at worst, ignored and secretly despised. Often he would look with envy at his friends attending all-black Howard or Fiske, wondering why he had been chosen to carry the burden of being a token black at a white institution. His only solace was that his old friend and roommate, Eddie Stoughton, had to endure even worse torments as the school's first black athlete. Further, both knew their community at home "valued us and sustained us and loved us."

Indeed, Roy's story is richly veined with older adults who encouraged and supported him along the way. Ironically, segregation meant that many of his high school teachers, unable to find jobs in colleges, were superbly trained. His band director, who had studied at the Sorbonne, and a French teacher, who had spent ten years in France, showed him a world beyond Raleigh. A science teacher encouraged him to consider a career in medicine, and a music teacher, who had been around the world and knew many of the great black musicians of the time, introduced him to the music and poetry of the Harlem Renaissance. And she gave him books—Richard Wright, James Baldwin, W.E.B. DuBois, and especially Ralph Ellison. "Reading *Invisible Man*, I too knew what it was to walk into a room and have people not recognize you were there or listen to what you had to say. It was very powerful."

The civil rights movement also brought with it a number of committed and caring adults. James Lawson, a student at Vanderbilt Divinity School, had been trained at Highlander and taught Roy "the tactics of reflection and social action." Edwin Mitchell, a physician, was an important guide, introducing him to strategic planning sessions, helping him to see from the inside how community organization worked, modelling for him a committed professional working coolly and effectively at fundamental social change. "So one began to see that there was a cadre of leaders and thinkers who saw far beyond Raleigh and connected us with what was going on around the world and around the United States, so one didn't feel so powerless."

But if high school was notable for the presence of committed adults, college was equally notable for their absence. His predominant feelings during those times were "isolation, insecurity, indifference, invisibility, and not doing well academically." Mostly there was "just no one to talk to about what was going on with me. There was no way to really understand what I was going through, and the old sources of support and guidance weren't there, so I had to count on me."

The problem was that "me" wasn't enough. He had never experienced failure before, and so naturally presumed that what was now going wrong was all his own fault. He began to blame himself. Unable to share his doubts with anyone, the buzzing of the demons grew louder. Was it because he was black? Was it really true, what they said?

He nearly quit that sophomore year. What got him through was the knowledge that no one in his family had ever quit anything, and he was not about to be the first. In addition, he had helped to form the African-American Association at Duke. The campus chaplain, Bob Ashburg, a white liberal from North Carolina, helped to support the Association and became one of only two important adults that Roy mentions during the college years. One evening at a coffee house where Fanny Lou Hamer was speaking, Ashburg narrowly kept Roy out of a fight with outside agitators. The two became close after that, and Matthews credits Bob with having "kept alive the ministry part of me." That was fortunate, for the only other figure, his major professor in sociology, while "right there" on racial and political issues, "couldn't identify with the religious part of me."

Roy also knew that more was at stake in his time at Duke than his own personal survival, and, despite the scars, grudgingly labels it "a defining experience." His primary lesson, which has served him well ever since, was not in the stated curriculum. "I learned how to wheel and deal and negotiate and manipulate in the white world."

Despite having been accepted at divinity, law, and business schools, Roy decided to take a job right at Duke, eventually becoming the equal opportunity officer and taking an M.B.A. degree there. By now he was married and a child was on the way. It was time to settle down.

Yet he looks back on those years as a hollow time. He feels he did not make a choice; rather, he fell into the work, driven more by a need to please others than by his own goals. The thrust of everyone else's dreams for him was no longer enough, yet there was no basis on which he could build his own momentum. Still in his young adult years, there yawned before him a chasm between a world others had built for him and his own not yet formed. It is this gap which mentors often serve to bridge. Yet Roy's early models—one uncle who worked in the post office, another in a dry cleaner's, another a railroad porter—could offer only limited help to him now. And the only mentors in his college world were white. There was no one to hold out for him a dream of who he might become as a black man in a white world. "I was working several jobs, trying to make a little more money. Just to survive. I didn't have the luxury of dreams and visions and all that at the time." Roy fell into the chasm.

"Freefall" is his own word for it. In part it was the times; in the late sixties, "everybody was doing it." But in part it was the particular rhythm of his own life—and the fact that "there wasn't much to dissuade me."

"For a long period of time I was doing a lot of alcohol and drugs because I just couldn't deal with the pressure and the little failures. I didn't know where I was headed, but it was down. I felt hopeless because pretty soon I wasn't sure I could make it without the drugs."

Moreover, the religious foundation so carefully laid in his early years seemed to have collapsed. He had experienced "a real crisis of faith" in college, as science and psychology seemed to relativize everything, including his childhood God. He "left the web" and stopped going to church on a regular basis. His guilt grew until it seemed to be his "main motivator." He felt guilty because of his desire for women, because he didn't spend enough time with his children, because he didn't attend enough to his mother's needs. And he felt guilty for leaving the church. "I was guilty about everything. You name it, and I was guilty."

But this was not simply a fall from grace absent any context, and one can find roots reaching well back into Roy's childhood. From the time the first neighbor bent down and intoned into the young boy's ear, "Boy, you're gonna be a preacher," he had felt a telling mix of entitlement and dread. He is keenly aware of how the story written for him from the time of his birth carried both gift and burden. He was Roy Matthews, *Junior.* When his father died, he found himself, a boy of only six, stranded on a gigantic throne. The obligation was there, but the source of power was gone. Understandably, a part of him quailed, rebelled against the expectation. Why could he not be a businessman, a lawyer, a doctor? Why must he take up this burden? More, knowing as he did from the age of twelve or thirteen what it meant to be black in this society, and feeling the cruel rub of dream against reality, there was little to hold him as the seams of his early home gave way.

When he was thirty-one, Roy and his family left Raleigh and moved to Cleveland where he took an administrative position in a community college. Despite his apparent success in the outside world, he was still wracked by guilt and a sense of failure. His continued dependence on drugs and his apostasy were a great shame to him. He knew he was becoming someone that he was not, and yet he felt trapped in his own rebellion.

His two children were entering school by this time, and he knew that even if he no longer attended church, at least they ought to. So he marched them off to Zion Baptist Church. The pastor's wife, Lena Gurney, saw in this young father, if nothing else, a promising Cub Scout Master. She signed him on—and somehow that did it. He began to realize that he mattered to the world, not because he had been told as much, but because it was right there in front of him—in the faces of his two boys, of the other children, of their parents who counted on him.

The Gurneys became powerful mentors for Matthews. As a "public minister" who had started a development bank, built a shopping center, and founded a retirement home, the Reverend Louis Gurney modelled religious commitment with a social dimension; and by her faith in his promise, Lena Gurney showed Roy the meaning of "saving grace." "She saved my life," he says simply, and recalls the story of the Prodigal Son. "For me the most powerful part of the story is when he's at the swine trough and the Bible says, 'He came to himself.' It just clicked that this is not who I am; that is who I am. 'He came to himself.'"

It was as though the melody of his life beneath the noise of the past ten years could be heard again. But this time, it came from the inside. This time, it was his own song. "The dream about the ministry finally crystallized for me; that's where I would find myself. I have not doubted a moment since then; that was the turning point." Roy Matthews applied to Yale Divinity School.

Roy found a new voice at Yale. The challenging readings and encounters with new perspectives brought his images of God under profound review. Although he could no longer accept the exclusionary elements of orthodox Baptist belief, he saw with fresh intensity his own story and tradition in the larger history of his people, and he learned again the power of his racial identity as if for the first time. But it was his internship that he most remembers.

He worked with the director of the Urban Service Mission, a remarkable woman named Rosalyn Williams, a short, massive presence of enormous spiritual power and a keen critical eye. "She is a very bright, intelligent, powerful woman. I was almost intimidated at first," he told us. "She was one of the best lay theologians I ever met, and the thing she loved about God was that God loved justice. For her, God's command to love one another meant to do justice. And even when she had to fight against people, it was because she loved them and she wanted them to be just. I thought that was very liberating. I mean, on one hand, you don't have to take it, and on the other hand, you don't have to hate people; you don't have to be enemies. You're doing this because you want to love them and love means being just to one another."

One time they visited a wealthy suburban church, trying to create connections in people's minds between the city and the suburbs, connections that went beyond dropping clothes for poor people off at the USM and making donations for food. "We pointed out that part of the problem between the suburb and the city was that their representative in state government voted on child care, education, and public transportation in ways that hurt people in the city because he believed he was protecting their 'best interests.' A woman stood up and you would have thought I had stabbed her with a knife because she thought I was attacking her personally, and I wasn't. I was just trying to help her see the connection." It was hard work. Their funding depended on suburban churches, and Rosalyn and Roy struggled often over strategy. "So I admired and respected her because she could give her life to that, which was something I couldn't do."

It was through dialogues with Rosalyn, both in her office and in a course she co-taught at the school, that he grappled in a whole new way with systemic change. "I was young and impatient, and I struggled with whether or not we were simply the troops out there who just cleaned up after the battle was over, putting on Band-Aids." He was beginning to see past the details.

"There were times when the board wanted her to be more pragmatic and focused on the budget, and she never bought that. If she went over budget for something that she believed was important, she found money, she found people, and they probably took a loss on it for a while till it got on its feet. She got a lot of flak for that, but she hung in there with it—like when she established a center where women who had been incarcerated would have some place to go when they came out of prison."

She taught him to celebrate the small victories, but also that without a grasp of the larger issues, it's hard to tell victory from defeat. "She had a rigorous notion of what incarnation was all about. So she would say, 'Well, what we have to do is see that there are indications of the Kingdom of God here and there, and we have to find those things.' And when we found them, we had to celebrate them; so there wouldn't be big, spectacular victories, but there would be small, subtle signs. If you weren't sensitive to it, if you didn't stay free of the proximate problems, you'd miss the whole picture. She was convinced that I had to look for those signs, and that when I found them, I had to really stay with them enough to understand what they were. We could not, in our zest to make things happen on our time schedule, fail to see that God was working in the lives of people in the community. She had to tell me that two, three times a week, and that was very helpful. And I began to look at things differently. Instead of seeing only the shoot-outs and drug deals and elderly people being held up in the community where I was youth minister, I began to see the kids grow and positive things happen with them, and it helped me reinterpret what it was I was supposed to do."

Roy reflects further on Rosalyn's vision of community: "Rosalyn believed that to be faithful to that call we needed to see it as a communal thing. We weren't Lone Rangers. We weren't good enough to go out there and simply solve those things by ourselves; we needed to communally address these things. And she wanted to create a community where blacks and whites and Southerners and Northerners and rich people and poor people could work together as a community to address those issues. That was very powerful and attractive for me, because I didn't know that was possible. I had the experience of the black church community, but this was a challenge for me, and still is. But it is now a part of my own project."

There were other struggles during Roy's graduate school years. The dislocation was hard on his family, and Rosalyn "was one of the few people I could talk to about my own marriage and some of the grappling I had there. She helped me to understand the importance of my being more communicative with my family about why I was doing this work and not just assuming that because they're my wife and family that they understand and have to buy into this." She confronted him on his own sexism and deepened his understanding of women in the Bible. His mother and grandmother had been enormously important in his life, but he had not previously recognized what that could mean for the contributions of women in church and society. Finally, what Rosalyn gave him was love. "I knew she understood what I was wrestling with. She didn't dismiss it. She didn't question my religious commitment. She didn't dismiss my concerns as being overly idealistic. She really understood, yet she didn't try to give me simple answers. She was a model for me of how a person of faith could live with integrity."

Out of this crucible of challenge and affirmation, Roy came to believe that racial and economic equality were tightly spliced, that until African-Americans achieved economic justice, social justice would elude them. Divinity degree in hand, he brought Passages to New York.

Roy's office is spare but elegant. A computer screen blinks placidly beside us as we talk. Behind the large oak desk, a window looks out on the edge of the neighboring brick building, slicing through the crack of light.

"What keeps you going?" we ask. "Don't you ever get discouraged?"

"I have the great fortune of loving the two things that I do for a living," he replies. "That's what sustains me." When the work goes well, he knows that his life is being well spent. He reads a lot, also, and feels encouraged by the work of people like Havel, King, and Mandela. One of his favorite films is "Chariots of Fire," and music is an important source of renewal. Further, Roy remains closely connected with his family church back in Raleigh, with the church where he served his internship, and his own congregation in Garfield. These networks ground his identity and sense of purpose. And despite mixed feelings about his college years, some of his old Duke friends have remained in touch, enabling him to retain valuable connections across racial and gender lines.

But all this has not been without cost, and he still carries the voice that would have sent him to medical or business school. His wife loves him deeply, but he also knows that part of her longs for a fine house in a suburb of Atlanta. Still, he has come to terms with these voices and reveals a particular kind of *noblesse oblige* as he talks about his gifts. "The kind of love and support and affirmation that I've received throughout my life—it almost boggles the mind."

The real costs are not so much in money as in stress, time, health. Both he and his wife had major surgery in the past year. And more poignantly still, he adds, "My daughter, who is at Fiske now, was in the ninth grade and then it seemed like all of a sudden I looked up and she had graduated from high school. So there have been costs."

At the same time, holding the tension between work and family has made him a better pastor, he feels. "I wouldn't have a clue as to how to be an effective minister were I not married," he says emphatically. He has learned in his marrow what it means to be faithful, what it means to struggle with a family and young children, what it means to really listen to people's suffering. His children have taught him well. "They have helped me to expand the room I have for other people, to learn what it means to make space for others." He pauses for a moment, reaching down for the words. Then, "I know that—not intellectually. Lived experiences tell me that."

On his wall is a poster of a father holding his young son up toward the sun. He looks up at it, speaking slowly. "When I was about twelve or thirteen, I began to realize that there were some things in my life that I would never get to do, no matter how hard I worked or how good I was. Yet I also knew that I was probably in a better position to see more of the horizon than anybody had been previously in my family. It was very, very painful to look around me, to see my friends, and know that as bright and as wonderful as they were, that was true of them too. Then I read about South Africa and realized there were whole continents and races of people who wouldn't even dream to have what I had."

He turns back to us, his face masking the passion beneath his words.

"I have sons now. I have daughters. And I don't ever want them to think like I did then. Because I almost quit. I almost just gave it up. 'Why do this? Why try?' That's why I understand all these kids in the inner city and in gangs—there is a terrible acceptance among them that they aren't going to make it, and that they don't deserve to make it. I understand what that is. And I look around me and don't see anybody from my neighborhood or my school—other than a few exceptions—who . . ."

"Well," we break in, "some would say that if you don't ever want your children to feel defeated, don't let them dream."

"Yeah," he replies, brushing that aside. "That's one answer. The other is to give them the courage that was given to me by my family and others around me to keep up the struggle. That's what keeps you sane and that's what keeps you believing that there is progress to be made. Progress is possible." Yet he has no formula, "no grand scheme in which all these things will fit." His only certainty is that there is a place for moral vision in public life.

"This is easier said than done," he adds, because he often gets it from both sides. He has always seen himself as a bridge between people, only sometimes it is he who must pay the toll. When he was in college, the Black Power and SNCC students viewed him as an Oreo for his stands on some issues. Likewise now, some of his more radical critics view the attempt to build links with the corporate world as a sellout. He is wary of the danger, but unwilling to back away from it. Others view his efforts to empower minorities as a threat to their job security. "It's easier to stand in one place or the other," he says with a grin. "But I can't do that, even though it's quicksand; you're always testing where you stand. I like that."

But doesn't he sometimes feel overwhelmed by the complexity, we wonder? "Surely I do," he replies, "but just as the problems are larger than we, so are the issues, the causes, the aspirations; just because there are ambiguities and paradoxes, doesn't mean we can't work with them." He almost seems to enjoy the uncertainty. "It is in the very unpredictability of people," he says, "that my hope lies. We don't know enough to be pessimists. I don't know what else to do other than keep going forward," he says with a grin. "For me to stop would be a sign of death. So the small victories will have to do. The small victories have to do."

Rosalyn Williams first met Roy in her office where he had come for an interview. "My impression of him was that here was a real jewel. He was very articulate, yet he wasn't out to impress you. He was being as honest as he could about himself. I liked the radical honesty in him and his willingness to struggle. He was replacing a young guy who I was in grief over having lost, and I never thought I would find another one like him to work with. So Roy was a good surprise." Then, almost parenthetically, she adds, "It helped me see that the waves of people who are coming into leadership just keep going on and on."

Although they worked well together, there were marked differences between them. "He's a black man who came out of a southern, black Baptist background, and I'm a black woman who came out of a northern, white Congregational background. We were bound together by our connection to the civil rights movement, but each of us had been weaned from different cultural experiences. So we didn't always agree. But that made our dialogues very interesting. We never really had any big confrontative moments; mostly ah-hahs, and we moved on from there."

"What did you want him to gain from the internship?" we ask. "I wanted him to have a fieldwork experience that pushed him to a new level of understanding," she replies. "His own understandings were already quite developed because he was an older student with considerable experience. I wanted him to be challenged, both in terms of his personal style and in terms of an understanding of what gifts he could bring into a community. The society in general is more and more desperate for good leadership, and Roy is a quality person. You just knew that to keep him sustained was going to be good."

We ask her to tell us more about the potential she saw in him. Somewhat warily, she responds: "Don't get me wrong about the way I say this. But he seemed to understand in a way that a lot of people who are culturally captive in this society don't. He had a great deal of empathy, and he allowed people of different cultures to be themselves. When I was young, it was a given that integration was the issue and that people across racial and cultural lines should get to know each other. By the time Roy came along, almost the opposite was true. Society had backed off from the hard issues of integration and everybody had a mindset of getting to know your own kind and coexisting. But Roy both knew who he was as a black man, and deeply cared about who other people from other cultural experiences were as well. And that was somewhat of an anomaly."

We comment that indeed, though white, we had felt comfortable with him. She responds, "And he didn't have to deny who he was to do that! That makes his leadership really rare in our society, which often wants to segment people and almost keep us apart in order to preserve cultural control. It seems less and less in the interest of the white community that blacks and whites come to terms with each other. When coalitions take form, there is subtle but significant organization against them—whether the issue is health care or anything else."

We ask her if she is getting more pessimistic. "Let me put it this way. I'm not getting more pessimistic in the sense that I'm less hopeful. But the encounters are less rewarding than they used to be; the realities are getting more dramatic that prove how hard and uphill the struggle is."

In the face of her sobering assessment, we find ourselves wondering about her unquenchable hope. Who has served Rosalyn in the way she has served Roy? She mentions Shirley Chisholm, then William Sloane Coffin ("who people fail to recognize as one of the wisdom figures of our generation because they have stereotyped him as an activist"), then Robert Moss, former President of the United Church of Christ, "the most important white guy I ever knew." A patrician Southerner, he might be one of the last people one would expect to form a bond with a black woman from the North, yet they formed a close working relationship. His extraordinary trustworthiness among people of widely differing worlds served to break down her own stereotypes about white men, and she feels that she still carries his spirit with her. But it was Dorothy Height for whom she herself was an intern.

We are in the corner office of the National Council for Negro Women. It is something like being in an elegant florist shop because it is the week of

Dorothy Height's eighty-second birthday, and her office is overflowing with what her secretary tells us is only a third of the flowers she has received. Dr. Height graciously greets us from behind her desk, and we are aware that she is at once both a grand presence and a woman with a clear sense of proportion — neither over- nor under-claiming who she is. In her role as President of the Council, as well as in her earlier work with the YWCA and the Delta Sigma Theta sorority, Dorothy Height has promoted business and vocational training for African-American women; she has been an advocate for women working in the "slave market" of domestic service; and she has helped organize food co-ops in rural areas. A sought-after speaker, she has served on numerous boards and councils at state, national, and international levels, and most recently sponsored a major effort to renew the extended black family as a powerful barrier against racism. Described recently as "perhaps the world's most prominent and effective voice for the empowerment of women of color, both in America and around the world," she still goes to work daily in this Washington, D.C. office.

"How did you first come to know Rosalyn?" we ask. She replies that a few months after the church in Birmingham was blown up, Rosalyn was speaking for a group of YMCA students when Height was the director of training for the national Y. "She did a beautiful job," Height recalls, "and I was interested because I had done a lot of that sort of speaking myself. And Rosalyn was interested in issues and concerns and systems." So Height asked her to join the student office, and brought her along to help with conferences.

For her part, Rosalyn remembers first seeing Dr. Height in a National Student Assembly meeting. Sitting in the audience, she looked up at this great person who was talking in front of thousands of people and thought, "She's the most brilliant person I've ever seen." As Rosalyn came to know her later, she learned what may have been the most important lesson Dorothy taught her. "I learned that she was just a normal human being like I was, who had a little guts and a little courage. When I had to preach the first time before a major congregation, I was scared to death, and Dorothy told me, 'I'm scared when I preach.' I said, 'you are?' That was really important to realize that it's no easier for our heroes to get up in front of thousands of people than it is for me, but they've got something inside of them that just goes into action."

"I also liked it that Dorothy had the silent courage to be a woman in the midst of all these men. One of the neat things about her finally getting the Medal of Freedom is that she used to hang out with that coalition, with Martin Luther King and Whitney Young, and had as much to say as anybody. Though

[97]

they always emerged as the leaders, she just quietly went about doing what she had to do. All those women who were pioneers became invisible people. And to survive being an invisible person is really something. That prepared me for the times when I become an invisible person." She laughs as she gives a mock cheer. "I'm in a great line of invisible people, yes, go get 'em!"

It is said that a sense of humor is a sense of proportion, and one of the things Rosalyn most admires about Dorothy is her sense of humor. Many of the black leaders had cadres who protected them, she recalls. "Like Jesse Jackson had five guys with him. So we decided—I was young and crazy—that Dorothy needed some lieutenants. So she took two of us to this black political convention, and we were supposed to follow her around so that she had a cadre just like Jesse had. Well, she was sitting up on the stage and they had a bomb scare. This other person and I got the hell out of there; we knew that they'd take care of the people on the stage. But afterwards Dorothy said to me, 'Where'd you all go? Some lieutenants you all are. We have a bomb scare, and you're taking off!' And to this day she teases me. She says, 'You've been anybody's cadre lately?' But I learned that you really can't imitate the ways of showing power that are available to others. When it comes down to it, you've got to be yourself."

Although Dorothy and Rosalyn shared a deep spiritual commitment, their friendship was not without conflict. "She had a different perspective on things, and a lot of times we didn't agree," Height recalled. "But what I liked was that we could sit down and disagree without being disagreeable. With her you could have a difference of opinion, you could test things with her. I find that very exciting. She was more like a younger colleague." Then she adds with an affectionate smile, "Every once in a while I'd have to say 'Just hold your horses,' and we would sit down and discuss whatever the issue was and plan a strategy." Yet "her wisdom was way ahead of her years."

It was while working with Height that Rosalyn began to feel she was bearing down on the purpose of her life. Hearing the stories of Africans working for national sovereignty, she came to see the civil rights struggle as part of a larger, global issue. Height was a central part of that expansion. "She taught me a lot about what institutional power is, what institutional racism is, and how to change structures and what that was like," says Rosalyn.

Where did Dorothy Height learn about that kind of power and transformation? Rosalyn had already given us a part of the answer. "One of the gifts of blackness is being connected to a sense of history, so that one's life isn't just for today but it's for the hundreds of years that went before and the hundreds of years that come after. When I start feeling sorry for myself, I remember all the way back to the first slave that jumped ship, to Sojourner Truth, to my mother who scrubbed people's kitchens all of her life, and my father who moved us out to Wellington—all those people paid a terrific price so that I can have the opportunities that I have. It made me feel like I was directly connected to that kind of genius. When you have that sense of lineage, it's really powerful."

Inspired by the testimony of Sojourner Truth, Mary McLeod Bethune, the daughter of former slaves, became a mentor for a host of civil rights pioneers, among them, Howard Thurman, Benjamin Mays, and Dorothy Height.

A Latin teacher had encouraged Dorothy to consider college, and perhaps that's why the poster announcing an oratory contest caught the young valedictorian's eye. The topic was the Constitution, the prize was a scholarship, and Dorothy won it. A quota on blacks denied her admission to Barnard, but by the age of twenty-two, she held a Master's degree from New York University.

She taught school for a time, then joined the United Christian Youth Movement in Harlem. To raise money, the UCYM Board decided to hold a major fundraising event on Wall Street. Wall Street? Dorothy and several other young people protested. The event should be held in Harlem itself. That was when she learned something of what she called "the balance between an ideal and reality." The treasurer of Riverside Church took them aside and patiently explained. If the event were held there, several potential contributors would be uncomfortable and might not make a contribution. "Our job is to get them to contribute so we can have a United Christian Youth Movement," he said. "It was a struggle," Height recalls, "but it was an important learning—to disagree with people and still maintain a relationship."

At a conference in England when she was twenty-five, she heard John McMurray, the political philosopher, speak. "He talked about capitalism and said that there are certain evils that seem to be built into it. If a system has evils, you don't need to do anything to it. They will destroy it anyway. If your system has to have discrimination, and it has to have unemployment, and it has to have war in order to exist, then you need to examine it. At the end, he told us, 'Go back to your own country, look at everything you can. . . .'"

His words stayed with her. Height wrote an analysis of the economic order, and for the first time, she saw that one could be critical of one's own system without being disloyal.

Shortly after returning, she joined the staff of the Harlem branch of the

YWCA. A month later, she was asked to escort Eleanor Roosevelt into a meeting that Mary McLeod Bethune, the widely influential black educator, was holding in Harlem. Impressed by Dorothy's composure, Bethune approached her after the meeting, asked her name and said, "Come back. We need you." Dorothy did, and Bethune put her to work on the Resolutions Committee, subsequently bringing her onto her staff. A year later, Dorothy was the Executive Secretary for Bethune's new organization, the National Council of Negro Women.

"Mrs. Bethune had an uncanny way of getting you involved," Height tells us. "She had very deep spiritual qualities, yet she was also an astute organizer and politician; she was always task-oriented. Yes, she drank tea and wore white gloves—but all that was superficial. The reality was, we were dealing with child labor, minimum wage, and working conditions."

But Dorothy also valued her mentor's sense of humor. "A sense of humor is extremely important. It helps you separate the things that are personal from the things that are not—and Mrs. Bethune had a great sense of humor. One time she was on a train in the dark days of segregation and the white conductor came through. He opened the door and said, 'Auntie, do you have your ticket?' She responded, 'And which of my sister's sons are you?'" Height later came to value this quality in Rosalyn as well.

In 1950, with Bethune's blessing, Height travelled to Haiti. Two years later, she taught social work in India for four months. These experiences further enlarged the international scope of her commitments; increasingly she brought a global emphasis to her work with black women, actively promoting links across the ocean.

Height takes a quiet pride in this expansion and attributes it to her having lived in diverse communities. "I have faced all kinds of discrimination, but I have known people of all backgrounds. At each stage of my life I've been in a more pluralistic setting." She sees deep tragedy in "the number of African-Americans who honestly have to say, 'I've never had a good experience with a person of another race, least of all a white person,' and adds, "I feel that I have."

"Mary McLeod Bethune? Howard Thurman? W.E.B. Du Bois?" Jim Jackson shakes his head. "I'd never heard of them before Roy introduced me to their names. But I've come to realize that they paved the way. At First National I've also got a tremendous mentoring network. I can name five or six people who have paved some roads and now are saying, 'Jim, I can see the potential in you; I want to work with you.'"

"What these mentors do, see, is teach you the rules. The rules aren't written anywhere; you can't go buy a book. It's from my mouth to your ear and you have to continue to pass it along that way. Roy's told us how to seek out mentors. He's given me the tools so I can play, and now I have to develop the skills so I can do the same."

He tells us that though he is still only twenty-seven, he is viewed by many of the new Passages interns as "the old man," a soubriquet he rather enjoys. "That's my responsibility—to make it a little easier for them. Because I was the first one to hire on, I told them what the hiring process is like, how to negotiate the salaries, and little things to look out for. Because someone's done it for me, I've got to do it for someone else, and Roy makes sure that you're keeping that at the forefront of your thoughts. It's invaluable knowledge and you can't express your thanks in so many words. Roy's a perfect person for this. He's helping scores of people to be the next generation of leaders, who will in turn help scores of others, and that's the key."

conviction

Developing Critical Habits of Mind

Sue Drucker has spent thirty of her fifty-one years working as an educator to expand public awareness of America's part in the larger global community. She delivers speeches, runs workshops, and counsels organizations around the world on the need for reordering what we value and how we think. She and her husband have co-authored a major publication on the global future.

We interview her in the cafeteria of the international apartment complex where she lives. A handsome woman with brown hair, a sharp nose, and soft, tired eyes, she speaks with gentle authority, punctuated by bursts of musical laughter. Six weeks before our interview, she fell and broke her right wrist. That was her writing hand, and she has found the experience of being unable to write both frustrating and instructive.

"When I have to use my left hand it does things to my brain," she says, and gestures with her cast. "It's as if I have to learn to activate new brain cells not used to being exercised." As she says this she grins at us to make sure we get the point. "Analogously, to think about the world from a global viewpoint instead of just our own ethnocentric or American interest viewpoint, we have to exercise new brain cells in some way, new patterns of thought." She observes that a "World War II mentality" still persists but points hopefully to a citizens' exchange program she sponsors that enables ordinary people to meet one another across national boundaries. We must stop working off of "old paradigms and notions of the world," she says, and begin establishing institutions that can deal with forces that are demonstrably larger than any individual. But it will take more, she adds, than "just heart to heart conversation." It will take *systemic thought*, an understanding of the larger patterns that shape and constrain us all.

Sue was not born knowing this. A lifetime of particular kinds of experiences conspired to teach her this insight. When her grandfather died after years of breathing coal dust in an iron foundry, his lungs were like concrete. To support the family, her father had been forced to drop out of school in the eighth grade and go to work in the same factory that had killed his father. Fortunately, as it turned out, the Depression put him out of work, and the young man found himself in the Civilian Conservation Corps, an experience that kindled in him the dream of becoming a forester. But the War intervened, and when Sue was a toddler, Arnold Kaproski was twelve thousand miles away on a Navy destroyer in the Pacific. Father and daughter scarcely saw each other for the next three years.

Under the economic pressure of raising a family in the post-war years, his dream withered, and Sue's father spent the rest of his life in the rust belt factory world where he had grown up. Yet Sue did not feel constrained by the financial hardship that forced both parents to work outside of the home, and she speaks of both parents with respect and affection. "They are very compassionate people. Even today they are still delivering 'meals on wheels' to those in greater need."

Growing up surrounded by extended family on both sides, she remembers gatherings that would fill the house, her father and uncles talking labor politics, her mother and aunts at work in the kitchen. "When it got late and we were sent upstairs, we would sit by the vent that came through the floor and listen to the talk that came from below." It was the political talk that most intrigued her, and a concern for the needs of one's neighbors was a consistent bass note throughout her childhood years.

At the same time, the fear of war was pervasive. She had never understood why her father had gone to war, and she felt abandoned and frightened. Thus, as she grew, she found herself torn between the deep patriotism of her Polish-American community and her own knowledge that the war had robbed her of her father and suffused her life with fear. Often as a child, when her mother was busy with her younger siblings, she would run off down the railroad track near her home to visit her maternal grandmother, "a very central figure for me." She remembers those times with particular fondness, times when she could feel special. Only later was she able to articulate what must have been at the time simply a vague feeling of incongruity: on the one hand this "central" person in her life spoke German and was clearly identified with Germany; on the other, "the world that I knew had gone off to kill Germans."

After the war was over, the fear was transformed into a dread of "the bomb," and she grew up feeling vulnerable under its shadow. When she was in the eighth grade, she won first prize with an essay entitled, "What to Do When the Bomb Falls." Once again, she felt caught in a curious contradiction. On the one hand, she clearly knew "the right answers" to the question. Yet on the other, she knew her answers made no sense. You should hide in the basement, she had written, "except that we didn't have a basement."

> I always had this feeling that I'd be somewhere else and I'd be running home and I wouldn't be able to get through the fence and then I'd get caught in the lilac bushes when the bomb fell. I knew all the right things to do, but I thought it was no longer doable. All these brave young men with their guns weren't going to be able to stop it. The bomb was too big. So that was a big source of questioning about the world. . . . and in this town one was not going to find answers.

The contradiction seems to have gone underground after that. Sue immersed herself in high school and later a small Catholic college where she came to appreciate the tradition of the Church's service in the world: "They were determined that people graduate with not only Catholic intellectual history, but also the social teachings of the Church." Again, her education had begun to raise questions.

One of those questions was a big one: "What is the purpose of my life?" As it turned out, she would not have to wait long for a clue. As she was on her way to her senior seminar one morning, the college president, who knew many students personally, stopped her in the hallway. "I have something for you, Dear," she said, and with a look of casual matter-of-factness handed Sue a notice about teaching opportunities in Africa. "This is for you." Sue glanced at the sheet of paper and almost without thinking, replied, "Of course." The reasons came later.

Her experience in Africa galvanized Sue's commitment. She had grown up with all the conventional missionary images of lost souls and starving children, but her encounter with the real Africa was transformative. Teaching school in a small village, she fell in love with the people and the land. Speaking their language, sharing their food, living in their homes, she came to know as human beings like herself, to see their traditions as "inherently fantastic and lifegiving."

Her village was within walking distance of the equator. It had no electricity, and a simple metal hoe was the most advanced form of technology available.

But shortly after she arrived, work began nearby on a satellite monitoring station. Changes came at blazing speed—people brought in television sets before electricity was available, children taught their elders to read, central government regulations encroached on tribal traditions. She experienced first-hand the terrific tension between the forces of modernization and the claims of tradition, between ancient tribal identities and emerging nationalism. "The globalization process was underway. But what would happen to human beings and the land in that process? What would be important to retain? What kind of values would be shaping this new global future?"

Bearing these awesome questions, she returned home where she was greeted by a huge reception. Most of her family and half the town turned out to welcome her and see the slides of her great adventure. At first there was intense interest, but the questions soon waned, and she realized that their misconceptions were so vast, their understanding so limited, that they literally did not know what further questions to ask. The room fell silent.

"It was clear," she says with an ironic smile, "that the family wanted it to stop. They were uncomfortable because everything I said was so far apart from what their assumptions had been that they couldn't go further—and that, therefore, I was somebody different too that they couldn't be comfortable with. I was aware of a huge gap."

Not long afterward, she fell in love with a man who shared her interest in Third World development. Mel Drucker had been training people for self-help projects in Latin America for years. A commitment to more than just a new relationship, their marriage "made it even harder to go home." Mel brought to their partnership a keen recognition of the need to understand the global complexity surrounding them from a systemic perspective. He recognized that despite the local value of many village cooperatives, without attention to how they integrated with "the macro economic system on a global level," little real change could take place because the villagers would remain at the mercy of forces that they could neither understand nor affect. Together, Sue and Mel started an organization called the "Institute for Global Initiatives," dedicated to developing educational materials emphasizing the emerging reality of global interdependence.

Their new enterprise flourished. Their publications reached a wide readership, a major book won them readers around the world and led to the formation of an international organization emphasizing global problem-solving. But with the success came new tensions. Both Mel and Sue had cut their vocational teeth in Third World villages. Both knew that it was finally the lives of these people whom they had first come to know and love as planetary family members that must guide their commitments. And yet with their recognition of global systemic interdependence came the knowledge that to address these issues "takes people who can move in other kinds of circles and affect policy at high levels—and that takes big budgets." Now, when she is speaking at a symposium in Russia or a conference in Geneva, she always tries to remind herself that she is speaking for the friends she made in Africa.

Sue and Mel have continued to receive sustaining affirmation from a growing network of people around the world who say, "Yes, we want to work with you. This is important." This community of confirmation matters greatly in sustaining commitment.

When we ask her what other sustaining factors steady her amidst all the complexity and ambiguity, she smiles softly, and then tells us a story.

When she was first in Africa, her project coordinator came to the village and asked how things were going.

"I replied, 'I don't know. The work is so big and this job is so little. I'm not really doing anything important.'"

"He just looked at me and then asked, 'Well, what did you think you were here to do, save all of Africa?'"

"That was a jolt. I sat back and said, 'Wait a minute. Yes, I'm only one teacher in one school. But this is one part of the picture.' So it was acceptance that this is part of the process of everyone doing their parts, and I had to find the part that was best for me."

She smiles, remembering those idealistic and hopeful years. "The ideals of young people are such that they need to see this Big Thing to do. But that's the critical moment to say, 'Of course, I can't do this whole picture myself, but I have to be a part. That big picture needs me, but I'm not the whole picture.'" She stops, shakes her head quietly as though seeking a way to explain it. Then goes on.

"I just think of plants often, you know? It's as if this plant comes into existence and it brings forth its seed and it spills those seeds into the ground and the thing continues. But if it didn't do that, the seeds wouldn't be in the ground for the next part of the process. So usually you have to see yourself over a long time span, and your life is just one single flower giving its seeds for the next part, the next stages. But don't necessarily expect to see the next stages bloom. It's for somebody else to see that flower."

It Matters How We Think

Most of us do not do a lot of thinking about thinking. Usually the work of our mind rumbles along without too much thought of itself. Inescapably, however, whether we are washing the dishes, pounding nails, or surfing a torrent of television commercials, our minds are active. Consciously or not, the human mind is continually composing patterns of order and significance from the myriad encounters, images, words, feelings, objects, smells, dilemmas, and surprises of every day. Consciously or not, the human organism is always organizing meaning.[1]

Meaning does not exist by itself; we create it. A tree may flourish apart from us, but the meaning of that tree does not. Whether we see it as a source of shade, a complex biological system, inspiration for a poem, or as a provider of match sticks, depends in large measure on who we are. Each of us constructs the meaning of that tree differently. In that sense, we are inveterate meaning-makers.

But the conditions of contemporary life assault our meaning-making capacity. The diversity of viewpoints and the complexity of contemporary conditions create an ambivalence that gnaws at the edges of our consciousness, eroding our conviction. Familiar ways of thinking no longer work. We try to understand, to make judgements, even to act. But when we do, like Raphael and Margo we find ourselves confronted by a maze of experts, explanations, and countervailing evidence. Faced by competing perspectives and partial knowledge, we hesitate. We often feel removed from the roots of things and barred from the power to change them.[2]

Sue Drucker does not feel powerless, however, and her story suggests that we are not at the mercy of those forces. She and her colleagues have learned how to make sense of diversity and complexity. They have learned how to make meaning in ways more fitting to the conditions of the new commons.

We have alluded earlier to the activity of meaning-making. In Chapter 1 we referred to the shifts in meaning-making required for the move from the old to the new commons. Then we described how the meaning of home is gradually transformed as we become more at home in the world, particularly through constructive engagement with otherness. Here we will suggest that although the evolution of meaning involves our feelings, it also matters how we think.

The people we interviewed are not immune to being overwhelmed, discouraged and bewildered, but they exhibit certain *habits of mind* that steady them in turbulent times and foster humane, intelligent, and constructive responses to the complex challenges that we face. While clearly hallmarks of effective people in many realms, these habits of mind are particularly germane to the problems of diversity, complexity, and ambiguity that we have described. They are

- the habit of *dialogue*, grounded in the understanding that meaning is constructed through an ongoing interaction between oneself and others;
- the habit of *interpersonal perspective-taking*, the ability to see through the eyes and respond to the feelings and concerns of the other;
- the habit of *critical, systemic thought*, the capacity to identify parts and the connections among them as coherent patterns, and to reflect evaluatively on them;
- the habit of *dialectical thought*, the ability to recognize and work effectively with contradictions by resisting closure or by reframing one's response;
- the habit of *holistic thought*, the ability to intuit life as an interconnected whole in a way that leads to *practical wisdom*.

These practices (the last two of which we did not find among our comparison group) are closely interrelated and developmentally sequential. Each is undergirded by the previous ones. Thus, dialogue underlies and permeates each subsequent habit. Interpersonal perspective-taking is necessary to achieve a full systemic awareness; and an awareness of how systems work is prerequisite to the full capacity for dialectical thought. As each habit evolves, the preceding habits are integrated but not lost.

Sue Drucker's story reveals all five of these habits at work. As a child, she was surrounded by and included in talk about the larger world. She learned that disputes, an essential part of the shaping of life, can often be understood and reconstructed by talking things through. From this early dialogue, Sue learned to take the perspective of others in a rudimentary way. Subsequently that capacity was deepened and elaborated through childhood reading, the study of literature in college, and her experience in Africa, where she made close friendships and came to know the world through the eyes of her hosts. The gap she felt upon her return marks clearly how the experience had changed her. Understandably, she was drawn to others who shared her transformed perspective—including the man who became her husband.

Through her late twenties, the larger aspects of her African experience came into focus. She grew able to see other cultures as systems, and consequently to take a critical (though not necessarily negative) view of her own culture. At the same time, her childhood ability to sense contradiction matured into a recognition that clashing perspectives are intrinsic to life itself. She came to see contradictions not as problems to be overcome but as challenges to help her think more profoundly and creatively. With Mel, she learned to value the tension between their commitment to the particularity and integrity of village life and the necessity of participating in abstract discussions of global economics. And finally, as her flower metaphor reveals, she knows that her own perspective is necessarily partial, yet she still longs to grasp things whole. In her recognition that she will never witness the final results of her work, we see a flash of the kind of long-term view that typifies the practical wisdom of many of those whom we studied.

The Practice of Dialogue

The practice of dialogue is foundational to meaning-making and to the moral life. Understood broadly as the underlying rhythm of a reciprocal exchange with our environment, dialogue is the central dynamic of human development. All human beings respond dialogically to their environments. Some are so influenced by the voices around them that they virtually cease to have an existence of their own, while others resist fiercely, sealing out all but the most resounding notes. The people we interviewed can hold steady in the face of complexity because they have learned to balance the dialogue between self and other well. They value settings where opinions are diverse and dialogue open.

An educator who is devoting the latter part of his career to addressing business and medical ethics enjoys bringing together interdisciplinary and interprofessional groups to focus on public life. "You might say," he told us, "that my way of coping with global complexity in all of its senses has been to call in others and say, 'Let's talk about this thing which is bigger than us all.'"

In Chapter 2, we described the "dance" between parent and infant and suggested that this primal dialogue is the very stuff from which a sense of "self" is born. Over time, it evolves into actual conversation[3] and is crucial to healthy development and the formation of commitment to the common good. Through shared talk we engage with voices different from our own and take them in, creating a diversity in our inner conversation that corresponds with the diversity in the outer world.[4] Over time, we gradually expand our repertoire of inner voices as our worlds expand. In effect, one might imagine a "self" to be an ecology of multiple voices and points of view, a kind of ongoing conversation generated by our interaction with a succession of environments. Thus, our sense of self is not only influenced by but actually constructed out of the activity of dialogue. The character of the self, therefore, is in part a reflection of the quality of those with whom we converse.

Accordingly, we asked the people in our sample about the nature of dialogue in their childhood homes. Over three quarters of them reported that when they were growing up, their families regularly ate dinner together. Some recalled lively conversations around the table. "My father was a conservative Republican, my mother was a liberal Democrat, and we read The *Washington Post* every day," Meg Powell, a physician, told us.

> I grew up with constant dinner table discussions about everything under the sun out of the newspaper. They really loved talking about things, usually heatedly, and both passionately believed what they believed. I learned from them the difference between arguing and discussing, because they were able to speak passionately but without animosity about totally different beliefs.

Meg now draws on this background in her work with health care systems. "I think my biggest skill is getting people who have totally disparate ways of looking at a problem into one room and agreeing on something."

By contrast, in the home life of most of the people of our comparison group there was a more limited ability to hold conflict well and to talk things out. Two were thrown out of the house by fathers, and one by her mother. Several of the fathers were silent, absent, violent, depressed, or forbidding, and there was little dialogue.[5] Some evidence suggests that people whose development has been inhibited—particularly the development of a sense of "voice"—came from homes often characterized by one-way communication.[6]

A handful of others who grew up in emotionally impoverished homes with little dialogue ultimately were able to become committed to the commons because enough positive dialogue was established in other ways. Elmira Frank, who has raised money for women's health clinics around the world, was quite clear about the lack of conversation in her own home. "Home was very difficult," she told us, "because there was no dialogue, no communication going on at all." Her mother did, however, provide her with a love of reading from the beginning. She began a dialogue with books, imagining conversations with the characters in them. This helped her to take the perspective of the other, a key habit of mind and gift to the imagination.

Many people quite deliberately incorporated external dialogue into their inner conversation. Here, Marsha Longstreth, a school administrator, describes her "advisory committee."

> I have a good and very diversified group of confidants that I turn to all the time—not just in times of crisis or conflict. I'm always talking to them about the work that I'm engaged in, about my own development, about their development, about the issues they're noticing. Some live on foreign soil, some are older, former teachers and counselors who are mentors, some former students in their thirties. They give me a different kind of barometer and view of the world . . . so that I'm just so enriched. I try to draw on all of it.

In this way, the habit of dialogue enables the voices of others to enlarge the self and opens the way for the practice of perspective-taking.

Interpersonal Perspective-Taking

In Chapter 3 we saw how constructive engagement with otherness enabled the people we studied to take the voice of the other into their inner conversation. The practice of compassion that these encounters both require and promote rests upon an early form of perspective-taking: the ability first to sense the feelings and respond to the concerns of the other, then to see through the other's eyes.[7]

Parents may model and encourage such perspective-taking in their children. In *The Moses of Rovno*, Douglas Huneke describes how Fritz Graebe rescued hundreds of Jews during the Holocaust. When Graebe was a boy and saw someone in distress or an unjust situation, his mother would often ask him "And you, Fritz, what would you do?"[8]

Through dialogue and constructive engagement with others, young people grow more able to sense, and to construct at least roughly, how the world may actually look and feel through the eyes of another. Such perspective-taking is fundamentally an act of imagination. The African-American theologian Howard Thurman writes of this act with awe.

[It is a miracle] . . . when one man, standing in his place, is able, while remaining there, to put himself in another man's place. To send his imagination forth to establish a beachhead in another man's spirit, and from that vantage point so to blend with the other's landscape that what he sees and feels is authentic—this is the great adventure in human relations. . . . To experience this is to be rocked to one's foundations . . . We are not the other persons, we are ourselves. All that they are experiencing we can never know—but we can make accurate soundings.[9]

The greater the care with which this form of perspective-taking is exercised, and the more perspectives that are brought to bear, the more accurate it may become. Todd North, the director of a multiproject community renewal program tells us,

When it's working at its best, you're hearing well and taking into account a lot of people's views and perspectives and trying to focus on an owned outcome. Think about that coffee cup [he gestures toward the coffee cup between us], and what you can see, and what I can see. We both can more fully describe what we're seeing if we both make contributions to its description, because there are things on that side of the cup that I can't see. There are going to be things that are obscured to someone else in the circle by shadows or lighting. So when we're trying to examine the whole of a new project, the most effective way is to draw on the contributions of where people of very different backgrounds sit and how they see things.

Perhaps the most difficult act of perspective-taking is to learn to see and feel the world from the point of view of those who have hurt us.

The director of the Passages program, Roy Matthews, whom we met in the first Interlude, described how deeply he had suffered as a child when his mother had to be away caring for white children. Subsequently, his experience in a predominantly white college cast a different light on his pain. "People would come up to me and talk in passionate ways about the nannies who had raised them, and say that the black maids and nursemaids were really their mothers because their parents just didn't pay them much attention. And I would listen to that, and I was just flabbergasted."

It enraged him—but he was also touched. He had heard stories of the alcoholism in the family that had taken his mother away, and she had conveyed to him the suffering of those children. He came to realize that "I had my stereotypes, too. I had my stereotypes about what white people were all about, and I had to come to grips with that. This is much more complex than any of us think."

As he came to this realization, the wall separating him from the white family grew more porous, and their suffering touched his own. At great cost, his network of belonging grew larger.

At work here is what Mary Belenky and her colleagues term "connected knowing." Connected knowers seek to "imagine themselves" into the other's position not simply by "effortless intuition" but by a "deliberate, imaginative extension of one's understanding into the other's position."[10] This imaginative extension is part of the felt connection foundational to compassion; it requires one not only to compose an image of the other's world but to experience the feelings of living in that world.

Critical, Systemic Thought

Critical, systemic thought is the capacity to identify parts and the connections among them as coherent patterns, to see oneself as part of those patterns, and simultaneously to step outside and reflect evaluatively on them. We heard this kind of awareness as Arthur Schwarz described his experience with inner city crack victims.

> I hate to say, "There but for the grace of God go I" because it wasn't God who put them there. It was broader society that destroyed these lives. Some guy's mother is in a prison for murder, and his father's a passing Celtics star who had one night with his mother, and all his brothers and sisters have different fathers, and his grandmother throws knives and meat cleavers at him, and he has a sister who seems to have her act together and tries to help him out, and she gets stabbed to death in a project stairwell. You know, if I was in a totally different situation, life would be horrible for me. I wouldn't know how to love. I would think love is hurting other people. You know, I might, too.

Clearly Schwarz has "established a beachhead in another person's spirit." He has imagined that world, and then included himself, asking, "How would I react if I were in those shoes?" But he has done something more. Instead of placing the blame on an arbitrary "God," he says, "It was broader society that destroyed these lives." In so doing, he rejects as insufficient an interpersonal framework in which one is either an innocent victim or the object of imperious fate, and steps onto a third entity, a system that he calls "society." This perspective enables him to locate problems within the frame of what several referred to as "the big picture."

From Interpersonal to Systemic Awareness

Systemic thought is crucial to managing complexity and seeing things whole. Developmental psychologist Robert Kegan argues that it offers a more adequate way to grasp the complex demands of modern life than the form of thought characterized primarily by an interpersonal view.[11] An interpersonal interpretation of the welfare problem, for instance, might see it as essentially a matter of personal fortune or character: to sympathizers, welfare recipients are simply down on their luck; to critics, they are lazy. While the interpersonal perspective holds a measure of the truth, it is limited and often distorted in the absence of a larger, systemic perspective. Seeing whole, we can recognize how the welfare system encourages certain harmful forms of behavior, or how the economic system makes welfare inevitable by creating a permanent underclass. Systems shape behavior in ways that may be invisible from an interpersonal perspective. By viewing problems as systemic in nature, we can conceive solutions that go beyond mere exhortations for individuals to work harder.

A Broader Framework

Ben Graystone, who has spent a lifetime designing public health systems, recalls when he "got" the concept.

> I went to the World's Fair in 1939 and there was a movie by IBM discussing complexity. A couple was planning a dinner party and saying "Well, who should we invite to dinner? Well, let's invite the Joneses. OK, fine. How about the Smiths? You know the Smiths don't go well with them, just the husband goes well. Maybe we'll leave the Smiths out." And they went on down to the next step below that. "Now who should sit next to who? Should we have fish or not? This one doesn't like this." They went on with this thing of designing the dinner party, discussing it as an interconnected set of elements — literally, the system. It was a wonderful way to show it. I remember it vividly.

By casting a particular problem in a larger set of relationships, systemic awareness imparts significance to what might otherwise seem an essentially random, "meaningless" event. What we see through an interpersonal lens as an isolated act of heroism, for example, may appear under a systemic analysis to be part of an evolving struggle for justice. Making this kind of link gave many in the sample an enhanced sense of their own efficacy in the face of suffering, injustice, and discouragement.

So when Arthur Schwarz said, "I hate to say, 'There but for the grace of God go I,'" he was resisting a spurious separation between his fate and that of another human being. Recognizing the larger system, he knew that the problem of crack cocaine was related to poverty and racism as well as to the inability to say "no." And because of this awareness, he could see his place in the system as well, thus recognizing that he was part of the problem, but seeing also how he could be part of a solution.

Training unemployed minority youth, Stefanie Green felt overwhelmed when 5,000 more factory workers were laid off. She realized she could not work just with minorities.

> It wasn't enough. There was just too much suffering, too much poverty, too much wealth, too much inequity. The whole economic system needed to be looked at. Capitalism can be made more responsible. It doesn't mean you are free to do what you damn well choose to do. There's no sense of the common good in that.

Viewed from an interpersonal frame, complexity can be overwhelming, but several of our interviewees, using systemic thought, actually found complexity to be the natural and appropriate expression of our world. Betty Russell, who builds intricate alliances among international relief agencies, told us,

> Complexity doesn't affect me negatively. I'm not cheered by it, I'm not glad it's complicated, but I'm not immobilized by it. Part of me feels like it's more realistic. I get more depressed by superficiality: people saying, "it's very simple—this is all we need to do." Then I feel there's avoidance coming into play.

An international educator, Samuel Kofi, finds the complexity of problems a natural outgrowth of their interconnectedness. If you're not working at a problem in a way that connects with other domains, it's a sign that you are not working at a deep enough level.

> I am always interested how the solutions of other problems fit into that singular thing you want to do. Supposing you are thinking about education. How does the environment, how does health, how does economics, how does religion, or the way you are going to comport yourself with your fellow man tie in? I need to see how it all comes out before I consider the solution to be a good one. If I don't see the root of it, and if I don't see how it spreads out to the people, I would say, it's not fundamental enough.

"Indeed," says Natalie Taylor Black, an economist and legislative advisor on international development policy, "sometimes it is the very complexity of a problem that may generate its own solution."

If you work out of a mechanistic or control model of how things work, complexity can be dangerous. But out of the organic model, the interconnectedness is actually healthy because sometimes by solving this problem, you also solve that problem. Problems can metastasize, but also solutions can metastasize in an organic system. So the challenge is to find the ways to pinpoint where intervention can use the dynamics of the system to bring health.

While a systemic approach may identify webs of connection in which a problem may be recognized, it is not a conceptually neat enterprise in which everything falls into place. Rather, it honors ambiguity by searching for meaningful patterns within the sea of what William James called "blooming, buzzing confusion" rather than walling it out.

Knowing this, and that most situations are fraught with ambiguity, Sr. Jeanne, a hospital administrator particularly concerned with the spread of AIDS, likes to "keep the door propped open," a metaphor used by several people we interviewed. "You can't be an isolationist; problems aren't confined," she says. "I'm frankly not sure that there is a solution, but I'm willing to work *as if* there is one."[12]

Cultural Consciousness

As perspective-taking is integrated with systemic awareness, cultural consciousness emerges. This is the recognition that we dwell in cultures—patterns of human behavior shaped by a particular community or population over time. Working in multi-cultural contexts, many of the people we studied developed a sensitivity that allowed them to reconstruct the world of the other with fidelity while simultaneously recognizing that their own understanding was incomplete.[13] This requires an openness to difference, for other cultures often seem inscrutable to those who hold their own cultural preferences as inviolable rules. Rachel Carbonetti, a diplomat with long experience at the United Nations, noted, "Though you're constantly reminded that you have your humanity between you, you also have great differences—in religious belief, cultural beliefs, educational backgrounds, point of view—that come from having been brought up in another part of the globe. And you can't forget it."

This cultural consciousness is more than simply a superficial "tolerance" by which one glibly confers value on another culture without engaging it. It requires acknowledging one's partial understanding of that culture, and tentatively presuming its worth while seeking to understand it better from the inside. Dr. Meera Gupta, director of a major international population program, describes a recent "country-specific" approach.

We need to understand the sociocultural setting of the countries so that instead of taking a message from here and trying to transport it somewhere else, our programs take into account why people behave and think in a certain way. They really should be tailor-made to the beliefs, issues and behavior of the particular community or of the country.

For people like Carla Andrews, an urban high school teacher juggling several points of view among her students on the Gulf War, this cultural consciousness was essential.

There aren't [only] two points of view on too many issues that I know of. They are very complex. And they get more complex when you think about the kind of places where kids come from, and that they come here with a script that has to do with their family experiences, their class background, their ethnic background, and their life experiences. We have kids who know nothing about war, and we have kids who are victims of war. We have an immigrant population that includes Salvadorans, Nicaraguans, kids from Ethiopia. This is a very, very painful experience for them because they had to relive their war experience as we talked about war and watched protests and demonstrations. We had to say to the kids who were antiwar, "There are people here with a different kind of experience." So it's not easy. We have to take these decisions a little differently than just arbitrarily talking about absolute right. Right in what context?

Yet while this kind of dialogue can be tortuous and complex, the people we interviewed describe moments when they not only persevere but even relish it because such intercultural conversations challenge and extend their grasp of the world and the problems on which they are working. They persist because in discovering the connections, they develop new avenues of possibility. Rather than buckle under the ambiguity of multiple perspectives, they thrive on it.

A Strong Moral Compass

Committed people understand cultural relativism, but are not paralyzed by it. Although their systemic awareness makes it difficult to see the world simplistically, they do make judgements about right and wrong. Although they resist making sweeping condemnations of people with whom they strongly disagree, they are fully capable of taking a stand. They exhibit a strong moral compass and can draw firm distinctions between what they welcome and reject, admire and abhor, uphold and resist.

Sam Cassidy, a man who would be described by many as an activist for peace and justice for over half a century, put it this way.

You just try and not be too fanatical—not insist that your way is the right way or that you know more than you do. But find the balance of how you can, on the one hand, drive ahead and agitate, educate, act, risk your life for truth as you understand it, but also know that your vision of the truth is limited. You try to listen to other people. You try not to be limited by too narrow an environment.

They do not shield themselves from their own critical eye.

Many exercise a fine balance between generosity and judgment that impels them to search for what may be worthwhile in people and causes they oppose. Sr. Clara Kennedy said,

It has always been important for me to try to see ways in which I could engage the opponent so as to educate and maybe change them. But I have also learned that the reasons why people oppose me or my beliefs are not always the reasons why I think they do it. I've realized there's more to people's opposition than is immediately apparent to me, and, in effect, there's no way I can ever really know all the reasons why they oppose me. So there has to be what Margaret Miles describes as a "hermeneutic of generosity" with regard to why they act and behave and believe the way they do.

When asked if even those she opposed counted in some way, she answered, "In some ultimate way, yes."

When we asked Jay LaDuke about how his work on behalf of native peoples brought him up against white people, he quickly corrected us saying,

First of all, you have to understand, I don't work in opposition to white people—I work against their opposition to us. Secondly, we have to survive in their world. We can live in a world within a world, but we can't do it and be isolated—we have to acculturate, not assimilate. And that's doable. Now, it's doable because the greater society is tolerant, and in fact does have a conscience, even though some of us are reluctant to say or admit that. But, in my state, for example, the public school system has Indian curriculum throughout now. Now, that's happened because a lot of Indians have demanded that and worked hard for that, but it's really happened because the greater society has allowed it to happen.

"So you see transformation on both sides?", we asked. "On both sides," he responded.

A systemic perspective has enabled them not only to see other cultures as systems of values, habits, and customs, but to turn the mirror on themselves and see their own culture *as culture* and themselves as products of a particular cultural history. "Look deeply enough through another's eyes and sooner or later they will fall on yourself," said a former Peace Corps volunteer. Asked how she came to see the limitations of her own culture, Sue Drucker responds,

> Maybe because I lived in another country with people of other cultures and beliefs and had to do such deep questioning about my own belief structures, and I did it at a deep enough level for a long enough time that I see the difference. I see what's happening but I don't know how to affect a whole country; and I think America right now is the country that has to be affected.

In sum, many of our interviewees are able to coordinate several cultural perspectives at once, including their own. Thus, they can appreciate what they find worthwhile and are open to what they may not easily grasp in another culture, yet they are forthright in their abhorrence of brutality regardless of where it is found. At the same time, they are conscious of their own cultural frame from which they are rendering the judgement. In effect, their appreciation of cultural difference does not invalidate their sense of a moral compass. On the contrary, their experiences appear to strengthen it by taking them across the boundaries and beyond the blind spots of their own tribal perspectives.

Systems with a Human Face

When Sue and Mel Drucker founded their institute, they did so in part because they knew that to make a significant difference they would have to work at a systemic level. But they remained determined not to forget the reason for their work—the friends they had made in the villages. As they mature, committed people increasingly recognize the strengths of both interpersonal and systemic thinking. They recognize that casting complexity into systems may do violence to some aspects of reality. Their felt sense of connection, however, helps to keep a human face on the issues and guards against the dangers of indifference to human suffering in the service of some abstract system.[14] Because of their direct experience with otherness, the people we spoke with know that, finally, no systemic construction is greater than the particular people within it. Speaking of the underlying commitments that grounded a lifetime of social action, Sam Cassidy said,

> Every individual is sacred. My work with people is always meant to be soul to soul. And I always try to relate it to my political convictions. . . . One tries to live with as much sensitivity and love to every human being as possible, and at the same time, tries to encourage the development of a society in which the institutions will be that way.

Dialectical Thought

Bringing a range of different points of view into dialogue with one another frequently provokes conflict; recognizing multiple value frameworks as legitimate in their own terms invariably leads to contradictions. Dialectical thought, as we use the term, is the ability to recognize and work effectively with contradictions, either by resisting closure or by reframing one's response to compose a more inclusive synthesis. It rests on the recognition that knowledge is not static but emerges out of ongoing interaction with the environment. Dialectical thinkers, therefore, tend to seek out a range of different perspectives—often, though not invariably, in the form of contradictions—because they believe that a synthesis can be formed which will be a more adequate representation of reality than can be achieved from a single point of view.[15]

Sue Drucker, who grew up amidst contradictions, learned that not all contradictions had to be resolved.

> My speaking brings me in front of other people who are maybe thinking about things in a totally opposite way than I am, you know, opposed to me. Which raises new questions. Or some people have thought about different facets of it and come from a different line of questioning. Or some may be very sympathetic but say things like, "Well, have you thought about it from this viewpoint?" So these are moments of growth for me.

We have identified two ways in which our interviewees seem to transform contradictions into "moments of growth." In one, which we call "flexible reframing," they identify the "frame," or set of underlying assumptions, of a particular approach and recast it. In the other, they seem to hold open the contradiction and dwell with it unresolved rather than forcing a synthesis for the sake of clarity.[16]

Flexible Reframing
The ability to hold and work with apparent contradictions depends on a fluid manner of responding to obstacles, persistent problems, and dilemmas. Flexible reframing includes standing back and examining the barriers to progress from all angles. Sometimes people do this intuitively, simply working "on their feet," and at other times it requires reflective assessment. Ben Graystone describes his approach.

You shift gears. There's a Chinese Buddhist guy who reads people well. Two of us came in. He said to this guy, "The trouble with you is when you want to do something and you come up against a wall, you keep hitting it and hitting it." Then he looked at me and he said, "When you come up against a wall, you take a look at it and you go around it, you dig under it, you go here and you go here and you go here and then you go someplace else." There are many different roads to Rome.

Working on behalf of the whole commons often requires one to take a different road to Rome, revising a hunch about what's going on and how best to respond. Our respondents appear to do this by referring to a "big picture" that enables them to walk around a can of worms and view it from several different angles. People spoke of the importance of having a grasp of such a "big picture," and yet no one could tell us exactly what it looked like. It seems more like a hologram—not static but more an ecology of interdependent systems, inclusive of many viewpoints, frames, and lenses. It demands more than a single image to describe it, yet it is held together by a kind of fluid grasp of the whole that enables "flexible reframing."

Flexible reframing makes it possible to shift to either a wider or tighter focus on an obstacle or contradiction, much as a zoom lens does in photography. Shifting back and forth from the problem to its context can yield insights from each. Don O'Neil, who drafted intricate state and federal environmental guidelines for the Bush administration, described it this way.

> I'm working on the details as well as every now and then trying to stand back and say, "What is the systemic issue here? What is the global thing I'm trying to accomplish?" It's hard to try to remember to do that. . . . I think the people who can do that, who can integrate knowledge of the details and . . . still have a sort of overarching sense of where you want to go and have a global picture, that's what life's about.

A related way is by breaking out of the constraints in which the problem or contradiction appears to be set. Chris Anderson, an engineer and senior executive who has designed innovative corporate structures to support workplace diversity told us that "it all comes back to getting the larger perspective, seeing how the whole thing works and then seeing how all the pieces play." He then described a familiar puzzle in which one is given three rows of three dots each and told to connect them with four straight lines without lifting the pencil from the page.[17] "You've seen the game with the nine dots? Well, most people try to solve it staying inside the dots. But you have to go outside the dots, and I think that that's one of the things that for some reason I've been able to do, is to get outside the dots. So I'm not a visionary, I just see the world differently."

Still another way our interviewees reframe is by recognizing the partiality of what they're working on and then placing that in relation to something more inclusive. Conrad Grudzinsky, an experienced teacher of teachers, said,

> I guess a strategy is to try to create a different kind of whole—a new kind of whole—recognizing the partiality. Once you recognize that the partiality is indeed partial, or a fragment of something, then to me the action is to say, "OK, what can we put it together with? It doesn't go together with what I thought it went together with, but what can we put it together with?

Holding the Contradiction Open

But some situations present contradictions that cannot be resolved by shifting frames. In such cases, our interviewees' systemic take on contradiction enables them to respond in a second way: they acknowledge the contradiction, but do not try to eradicate, hide, or force it into a premature solution. In effect, they simply hold the contradiction open.

They may do this in several ways. Sometimes they engage with the contradiction directly, abandoning the expectations, but not the hope, that the contradiction may eventually resolve itself. Joel Rosen, a lawyer who spent two years working through city and state bureaucracies to relocate a center for at-risk youth explained, "The way I deal with being overwhelmed is to return to the source of the greater understanding, to see the contradiction in a larger context, and to sort of let it be and let it flow. Usually it settles down, and then there's a greater integrating point, in the future if not now."

When the contradictions are held open in this fashion, people can be brought together to discuss the problem in the hope that the contradiction itself will become the catalyst for a dialogue from which some common ground can emerge, if not a full solution. Some were able to use this approach, not just for external problems, but in self-examination as well. Barbara Fox, director of a social service agency, reflected:

> I try to have a really broad mind, and I try to look at things from all positions. I may not want to accept it, but I can see when we should be doing things differently. So I recognize our limitations, and then I'm willing to talk to other people and say: "How can we work together to do this particular task?" And I will always listen to what others have to say.

Finally, some of our interviewees may hold open contradiction through a recognition of paradox and respect for mystery. This is an essentially spiritual stance that rests on the understanding that contradictions sometimes represent polarities held together by an only partially understood, yet underlying unity.[18] This stance turned out to be most common among our older interviewees, corresponding to theories of faith development which point to the emergence of not only an awareness but trust in paradox after midlife.[19] As Natalie Taylor Black, the legislative consultant, put it,

> It's this two-sided thing going on all the time. You're holding the problematic nature of it and there's mystery, but there's also this incredible potential for transformation. The dynamics of that are mysterious, but I've seen things be so powerfully transformed for good without anybody controlling them or wilfully making it happen. What I've learned is that there's sort of a stance of openness and trust and vulnerability that, if you can live it appropriately, seems to keep space in the process for these transformative things to happen, not because they're being made to happen, but because somehow it's possible for them to happen.

Practical Wisdom

We have noted previously that when people age well, they make meaning in ways that are at once more finely differentiated and fully integrated. It is clear that the elders in our sample have aged well. Over the years, they have developed a kind of practical wisdom, an ability to see the big picture without missing the details, to recognize our connections to one another while acknowledging our distinctness, to celebrate the whole without losing a grasp of the particular. Each habit of mind contributes to these capacities.

Because they appreciate the importance of dialogue, they listen well, attending to the particularity of each speaker, yet reaching for language that connects, creating a conversation. Because they can take the perspective of others, they feel both the radical uniqueness and the fundamental humanity of people different from themselves. Because they recognize systems, they are able to link immediate problems to larger, global issues, and to take a broad-based, long-term stance. With a bird's eye view on the partiality of their own work, they can see themselves as "one among many," and carry a sense of both greater humility and enhanced responsibility. And because they are dialectical thinkers, they are less vulnerable to simplistic explanations or universalistic bromides; they know that reality is constantly emergent, and that we bring truth into being through dialogue. Thus, while seeking to apprehend some larger whole, they know they never grasp it fully. It is this impulse, both open and integrative, that drives their work toward a common good, a commitment to a more inclusive sense of the whole, while refusing to settle for a premature, false, or sentimental universalism.

So they are ferociously practical, leery of theoretical meanderings or ungrounded schemes, emphasizing that what finally matters is "making a difference" through their work. They are skeptical of what one person referred to as "all that BS on the table that has nothing to do with the real battles." Said another, "We have to embody [our conviction]—physically and visibly—and not just talk about it. To me, you engender commitment when you demonstrate that you are willing to follow through on what you said."

When we asked some of the older interviewees what they understood wisdom to be, Sam Cassidy commented,

> I think wisdom, in part, is having a perspective in which you understand, first of all, that you're part of the whole world, everybody and nature, and secondly, that despite the fact that you are inspired and energized by being part of all people, on the other hand you're very limited. In one sense you know everything by being at one with nature. But in another sense you know how limited you are in your own understanding.

Then he paraphrased George Meredith: "A truly wise person is one who understands that the things that seem to separate us from all our fellows are nothing compared to things that unite us with all humanity. And I understand that," he said, adding wryly, "but I don't live up to it."

We have detailed five forms of thought that appear essential for people to stay steady in the face of diversity, complexity, ambiguity, and the challenges of the twenty-first century. We have argued that it matters how we think. But *what* we think also matters. The content of our thought is fully as important as the form. In the next chapter, beginning with the story of Rosalyn Williams, we will examine the role of images, stories, and symbols in the formation of commitment to the common good.

courage

A Responsible Imagination

Through a Lot of Fire to a Place at the Table

In her first year at Penn State, Rosalyn Williams went to babysit at the home of Bob and Ellen Thayer, pastors of the First Congregational Church. As a young black woman who had grown up on the only black street in a white suburb, she had babysat often for white families. Always it was expected that she would eat in the kitchen while the family dined in the dining room. When Ellen asked her to help set the table, Rosalyn automatically set her own place in the kitchen. This time it was different.

"Ellen is just a very natural person, and I think she thought I was really acting out. She said, 'What is this?' I said, 'That's my place,' and she picked it up and moved it into the dining room, and I just was really stunned by that. Then she asked me how I liked my steak. I didn't have any idea how you'd answer. I said, you know, 'Cooked'!"

Shortly after that, Martin Luther King came to speak at the Thayers' church. Rosalyn went home afterwards and read *Stride Toward Freedom*, a book she describes as "the single most influential book I ever read." For the first time, she realized that she mattered, not only to herself and her people, she mattered to America. "King not only said that we count, but that we count most profoundly because we hold clues to the soul of America, to redeeming the soul of America."

These events marked a turning point in Rosalyn's life—between a time when she saw herself essentially as a passive participant and a time when she had a sense of "peership and expectation." Yet they became important in her ongoing imagination only because they were resonant with elements in her earlier experience. How did she come to babysit in that home? What enabled her to hear the power of King's words?

There was a Woolworth's not far from where Rosalyn grew up. It was her mother's hope that if Rosalyn worked hard and behaved herself, she might become the first black salesperson in that store, rather than "just bust suds" as she herself had done all her life as a housekeeper and laundress. That would have been a step forward, for no one in her family had ever graduated from high school. In those pre–Civil Rights days of the late 1940s, her mother was a realist.

Her father, on the other hand, was not. He had always wanted to be a dentist, yet was forced to settle for stonemasonry; an accomplished golfer, he was denied membership in his own town's private country club. He had moved his family out of the city into the suburb of Wellington, where he knew Rosalyn would have a chance to attend better schools and understand the white middle-class lifestyle. Rosalyn recalls how he used to have her strut around and practice being a lawyer.

The differences between her father and her mother came to a head when Rosalyn was ten years old, and they were divorced. Rosalyn lived with her father for two years until he tragically died. "I felt a lot of the pain that anybody feels coming from a dysfunctional and broken family, especially as split as ours was and as different as our parents were—and because my main parent died on me," she says.

Now in her fifties, she believes that those "earliest myths" have ongoing power in her life, stirring her feelings about abandonment and loss. But they also give her greater sensitivity to "the people who get done unto," who feel themselves abandoned, "not only by people, but also by dreams and ideals—like prisoners, and kids who I think we're just stockpiling on waste piles and giving up on and not creating a useable future for, and AIDS patients who are lying in the back wards of hospitals alone. I have a sensitivity to 'accompaniment' because I really understand in my gut that feeling of being left."

A year after her father's death, while on a class hiking trip, Rosalyn took a bad fall, slamming into a tree and dislocating her hip. Bedridden for the next three years, she benefited from her father's foresight, for the town provided her with individual tutoring and a telephone link to the classroom. Through the tutoring sessions, her teachers discovered her potential and encouraged her to go to college. It was also during this time that, though unable to walk, she became involved with a local radio show and cultivated a public voice, a voice with which she became a folk singer by avocation, a choral director, and finally a powerful speaker.

Despite her accomplishments as a high school student, Rosalyn encountered the inevitable racism. She never quite understood, for instance, why her friends did not invite her to join the Order of the Eastern Star, and she was painfully aware of the abuse endured by one of her best teachers, a Jew; his experience, she knew, could have been hers. All in all, she says sardonically, "my own self-image in those years wasn't too terrific."

At the same time, however, Rosalyn had begun to develop a sharp sense of irony and a keen eye for the contradictions around her. Juxtaposed with words about liberty and justice for all, she saw actions denying these things to some. Once, at the height of the Little Rock crisis, her high school history teacher took her aside and asked if she would be embarrassed if they discussed the events in class. "Well, I'd been watching scenes of black kids being taunted and chased with broken Coke bottles; I just looked at her and said, 'I wouldn't be embarrassed if you wouldn't be embarrassed. It's the white folks who are acting up!'"

In her early teen-age years, an incident occurred which she experienced as personally humiliating, but which she later came to recognize as the systemic oppression of both class and race. Every Christmas, the members of her church in Wellington wrapped canned goods in white paper and brought them to the altar for the poor. That year the gifts were given to her family. "The kids all came over and sang 'Hark the Herald Angels Sing' and dumped this barrel of White Gifts," she told us, "and I was so humiliated." But it was worse when they opened the presents. That year the sweetener in cranberries had been rumored to be carcinogenic, and almost half the gifts were cans of cranberry sauce.

Shortly thereafter, her mother and stepfather sent her to a different church. There, she met a number of foreign students from the university—African, Indian, Filipino. A Nigerian medical student told stories of African life, and she began to glimpse this part of her heritage.

Rosalyn joined the youth group and choir and the pastor recognized her in important ways. Unlike the school, church proved to be a place "where most of the time I felt more equal and could play a lot of leadership roles." She feels that "everything I've done since then has really emerged from those contexts."

Though her family feared she was becoming uppity, she went to college. She majored in History, and shepherded by the Thayers and several mentors whom we met in the first Interlude, Rosalyn's life dream began to take form. She aspired to write a new sociology and to touch people in ways that gave them skills, power, and possibility—"to give that gift back."

In the spring of her senior year, she stood in the hot sun near the front of the huge crowd, listening to Martin Luther King's great speech at the March on Washington in 1963. To her right stood an old man, a portable radio pressed to his ear. "Go on, Martin. Go on, go on!" she heard him urge—and watched the tears flow down the deep furrows of his creased, brown cheeks. "We've done it!" she said, and went to bed that night genuinely believing that the world would be forever different. A month later, the church in Birmingham was blown up, "and the reality sank in that this was going to be a lifetime struggle."

Upon graduation, she took a job with the YWCA and came to know some of the most influential moral leaders of the time. On a trip to Asia, she found herself sitting opposite Indira Gandhi, not three feet away. When her chance to ask a question came, she asked, "How would you like to be remembered?" Gandhi smiled, was silent a long moment, then replied, "When I was a little girl, we used to sleep out under the sky on our veranda, and my father, the great Nehru, used to look up at the stars and say, 'Do you see those stars? Those stars, they are free. Do not ever rest until your people, like those stars, they are free.'"

It was, she says, "a goosebump moment," and the message sank in like a coin in a wishing well. Gandhi's personal answer to Rosalyn's question enabled her to see this great woman as a fellow human being, and "raised the question about what my own response to challenge or greatness—or my evasion of it—was really going to be."

The lesson has remained with her, but so does the awareness that she is surrounded by seemingly intransigent injustices. She knows that there are people who are constantly struggling and repeatedly defeated, and she acknowledges her anger. Though the anger is personal, she knows it is also collective—a function of an entire set of interlocking systems that oppress.

It is frustrating that even the churches with whom she works, particularly the white churches, have a hard time hearing it. "They have very little way of dealing with black anger. So the minute you begin to express it, even if it's very intellectual, people try to talk you out of it. In the church, which ought to be the place where people can really express their feelings, confess their feelings, and forgive them, it doesn't happen because it never gets on the table. I just don't think that you can ask people to repress their real feelings, or even their forgiveness if that's what's happening. Church is the place you're supposed to be able to practice that."

In counterpoint, she describes her work with the Urban Service Mission as "mobilizing communities of caring people into changing their behavior so that we can have a different world." There can be, she tells us,

"moments of power"—a time when your own integrity gets in sync with something that you are to be or do and touches base with a kind of sychronicity with others and with the world. Those moments are enough to enable you to get through the other parts as humanly as you possibly can. We can create those kinds of moments— economically, politically, socially. So my life work, as I struggle with the issues of public policy and all that, is to find ways not just to get Bill HR 476 passed, but to en- able people whose lives depend on that to have moments of power that enable them to do that kind of advocacy for themselves.

Underscoring how her own struggle to create such moments relies upon the company of others, she says, "I used to think that everyone could live in peace, but I've decided that's not hope; that's wishful thinking. So what I believe now is that there can be communities of faithful folk who laugh, pray, and sing to- gether and who tap into great moments of reality and the spirit of life that fuel up the engines for you to go back out into the world and do what you can."

As she reflects further on the nature of communities of faith, it is clear that she has a "lover's quarrel" with her own. "The Navajos talk about people who operate off the artifacts of the faith rather than the real, vibrant stuff. The church is too often frightened and operates out of a lot of artifacts." Then quot- ing a mentor, she says, "The church is here and there, now and then." Despite the failures of the church, she explains, she holds a bedrock conviction that re- ligion as much or more than any other institution can shape attitudes—atti- tudes about love and justice and who counts in this world.

She believes that religious communities can be communities of hope. "If my hope dries up I need you to be hopeful. We need to talk so that we can strate- gize together and celebrate our victories—weep and rage at what's wrong and nurture it. I think we've got to build whole new networks, liturgically based, where we also acknowledge that all this isn't just us alone, but that we're tap- ping into some power in the universe that is groaning with us."[1]

But the sheer tonnage of the task often leaves her feeling her limitations. "There are lots of days," she says with a small laugh, "when I just don't want to get out of bed in the morning."

Asked what sustains her during the hard times, Rosalyn speaks of the importance of memory. Paraphrasing King, she says: "Remembering the saints stiffens your weak knees and lifts up your drooping head. In black culture, telling the stories is much more important than it has been in the white community. In our present society we have to find a way of remembering. The Bible is full of that metaphor. Just before Micah's injunction to 'do justice, love mercy, and walk humbly,' God is contending with Israel 'because they've lost their memory.'"

We ask her if there are any particular images or symbols that sustain her over time. She immediately responds that there are two: music and meals. "I don't know what I would do without music. You can tell all kinds of truths with music that you can't with words, and I've watched the way it transforms community. In our Western society, I think we're too verbal. So powerful symbols and music of all sorts that make connections beyond words are real important."

Meals. She mentions her experience with the Thayers. "From my various families I have learned that home is where I'm invited to the table. Home is pretty critical to me because of my upbringing—the big myth I strive for." She pauses and then quotes Douglas Meeks: "Home is the place where there will be a place for you at the table, what is on the table will be shared, and you will be placed under obligation." Continuing, she adds, "Communion has always been really important to me, because it's a leveller. There's nobody with any more sin or less sin than anybody else when you're around that table, and the whole world is invited there. So the breaking of bread—I think that's when intimacy emerges."

The Thayers have remained companions to her over the long years since Ellen first brought Rosalyn to the table. "They've really just been there," she says. "When people pour themselves out for you, that really is home and family; it teaches you the miracle of transformation and makes you really understand what could happen if you could pour yourself out for somebody else. But it's not a sloppy agape; they've been a real tough kind of wonderful, challenging presence."

Toward the end of the interview we ask, "What has enabled you to recognize your own limitations and still speak out and act with the courage you do?" Her reply leaves us both in silence.

I came through a lot of fire. I was born in the time when I saw people put everything they had on the line for an idea, that idea being freedom and justice. I saw people go down and die, go to prison, and bear scars on their body and come out with the same faith and energy and belief that they were a part of something nonetheless. And out of my own fire—trying to figure out who this black woman is and what I was called to do in the timing of my time—I can connect to their story.

Rosalyn Williams has come through a lot of fire, connected with the larger story of her people, and experienced transforming moments of power that enable her to work on behalf of the common good. For many, hers is a story of courage; yet even when they are contending with formidable opposition or danger, people like her do not typically describe themselves as courageous and sometimes resist being described so by others.[2] More often they describe themselves as simply doing what must be done. "Courage? It's not courage," one person said. "It's just where I should be." Just as someone who plunges through a wall of fire to pull a friend to safety sees the friend more than the danger of the flames, committed citizens likewise tend to understand themselves as simply acting in a manner congruent with their perception of reality. "Courage" from the French "coeur," meaning "heart," suggests that committed lives have heart—not mere sentimentality, but rather the strength and grace of a seeing heart that, joined with an open and informed mind, can apprehend reality in a manner that seeks not to deny but rather to engage central challenges of the twenty-first century. What is the nature of that courageous heart and how has it been formed?

The Formative Power of the Imagination

Public awareness of the power of the human imagination to shape the reality of our common life is increasing. There is growing concern about violent and degrading images in the entertainment media, volatile language in talk radio and in political and religious rhetoric, sensational television newscasting about violent acts and their effect on children, and the misplaced hungers of an advertising saturated culture.[3]

There is also a growing awareness of the need for more adequate language—images, symbols, words, and ritual—to grasp, name, and responsibly communicate the realities of the new commons. Spawned by the development of technology, such images as "cyberspace" and "the information highway" did not exist in common discourse until the development of the Internet. Similarly, our social, economic, and political language is being pressed to generate better images to describe the intensification of our interdependence within the new commons.[4] "Global marketplace" and "interbeing" are terms necessitated by our evolving experience.

Two questions, therefore, that we bring to our inquiry are, "What images,

symbols, stories, and songs elicit and instill the strength and grace that characterize the quality of citizenship needed in the twenty-first century? What clues
can we harvest from committed lives about the sources and character of images
and language necessary to apprehend the reality of the new commons, to act
responsibly and prosper within it?

Imagination: Process and Content

Philosophers and psychologists have long shown that what we apprehend as
reality is continually being filtered and interpreted, composed from our experience by means of the imagination. When we perceive things, we do not take
them into our minds "just as they are." Rather, we compose them into internal
images. Wrapped in the senses, these perceptions, or compositions, become
the stuff of feelings, thought, and language. The human mind is not a simple
copier but rather an incessant composer, and this composing occurs through
the process of imagination.[5]

Samuel Taylor Coleridge identified imagination as the highest power of the
knowing mind. The process by which we reflect and learn, imagination participates in reason, sensing, judgement, understanding, and conscience.[6] The
German word for imagination is "einbildungskraft"—the power of shaping into
one. As we seek meaning and purpose, imagination is the power by which we
sort and shape into one the disparate elements of our world, using images, symbols, stories, theories, and rituals. Thus the process of imagination permeates
the habits of mind we discussed in Chapter 4, and may be understood, in part,
as a "meta" habit of mind.

It is important to distinguish imagination from fantasy, since we are prone to
conflate the two. Fantasy is the activity of mind by which we associate, com-
bine, and juxtapose previously uncombined things. It keeps the mind open and
limber; it can entertain; it can be a means of experimenting; it can help us do
the important work of building new wholes. But fantasy need have no necessary relationship to "reality" and hence it can end in its own subjective pleasure
or horror.

Imagination incorporates fantasy, but as Coleridge, Blake and others have so
clearly seen, its highest function is to find relationships that are truthful. The
work of the imagination is to create the real.[7] The imagination seeks to put
things together which belong together. And this belonging has significance for
us because it illuminates the mystery of how life is.[8] As morality is oriented by
truth, thus imagination has an inherently moral and ethical function. Clearly,

then, the work of imagining cannot be consigned to children, artists, and idealists alone; it is something we are all constantly doing. Since the images we take in, along with the images we compose, serve to define "how life is," they also determine how we act. The quality of a society is dependent upon the strength of its imagination of the world and the meaning of citizenship within it.

We do not adequately grasp the significance of the role of imagination until we recognize its influence over both how we think and *what* we think. Although in this chapter we focus primarily upon the *what*—the *content* of thought—how this content comes to shape our lives and our commitments cannot be understood apart from a respect for the *process* of imagination.

The Process of Imagination

The ongoing process of imagination occurs at the edges of our present understanding, where we work to move beyond current knowledge and give form to our emerging experience. For descriptive purposes, this process may be subdivided into five phases, each flowing into the next. Continuous and cyclical in nature, the process can "begin" at any of several points.[9]

Conscious Conflict. This phase arises from what many of our interviewees described as a sense of contradiction.[10] We become curious, or troubled, even devastated. Something is amiss, dissonant, or won't work. Unless we are subject to an environment in which we are systematically distracted, the conflict between an assumption about the world and a perception with which it clashes motivates us to sort out and clarify the dissonance. Among those we interviewed, several recalled times when a sharp sense of contradiction set them thinking. Often they had witnessed an injustice which violated their earlier assumptions about fairness.

Pause. Once such a conflict has come into view, but before it is resolved, we need to pause. This is the time when we "put it on the back burner," "sleep on it," or turn to contemplation-meditation-prayer. This pause may be brief or lengthy, but it is not an attempt to escape from the conflict. Rather, it allows for a kind of underground scanning. Bachelard describes this phase as a time when the mind is asleep but the soul keeps watch.[11] The people we interviewed often spoke of "taking time," and more than half of them reported some explicit form of pause as an important practice. Rosalyn, for example, described a discipline of journal writing and prayer. One man, a scientist, distinguished between times of loneliness and times of "aloneness." He said, "I am a disaster at meditating, but these alonenesses allow you to do things. It's a place where things come together and you can work with them. Very frequently we are ruled by partialities, but if you become less ruled, you begin to create."

Image-Insight. Indeed, the gift of the pause is an "ah-ha!" An image (not necessarily visual) lends its form to hold a new understanding that simplifies and unifies the previously disordered and unmanageable fragments of our experience. The image, which may emerge from within or be borrowed from without, crystallizes a new insight which presents itself to us with the force of reality. As when Rosalyn used the images of music and meals, the people we interviewed called upon both ordinary and extraordinary images to name and convey the truth of their experience.

Repatterning and Reframing. Unless one finds connections between the new insight and lived experience, the new insight will languish. A process of repatterning and reframing connects the "ah-ha" to our lives in fitting ways. The new image-insight becomes a symbol, a key to recomposing a whole pattern of meaning[12] and understanding, much as "a place at the table" has become a symbol by which Rosalyn recomposes her experience of family, making critical connections between communion and community.

Interpretation in Dialogue. If the new insight is to live in the world, it also needs to be articulated and acted upon in the midst of an interested public—in verbal and/or other forms. This serves two purposes. First, our inner process is brought to completion and we are able to "own" the new insight. Second, the adequacy of our imagination can be tested, protecting ourselves and others from the limitations of our own subjectivity.

As the inspector in an Agatha Christie mystery says: "If five people were to completely agree in their account of events, I would be suspicious, very suspicious indeed." Each mind composes the facts somewhat differently, and we can be attracted to misbegotten and ill-fitting images. More, every image has both strengths and limitations. Thus we human beings must always be playing detective, testing our perceptions—our imaginations—with each other in our quest for truth, seeking a shared sense of "reality" upon which all can agree. As Lily Tomlin had it, reality is "a collective hunch."

Accordingly, we are dependent upon trustworthy communities of confirmation and contradiction who can affirm that "Yes, life is like that" or respond, "No, that interpretation is inadequate, perhaps even dangerous." This is what Rosalyn recognizes when she seeks to create a community of ongoing dialogue in which to rage, strategize, keep up hope, challenge, and celebrate.

The Content of Imagination

The moral life, then, may be understood, in part, as a search—shared with others—for appropriate images by which to interpret our sorrows and our joys.[13] From our earliest waking into life, images are planted at the heart's core. One by one, layer by layer, a myriad of images seek a pocket in our meaning-making and vie for our allegiance.

Over time, as we interact with the natural and social world, we develop the capacity to take objects, people, places, actions, language, and ideologies into the self, into the mind, into the heart, and to imagine them. We shape and order them into the one reality we thus come to trust. In this process we are necessarily dependent upon the nature of the images available to us. From this constant imagining, we learn who we are, what our world is like, and what will be asked and allowed.

In Rosalyn's family everyone learned as a part of inherited folklore "little adages that were meant to explain life and to keep you in your place." One she remembers was, "Facts is facts and figures is figures, white folks is white folks and niggers is niggers." Reflecting on this now she says: "You know, you grow up your whole life hearing little things like that, and it really shapes your self-concept and breeds a lack of expectation, community, and peership. It was a joke, but it conveyed a reality."

How might Rosalyn's life have been different if a different adage had been placed at her core?

A Conversation

At one point during our study, we convened several of our interviewees to learn more about the sources and character of the images, symbols, stories, and concepts that informed their commitments. The conversation was wide-ranging.

Reflecting on her experience, one person mused that for better or for worse, Disney has been a primary shaper of the moral imagination of at least two generations, creating mass accessibility to such stories as *Snow White*, *Pinocchio*, *The Lion King*, and *Pocahontas*.

Sr. Clara Kennedy recalled that her decision to join a religious order was made in dialogue with three primary images. At the time, she was not so much without direction as with too many. Holding in her heart the image of a friend who was dying of cancer, she took a long walk through New York City, immersed in questions about the possibilities and limits of life. She looked up and found herself beside a statue of Prometheus chained to a rock. Nearby was a synagogue with the familiar inscription: "Do justice, love tenderly, and walk humbly with your God." The three images came together in what Rosalyn would describe as a "'moment of power,' when who you are gets in sync with what you are to be or to do and touches base with others and with the world." Recognizing that responding to the call to religious life can be powerful, complex, and costly, she remembers thinking, "Yes, if you steal fire from the gods you pay for it, but it's worth it." Shortly thereafter, she joined the Franciscan Sisters, and has served as a teacher and scholar in both the United States and Latin America.

David Bradley, a journalist committed to delivering stories about Third World realities to First World peoples, ironically resisted the notion that images and stories might shape his sense of self and commitment. But as the conversation took some imperceptible turn, he began discussing a photograph that had been widely circulated in major print media a few weeks earlier. A child in Somalia, naked and starving, has collapsed face down on the road to the feeding station. A few feet behind the child, poised on a rock, a vulture waits.[14] With aching dignity, Bradley, who had become a father for the first time during the previous year, wept as he discussed the power of this image and its complex meaning for him. In Bradley's imagination, the child in the gaze of the vulture was a symbol of every child, including his own. He spoke movingly of the struggle to choose wisely between his commitment to his son, who he knows now plays on a planetary commons, and his commitment to all children of a now global generation.

Images implanted in the soul, at whatever age, can disturb, delight, move, haunt, and compel. Sometimes we are conscious of the images at play in our formation; more often, at least initially, they capture us unawares.

Sources of Images

While all experience feeds the imagination, two particular spheres of image and language were salient in the interviews—family and religion. Though we did not hypothesize that this would be the case, we should not be surprised by these patterns. Images gain power when they are deeply and broadly *resonant* with our experience.

The experience of family is powerful throughout our lives and for good or ill, inevitably shapes the imagination by which we live. At its best, religion is not a single facet of life, but rather a culture's way of interpreting the whole of life. Religion can serve as a primary source of story and symbol, orienting or distorting life commitments. Interdependent with these two powerful spheres, a myriad of images from the whole world surround can shape or misshape commitment. We saw, for example, how images from nature, the media, science and philosophy, the arts and literature can either nourish commitment—or numb and crush the spirit. We turn now to a consideration of the images in these three interrelated spheres—family, religion, and culture in general—that had positive power in forming commitment to the common good.

Family as a Source of Images

Family Moments as Icons
Among the many examples of powerful images rooted in family experience, a particularly dramatic one came from Stefanie Green, who works with minority unemployment and teaches Economics in urban settings. When she was a young child, her father, a sociologist, was a missionary in Burma when war broke out. Her parents were advised to evacuate, but, committed to the people there, they chose to stay.

> The soldiers came tearing into our house. My parents had put tea on the table to welcome them and to say, you know, "Have some tea." They said, "We want money," and my father said, "We don't have money, but we have tea." And the guy was going to kill my father. He got a clip of bullets out, and then dropped them. And my father, being a very courteous man, picked them up and gave them back to him. [Laughs] The soldiers also wanted my grandmother's wedding ring and so they filed it off. All that must have had a lot of impact on me—I was confused and didn't understand, and yet I did understand.
>
> My parents had given us each a toy to give to them—this is interesting to have thought out—and my brother handed the soldier his Teddy bear. The soldier patted him on the head and said, "Don't cry, I have a little boy at home, I know how it is."
>
> My parents were setting us up to have a human response to wild, crazy, tired, and hungry people.

Another, Reeve Hess, who founded a multi-class organization that links economic reform with global peace, was six years old when she accompanied her mother to a crowded country store where the townspeople registered to vote.

> There was a black woman in front of my mother in the line, trying to register. I didn't know what she was doing, but when it came Mama's turn, she told them that she

wanted to take a reading test too. When they told her that she didn't have to, she said that if the woman in front of her had to take the test, so did she. So she stands there reading part of the Constitution or something. But all I remember is knowing she was doing something really, really bad [laughs] because all these people just got totally silent and were staring at us. That is the only time I remember my mother being political at all.

In a less dramatic and more common example, a director of a health agency remembers that in the years of her childhood there was a neighboring family whose children were mentally disabled. Every other Sunday her mother took dinner to them; on the alternate Sundays, her aunt provided the dinner. Together, mother and aunt helped to weave a reality of connection and responsibility that embraced the wider community.

Like the "public parents" we described in Chapter 2, these immediate family members became images of connected, compassionate, and practical participation in the life of the commons, anchoring perceptions of "who we are" and "how we do things."[15] These kinds of images challenge simplistic assumptions about people being merely winners or losers and impart a more complex understanding of human purpose and responsibility. They provide an alternative to the imaginations of individualism and fortified tribalism.[16]

Family Lore

Along with the stories of immediate family members, we also discovered a good deal of powerful family lore, sometimes going back several generations. For example, R. Lowell Rankin, co-founder of a major relief agency, remembers a story his grandmother often told.

As a little girl, she would peep from her window at the trains as they rolled past. One day the cattle train stopped as it often did to water the animals. But this time when the doors rolled back, instead of cattle, human beings poured out. Crammed together in box cars, whole families of Native American people were being shipped west from their homelands in the East to the parched hills of the Dakotas. Like the cattle before them, they were being let out to water. Later, on a trip to town, she was running down the boardwalk, when she tripped and landed in the mud. Looking up, she saw towering over her, the figure of a huge Indian man. Smiling, he bent over and gently picked her up, putting her safely back on her feet.

The disparity of these two scenes never left Rankin's grandmother, and years later, after a lifetime of work with Native Americans, she would tell these stories to her grandchildren as they sat in "the Indian room," surrounded by hand-woven baskets, headdresses, blankets, carvings—all gifts from people so different from her own.

"My grandmother was a very strong example. It was as though I thought 'she served the Indians, I might as well serve all of Africa'!" he observes, chuckling at his childhood grandiosity. All four of his siblings went on to work on behalf of the larger community—in law, education, and as public trustees.

Another piece of family lore came from an African-American, Cecil Baldwin, who has exercised exceptional leadership in several institutions and is now well into his seventies. As a boy, he was often told this story about his great grandmother's cousin, a slave.

> Fathered by the slave owner, she worked as a young girl in the master's big house. One night, she and other household slaves were sitting at the top of the stairs listening to the master talk in the parlor. They heard him say, "As of tomorrow, the slaves will be free." At dawn the next morning, her mother who had been a slave at a farm down the road, rapped on the door and said, "I've come to get my daughter." The now former master said, "Let her remain here," suggesting that she might now stay on and work for pay. But the mother responded: "No, the bottom rail's on top now, and I'm taking her home."

"That kind of lore was central," he says, recognizing that though he had not thought of the story for many years, it had been stored in his soul across seven decades and served as a plank in the platform of his personality, lending its strength to his own self-definition and expectations.

Family Exhortation

Metaphor and story also appeared in family conversation and exhortation. When images are offered as admonitions, they appear most influential when they are congruent with the lived example of the person who admonishes. A Hispanic woman who has made significant contributions to public health in both the military and public office remembers her mother, a dedicated and respected community leader, saying, "Don't be a 'buche pluma'"—a showy bird which doesn't produce. An Episcopal priest who has led her parish in addressing the problem of guns in urban settings remembers her father saying shortly before he died: "Remember always that human need is infinite, and that the number five bears the same relationship to infinity as does the number five million. Therefore, wise persons are going to make conscious decisions that have a qualitative impact on infinity rather than a quantitative one."

A physician in a city hospital remembers going in and out of Washington, D.C. with her mother, driving through the wealthy and poor sections alike. "I remember when we drove through the poor neighborhoods, she talked a lot about our responsibility to do something about that. Her response was to pray for the people there. My response was to go into medicine and try to do something about it."

Religion as a Source of Images

The Complex Nature of Religion

Although we wanted our sample to reflect the religious pluralism that characterizes our society, religious commitment *per se* was not a selection criterion, and our stance regarding religion is complex.

We began with two contradictory hypotheses. On the one hand, we recognized that religion at its best can be a significant cultural source of symbols, stories, rituals, and beliefs presumed to provide an ethical orientation to human lives. This is not to say that all religiously inspired action is either moral or serves the common good. It is only to say that religion always has an ethical valence, because it is a response to the ancient moral question, "How are we to live?" People in our sample, we surmised, might have been influenced by religious traditions and practice.

On the other hand, it seemed equally plausible that they might not have. In a time of significant cultural pluralism and the re-examination of fundamental values, religion itself is undergoing critique and revision. Subject to the doubt, relativization, and marginalization that has accompanied the rise and dominance of the scientific paradigm, religion has been displaced in the lives of many by a kind of "secular faith," often oriented to centers of influence indifferent to religion. Prompted by the same forces, other people have sought out religion as a defensive and even hostile form of re-tribalization, directly contradicting a sense of commitment to the larger whole. One could presume, therefore, that people committed to the common good—aware of cultural ambiguity and the importance of a critical perspective—might be particularly subject to secularization, actively distancing themselves from religion. Further, some people simply grow up and live in contexts where religion, by happenstance or intention, plays little or no apparent role.

Religion Wasn't Far Away

In fact, we found that in the majority of the people we studied, religion played an important role in the formation of commitment, a finding similar to those of other studies.[17] When asked if religion played a part in their lives, 82 percent said that it had. Most said they were influenced by religion when they were young—though the degree and form varied dramatically. Currently, over half are affiliated with some community of religious faith and an additional quarter classify themselves as unaffiliated, yet "spiritual." Some 18 percent do not consider themselves religious.

For some in this last group, religion appeared to be an influence in indirect or partial ways. For example, although he has no religious affiliation or practice, and his family was in no way religious, one man mentions that when he was an adolescent, he shared important conversations over some period of time with a local minister. Nevertheless, to describe these few as religious or even spiritual would violate their own understanding of themselves.

Looking at the sample as a whole, we conclude that while people committed to the common good may or may not be religious in terms of either affiliation or practice, in the process of their formation and ongoing lives, religion has not been far away. What do we mean?

We use "religion" here not in its narrow ideological sense but rather in the broader sense conveyed by the word "faith." In contemporary usage, faith is often used synonymously with intellectual belief, dogma, or creed; yet when the phenomenon of human faith is examined across cultures, faith means something much closer to trust. In Sanskrit the word for faith is "sraddha" from "to set" and "heart." In this sense faith is an activity of setting the heart.[18]

Whether expressed in religious or secular terms, having faith may be understood as the activity of making meaning—composing and being composed by what we trust as ultimately true and dependable. Thus, faith is not just something that religious people have. Faith—meaning-making in its most comprehensive dimensions—is something that all human beings do in the everyday dialogue between fear and trust, hope and hopelessness, power and powerlessness, alienation and belonging.

In Chapter 2, we described the ongoing life task of composing and recomposing a trustworthy sense of self and world—a process dependent upon communities of belonging that offer developmentally fitting elements and provide the appropriate mix of support and challenge. A critical part of what communities and societies provide—by intention or default—is moral content. That is, they provide the actual material—images, stories, symbols—that constitute the imagination by which their members name and know life itself.

It is said that faith is "meant to be religious." Faith seeks a language, a *shared* system of symbols with which to interpret the whole of life. If imagination is the process of "shaping into one," religion may be understood, in part, as the distillation of shared images, powerful enough to shape into one the chaos of our experience. In other words, stories, habits, and the rituals of the everyday are the content of the imagination by which people know who they are and what they are to do in the world. It is the work of religion, in concert with the whole life of the commons, to do that well.

Therefore, as a research team, we have been interested in understanding the faith by which committed people live—how they make meaning, how they construe life as a whole, how they imagine the relationship of self, world, and cosmos, the seen and the unseen. By these definitions we can say that for most people in the sample, religion has either played a direct, explicit role or has been an influential feature of the wider ecology of their lives. We cannot say that all of the people we studied have a religious imagination, but we can say that they are characterized by an imagination, a faith, that seeks to be responsive to and respon-sible with the whole of life. It is the character of this "faith"—or consciousness—that sometimes causes them to be regarded as courageous by others. In a culture plagued by fragmentation, meaninglessness, or narrow self-interest, those who work to see a larger whole and act on its behalf are deemed courageous.

Revising Boundaries Outward

"God is always revising our boundaries outward," wrote the Quaker philoso-pher and mystic, Douglas Steere.[19] Whether they would express this in theistic or other terms, the people we studied would tend to concur.

This kind of enlarging revision has sometimes occurred at the cost of a sense of betrayal. Perhaps, for example, in their adolescent years or at another time when their own spiritual, communal, and moral sense was expanding, some were a part of a religious community which placed strictures on belonging. If this meant exclusion or denigration of one's own self or others, the person was likely to experience this as a betrayal of the essence of religious sensibility—the capacity to embrace the truth of the whole—which was at once professed and denied by the community. This kind of betrayal drove some away from religion. Yet in their resistance to a confining and distorting religious formulation, they simultaneously preserved a sense of spiritual and moral fidelity.

On the other hand, when religious understanding and practice could be continually reframed to fully respect those from beyond the tribe and to support participation in the complex diversity of the commons, people found in religion a strength of spirit and imagination that encouraged commitment to the common good. For these the encounter with otherness enabled them to reimagine their own spiritual and religious experience, sometimes drawing them into a more profound understanding of their own deep religious root system. In many cases also, that encounter with otherness has given them meaningful access to the symbols, stories, songs, and beliefs of other religious communities. Thus they remain religious, but not in a provincial or narrowly tribal sense. They seek, and some have found, spiritual-religious communities with whom they share ways of making meaning that they can hold with integrity in a complex, multi-cultural world.[20]

They practice a critical-systemic faith which helps them hold steady even as a spiritual sensibility of awe and participation deepens. A spiritual-religious sensibility is a part of what enables many of them to tolerate the complexity and ambiguity with which a commitment to the commons must contend. Thus one person, for example, spoke of how both his experience of Jesus in his Roman Catholic upbringing in the Midwest and his experience of Shiva in his more recent experience in India inform his understanding of life. Though he used to keep them separate, he told us, "they have begun to talk to each other."[21] His boundaries have been revised outward.

Images of Interdependence

If the people we interviewed speak of God, the Holy, or a sense of sacred presence, they tend to do so in ways that suggest a principle of interdependence.[22] Said one man, "Sometimes we tend to fall back on God and assume He will walk our walk. But I think we've got to do the walking ourselves, with the understanding that we have a copilot." Chris Anderson, an engineer, told us that his early religious experience had taught him to see the universe as ultimately harmonious. It had provided the critical backdrop that enabled him as a corporate executive of a major company to build more integrated systems. Always deeply confident that there was some way that things could work more effectively as an interdependent whole, he had forged new relationships between finance and manufacturing, and developed benchmark models of managing diversity in the workplace, transcending narrow patterns of departmentalization and socialization within the company.

This sense of the interdependent nature of all of life also appeared in the desire of many to hold religious and public commitment within a single frame: One spoke of John Calvin—"the minister as politician. His combination of piety, intellect, church leadership, and the attempt to be a public leader. . . . That for me is the Puritan synthesis for which I remain perennially homesick without any apologies." Another admires Bill Moyers who "carries theology and moral analysis into the exploration of public issues with a great variety of public people." Still another was inspired by an archbishop in Latin America who had transformative influence in political life, "a man of such spiritual force and intellect—this combination, which you don't see very often, of tremendous spirituality and yet hardheaded realism."

Most of those for whom religion is personally meaningful, wrestle with ambiguity, not only in the new commons as a whole but also within their religious community. Stefanie Green, for example, struggles with the hesitancy of the church to grapple with some of the issues she believes are integral to the life of the new commons.

> I've had trouble with the tradition for some time now because it is so male oriented. And I grapple with my faith as a Christian. But I really do see Jesus as a very radical person who was speaking to the poor and the disenfranchised and giving a word of hope to them, and that gives a word of hope to me too. Lots of times I feel that I'm very much on the edge of the church, and yet I'm in such good company.

The Combined Power of Family and Religion, Story and Community

"Good company" captures something of the combined power of both family and religion. It appears that when these spheres function well and overlap, they steep the human imagination in traditions of community and story, "peopling the imagination" with a great company of others who share a common suffering and aspiration. Good stories told in trustworthy company confirm us in the knowledge that we are a part of a vast drama of life that both holds and depends upon us. Craig Dykstra, a religious educator, has written that "storytelling in its many manifestations, invites the teller and the listener or reader to an intellectual adventure that weds our deepest powers of imagination, emotion and intuition with our powers of reasoning and assessment."[23]

A man who was the entrepreneur and CEO of an internationally recognized company that has become a model of progressive, socially committed business practice told us that when he was a boy, his family enrolled him in Hebrew day school where he learned that he was a part, not only of a family, but also a people. Were there any stories or images that were important to him in those years? He responded:

> Well, obviously, the Purim story, with some mean old king that was oppressing the Jews. There was the Passover story and the Exodus story. I think part of my expected life story was what I got from the Middle Peninsula Jewish School. When I was really young, there were the stories of how Judah Maccabaeus saved the Jews, and that was influential. I had dreams of being a Judah Maccabaeus.

In a similar vein, Susan Jay told us:

> I grew up with the idea that Christianity meant that you acted out of love and compassion and it was systemic social change that was required. It was always so clear to me that my parents and grandparents were living it out—this fusion of politics and religion. The overarching metaphor was to be someone building the kingdom of God, and everyone had dignity, worth, gifts, and talents, and the script was to find your particular way, whatever it was—carpenter, homemaker—everyone had a role to play. And the motive for doing that was joy. That's what it meant to live well.

A World of Images and the Challenges of Committed Lives

The imaginations of the people we studied draw upon a world of images. The natural world, literature, music, film, theater, visual art, and other media such as newspapers, magazines, and radio were all mentioned as wells of important and memorable images.[24] Principal among these was literature of all kinds—from poetry to philosophy, biography to novels. A remarkable number referred to themselves as "voracious readers." Said one who now works to address the quality of television for children, "As a child, you couldn't give me anything I wanted more than a book." The natural world appeared also as a particularly fruitful source of meaningful imagery.[25] References to television as a source of significant and positive imagery were surprisingly sparse, given its pervasive presence in our society; but there is some evidence that it can foster awareness of a wider world.[26]

Looking across all of the images people mentioned, we began to discern certain patterns among them that directly addressed central challenges of the new commons. Notably, *images that give form to a positive, connected, and centered sense of self* enable people to withstand personal, commercial, and political assaults on their self-esteem; *images that reveal the world as it is* along with images of "what should not be so" fuel the strength to engage the complexity and moral ambiguities of the new commons; *images that convey the overcoming of obstacles and discouragement* engender hope; and *images that hold a sense of paradox and mystery* enlarge the mind and sustain energy and spirit over the long haul.

Images of a Positive, Connected, and Centered Sense of Self

Committed citizens employ images that give positive form to their own sense of self. This was particularly important for minorities. Just as Rosalyn learned through Martin Luther King's imagery that she counted in this society, so too did a young black man in the sample find voice, pride, and a deepened identity as a teenager when he discovered the works of black poets like Langston Hughes, Countee Cullen, and Sonia Sanchez. "Man, that stuff hit me. It just resonated with me. The connection was so profound to me that I just read through the night."

But forming an identity is a struggle for those of the majority as well. A researcher and writer devoted to the issues of children, poverty, and the arts says: "I was seen as a 'watercolor' child all through high school. I've worked hard to find more vibrant colors. I have no desire to be a strictly watercolor or even a tempera personality. I have oil paints in my soul."

Tim Lloyd, born to an upper-class white New England family, tried for years to shed his privileged identity. Then, fresh out of college, he found himself considering a job in Alaska. Once again trying to run away from an integral part of himself, he realized, "I'll never be able to get far enough away." Yet in his imagination, he fled in the other direction to Spain, picturing himself finally at the far end of a road to nowhere, out of money, down on his knees in the mud. Even then, he knew, he would still be only "one panhandled dime" away from a phone call and all the resources he needed. Barring amnesia or catastrophic social collapse, he would always bear some measure of privilege. It was then that he was able to say to himself, "There must be some meaning to this heritage from which I cannot escape." The answer that came to him was, "That's it. No one should be down on their knees in the mud; I have had the privilege of being raised to stand up and do things." The moment became an important touchstone in his imagination. He has subsequently given his energies to elected legislative office and innovative educational leadership, providing people at the margins of society with access to the political-economic franchise because, as he puts it, "Education done right, does this for people."

A part of the positive image of self reflected in committed lives is a sense of connection and right proportion, often cultivated, we found, in contact with the natural world. A leading business consultant remarked provocatively: "The graven image I worship is my boat."

> It takes on all kinds of symbolic importance. A transportation to heaven. A place where my children and grandchildren come together and great relationships evolve as generational differences collapse and everyone has to depend on everyone else. The boat is filled with years of those memories and that kind of spirit. You are a part of nature. The idea of holism is manifest on the boat in the most intense kind of way. Not just the boat and the water but the human beings and everything. It's a microcosm of holism. Everything connected and interdependent and multifunctional and emotional and rational and spiritual. It's related to hubris (what it takes to go out there) and humility (because you're crazy if you are not humble before the elements).[27]

In a complex world, people of commitment need to learn to hold steady while engaging turmoil. A woman from India shared a story that helps her to do this.

> There was an Indian king who tested his new disciple by saying that if he was serious, he was to walk with a lamp filled with oil all the way through the palace. The disciple did so and returned saying, "Here, I haven't spilled a drop of oil." The king said, "Well, did you look around the palace?" And he said, "I was so busy watching the oil, I didn't." The king replied, "Well, go back there and balance the oil, but now look and see what's around you as well."

"That, I feel, is a lesson of a lifetime," she said, "to operate out of a sense of serenity in the midst of storms."

Images of the World as It Is

One of the features of committed lives is a willingness to work to understand things as they really are—to recognize manifold complexity and diversity and to seek out "right images" that can help to make sense of often unwieldy interdependencies.

Steven Rhode, a physician who has received recognition for his leadership in state and national mental health systems, remembers that when he was growing up before the age of TV, he and his parents would regularly listen to the radio program, "Grand Central Station"—a series of engaging episodes, focused on many different lives, each life drama beginning in Grand Central Station. Four decades later, he could still recite the opening, complete with sound effects.

> Day and night great trains rush down the eastern bank of the Hudson River, flash briefly past the long, red row of tenement houses south of 125th Street, dive with a roar into the two and one half mile tunnel that burrows beneath the glitter and swank of Park Avenue and then (a big hiss of locomotive steam) Grand Central Station!— crossroad of a million private lives, gigantic stage upon which are played a thousand dramas daily.

This inclusive and evocative image of the commons appears to have helped cultivate the soil from which an imagination embracing both the complexity of a whole city and the particularity of individual lives could grow into a commitment to the mental health of a whole society.

Recognizing that it is important to choose carefully and strategically which images of the world one uses, R. Lowell Rankin commented that the relief organization with which he works is careful not to use pictures of Third World peoples that portray them only as hollow-eyed and starving. Rather, they portray the "other" as participating in their own development. If they convey only the first, he tells us, people stop giving when those in need "start talking back."

What Should Not Be So
When asked for images that sustained them, a surprising number of people spoke, not of dreams of justice, but rather of specific injustices and examples of cruelty and suffering that they had seen. These images seemed to serve as powerful icons for what should not be so. Some of these came from theater and film. For example, a white man remembers being exposed to racial oppression through a play called "In White America," which he saw as a teenager with his father. And a woman who now works on behalf of families and children vividly recalls the impact of a rape scene in the film "Two Women." "I came home and looked at my daughters with a deep but inchoate feeling about how vulnerable women are."

A stateswoman and legislator told us that she often thought of a line from Pericles: "'We [must] obey those unwritten laws which it is an acknowledged shame to break.' 'Acknowledged shame,' she mused. You've got to have a consensus that certain things are simply not done."

Images Engendering Hope

One of the people we interviewed, Don O'Neil, an M.B.A. working in the executive branch of the federal government said: "The place to be effective is that area where there's pressure from all sides and you're sitting there trying to find the common ground. You're trying to find the link between the doable and the desirable."

This is the stance from which committed people cultivate an imagination that engenders hope. By developing provisional models they envision alternatives to prevailing but inadequate views. Their imagined alternative has about it a sense of greater adequacy—more dependability and ultimately more practicality—even if it is difficult to achieve in the short run.[28]

It is our perception that committed citizens can imagine alternatives and believe that change is possible because they have seen it happen in ways that suggest that ongoing creation is a principle of life. Thus, they have a storehouse of images that anchor persistent hope and a conviction of the possibility of transformation. Peteris Zieds, the Latvian-born biologist we met earlier, recalled his first days shortly after the end of the World War II. Separated from his family and fearing that they had been lost, he began taking courses at the University of Freiburg, a city which had been largely destroyed by carpet bombing.

> The shortcut to school passed right through the ruins. One day as I was walking there I saw this incredible tree growing right in the midst of it all. And I was totally flabbergasted. And I passed by a second and third time, and it was growing very fast. In two weeks it had grown considerably. I thought to myself, "There's all these ruins around, and we have done it, we humans. My life had been ruined; people's lives had been ruined. But that tree is stronger than what we have done." I was so intrigued, I went back and I said, "I have to find out about that tree. What is going on about that tree? Or trees in general and life." And then I found that the tree was the ailanthus, it is "the tree of heaven." They tend to grow when everything else is destroyed; they are able to grow rather fast, and they spread nicely.

Notably, certain institutions served as images of hope. Since people committed to the new commons think systemically, they are almost invariably concerned with the health and viability of institutions. They need images of institutions that they can affirm and point to as signs of possibility. Several saw the existence of the United Nations as a source of hope. "There are 159 nations sitting down together, and at least at some level trying to communicate. That's the most hopeful sign in the world. That's a thrilling direction. All the ingredients are there."

Holding Paradox and Mystery

Grappling as they do with complexities that ask them to hold paradox, people in the sample sought images (not necessarily visual) that were expressive of the same elusive understanding. Susan Jay told us:

> I was at this conceptual problem in my dissertation of how you talk about the tragedy and keep hope alive at the same time. Then it hit me. Reggae does that. The blues do that. That music embodies at the same time the memory of how much has been lost with the hope for the future and the delight in the present. It's all there. You don't get the deep joy without the suffering. So listening to that music was critical. And I've found it in black women's novels, too—like Mildred Taylor, for example. They depict the complexity of human goodness that I had known in my life but I didn't find reflected in novels written by many whites. Those are my scriptures. I mean, that's the place where I find the guiding stories that get me through the rough parts. In these stories, I see my own racism, but I also see my own strengths."

With paradox comes an opening into mystery. The people we interviewed typically speak of being connected with a sense of life larger than their own. They talk thoughtfully, carefully reaching for words and images to name what cannot be named. Sometimes they describe it as cosmic and evolutionary; sometimes they use their own traditional religious or spiritual resources; and often they draw on the broader literature and across the wisdom traditions.

A man who builds educational models to prepare youth for the changing future puts it this way:

> I do think that there is a power that is intimately bound up with our existence and the universe. And it's part of the puzzlement of life to be engaged in the fascination of having different ideas on what that power might be like ultimately. I think it is a caring power that informs our relationships and enables us to realize the best that we may be capable of as a species.

An attorney who has worked with complex real estate and financial issues at city and state levels spoke of "an evolutionary, cosmic reality that I feel strongly connected with. . . . I know there's a process going on that I'm a part of. I feel a connection with some of the Christian symbols, and I also find strength in the masses of wisdom of the great ones."

This sense of shared participation in an interdependent reality that fades into mystery is mediated by metaphor. In the reflection of another we hear a deep conviction of commonality conveyed by the metaphor of "quanta." When we ask him, "Is there any sense in which you work even on behalf of those you oppose?" he responds:

Well, there are two things. One thing I regret to say, I am fatally impatient with people who don't think my way. However, I think there is also another characteristic that I have. I can see the other way as well. I look for a side channel. And very frequently I find, "Oh, we are speaking about the same thing, even though we are fighting." Then you realize that although there is adversity, actually there is the sincerity base which goes down and into where they meet at the common denominator. And those common denominators, though they may be abstract and less and less defined, are the quanta in which we all work.

The Responsible Imagination

As theologian and ethicist H. Richard Niebuhr observed more than three decades ago, in a world which is becoming more conscious of the radical interdependence of life and the manifold interactions which constitute all being, the moral imagination is necessarily a responsive and responsible imagination, constituted in dialogue, capable of answering.[29] People committed to the common good strive to practice this kind of imagination. The word "responsible" comes from the Latin *respondere*, rooted in the Indo-European *re-* meaning "turn" and *spond-eyo*, meaning "promise." Committed citizens have the capacity to turn, to notice, to be affected, to be informed, to form bonds, and to make promises.

The people we studied appear to compose reality in a manner that can take into account calls to help, catalyze, dream, work hard, think hard, and love well. They practice an imagination that resists prejudice and its distancing tendencies on the one hand, and avoids messianic aspirations and their engulfing tendencies on the other. Their imaginations are active and open, continually seeking more adequate understandings of the whole self and the whole commons and the language with which to express them.

Their practice of imagination is responsible in two particular ways. First, they try to respect the *process* of imagination in themselves and in others. They pay attention to dissonance and contradiction, particularly those that reveal injustice and unrealized potential. They learn to pause, reflect, wonder, ask why, consider, wait. One, reflecting on his own period of confusion and discernment said: "Whoever has to strike lightning has to remain clouded for a while." They also learn to work over their insights and those of others so that they "connect up" in truthful and useful ways. They seek out trustworthy communities of confirmation and contradiction.

Second, they seek out sources of worthy images. Most have discovered that finding and being found by fitting images is not only a matter of having access to them but requires discretion and responsible hospitality—not only to what is attractive but also to what may be unfamiliar and initially unsettling.

It has been rather boldly suggested that two images now dominate the human imagination, the mushroom cloud and the Earthrise—the image of Earth as seen from space.[30] Both are products of a partnership among nature, technology, and the human imagination. Each is an image of a possible future. One is a metaphor for despair wrought by the specter of political, economic, or ecological holocaust, and the other a metaphor for hope wrought by the vista of a blue-green, borderless, interdependent, life-bearing sphere called home.

Living with these images, the people in our study appear to know that two truths must now be held together—that we have the power to destroy the Earth and the power to see it whole. But unlike many who seek escape from the potent tension this act of holding requires, these people live in a manner that conveys a third and essential power: the courage to turn and make promises, the power of a responsible imagination.

In the Interlude that follows and in Chapter 6, we see the struggle with human strength and fallibility that committed people experience in the course of promise-making and promise-keeping.

introduction to the second interlude

Like the first, the second Interlude is a story of how people committed to the common good recognize and live out their interdependence with one another. Based on extensive interviews in a real community, this story is about a network of people, all of whom live and work in one of our large cities, each in a differing role, each a part of a shared ecology of commitment. Struggling with human and material limitations of all sorts, they nonetheless seek to bring an alternative imagination into a community long since left behind and out.

Evansburg

*It's this community who are the ones I talk to, spend
time with. We share our frustrations, our joys, our sad-
nesses, our successes. They're the ones who ask, "How are
you doing?" and keep you going. We always joke about
our boards and our networks, that we're all interrelated.
The discussions that we have when we get together over
beer or a cup of coffee are often about neighborhood issues, our schools, our kids, zoning issues. We have to
check ourselves every once in awhile and decide to talk
about something else, like, "Wait a minute, let's get off
this!" But that group, because we all work together,
there's a lot of strength and joy.*

JESSICA BASOM

Seen from above, the Fremont neighborhood nestles a mile or so west of the
great dome that marks the top of the old city hall in downtown Evansburg. But
between the dome and the neighborhood, the raised concrete sweep of I-460
cuts like a cleaver through the arteries that once connected downtown with one
of its most exclusive suburbs. As we drive through early rush hour traffic due
west from the Evansburg Hyatt, the high rises rapidly fall behind, eventually
deteriorating to a strip of tired houses withering under the concrete shadow of
the Interstate. The street comes to an abrupt halt, and we are forced through a
maze of turns and beneath an underpass, finding ourselves suddenly on a quiet
street, lined with trees and rows of one and two-story houses, some neatly
primped, others peeling and boarded up.

On one corner, a particularly commodious three-story Victorian home, freshly painted a pale and regal yellow with tasteful brown trim, dominates its neighbors. The house, we are told, has a story.

Built around the turn of the century, the old Chickering House was one of a number of elegant homes planted on the outskirts of this booming railroad hub as prosperous industrialists sought escape from the smoky tangle of the inner city. Over the years, the surrounding area sprouted row on row of prim homes for skilled workers and middle-class professionals, forming a suburb as tidy as a bookkeeper's garden. By the time of the Second World War, virtually all of the present houses in Fremont were in place and, surrounded by successful factories and businesses, this community of some forty thousand Irish and German workers looked forward to a fertile future.

But something went wrong. The rust on the nation's midriff reached Evansburg, the large employers began to pull away, and in the three decades following the war, over one hundred businesses left the area. Thousands of jobs went elsewhere, and those who could, followed them, selling their homes to absentee landlords, or renting them to new, less affluent immigrants: whites from the neighboring mountains, blacks displaced by the Interstate, and more recently, Hispanics. During the 1980s, three banks closed, four public schools were consolidated, two churches moved away, and three Fortune 500 corporations abandoned the area, leaving behind over two million square feet of vacant space. The Chickering House was sold and resold, and finally divided into rental apartments by an owner who lived fifteen miles away on the other side of the city. On adjacent streets, as renters replaced owners, paint started to peel, windows were boarded up, and one after another, houses began to empty altogether. Every month, on every block, thousands of dollars in rent payments streamed out of the community. More thousands were siphoned off in utility payments, and still more went into the pockets of business owners who would no longer locate in Fremont—owners of supermarkets, automotive supply shops, banks. City priorities followed them, leaving behind cracked pavements and potholes. Young people left as soon as they finished school, draining any lingering hope for future recovery. The few youth and little money that remained seemed destined for the underground criminal economy. If the neighborhood were a patient in the emergency room, it would be obvious that the first task was to stop the hemorrhaging.

In the midst of it all, the neighbors on either side of the old Chickering House woke up one morning to the sound of motorcycles. A gang, it appeared, had moved in. Before long, a tangle of barbed wire grew around the house. From behind it, two ferocious Dobermans snarled and frightened children on their way to school. An occasional empty syringe appeared in the gutter, and finally a concrete block wall with gun holes went up around the front porch. It was said that the rooms inside were painted black so shadows would not show, that shots were randomly fired through walls and windows, and that a man had been killed on the second floor. Slung over the peeling neoclassical lintel of the porch, a crudely lettered sign read: "Renegade House."

Turning south, we skirt the grounds of the old Civil War arsenal, a technical high school since 1916, and pull into a parking lot, once the playground of a now abandoned junior high school, housing the office of "Fremont Neighborhood Investments," locally known as "F.N.I." An early morning rain is falling, and with relief we note that the visitors' spaces are closest to the building. We feel welcome. Scurrying across the asphalt, we duck under an incongruous yellow stone arch and through the glass doorway, just in time for our eight o'clock appointment.

On the building directory are listed the programs: Neighborhood Daycare Centers, Self-employment Training, Credit Circle Enterprises, Casa Nueva, Special Needs Housing, Youth Interest, Housing Rehabilitation, Volunteer Operations, Property Management, and Home Ownership. The walls are studded with framed citations—for exemplary service to children and families, neighborhood development, local initiative, and a daycare cooperative. They come from the state senate, the city government, the mayor, and local community groups. Two plaques side by side cite innovative urban development and historic preservation. "That's a neat balancing act," we comment to ourselves and turn to another pair of plaques, these with photographs of people on them. One is a lean Spencer Tracy, complete with clerical collar, the other, a wiry, electric face with snapping black eyes, open and ironic, and a terrific smile. "He almost looks Asian," we are thinking, when we are interrupted by a pleasant-faced young African-American woman who informs us that Mr. North will see us now.

"Are you always in the office this early?" we ask.

"Nope," he replies. "I used to be here by seven-thirty. Would you like some coffee?"

Todd North is unassuming, softspoken, and looks ten years younger than his thirty-nine years. It's hard to believe that he has been running F.N.I. for nearly a decade. He seems an unlikely figure for the position, yet after hearing him speak in his steady, savvy way, we begin to understand how it is that despite years of declining economy, he has been able to parlay a small local investment program into a corporation capitalized at over a million dollars, responsible for a host of social services, from battered women's shelters and day care facilities to tree planting projects, teen fathers' training groups, and a nationally recognized home winterization program.

"When F.N.I. started," North tells us, "we simply wanted to address poverty. The housing was bad, there were nonresident landlords, the population turnover was terrific. We needed to reclaim the whole neighborhood."

One of the first moves was to purchase and rehab the "Renegade House."

"We knew we had to win credibility in the community. We figured if we could tackle that house, we could do most anything," Todd says, with a grin like a bulldozer. It was a smart move, at once lancing a boil and mobilizing community support. But he also knew that it was more drama than substance. Real economic development meant that "we needed to invest in people and programs for people."

Todd and his colleagues began by renovating vacated houses, using builders from the local high school vocational programs, caring for details that maintained a sense of identity for each house, and celebrating every restored home with invitations to the whole community to attend an "open house" complete with balloons, ceremony, and awakening hope. In the process they discovered that when one house was restored, typically two other properties on the same street would be improved. As their involvement in the community deepened, they began to see a whole network of related needs.

For example, fully a quarter of the households in the area were headed by single parents—many of whom had to give up jobs or work erratically to care for their children. It was clear that if the community were to use its resources well, better day-care facilities were essential. The logical response was to build a central day-care center for the whole community in the nearby industrial park. But as North and his colleagues listened to the people themselves, they began to realize that there were underdeveloped assets to meet this need already in the neighborhood. Day-care was virtually a cottage industry, but it was haphazard and largely substandard. Convinced that the most important thing was to stanch the flow of money out of the community, they decided that rather than hire outside contractors to build a new facility—and outside professionals to staff it—they would identify local women who could care for children. By providing them with training and support, and subsequently helping to rehab existing houses for sites, they were able to strengthen existing local day-care providers and develop new ones right in the neighborhood where they were needed. "Had we stuck with that initial interpretation," says North, "we would probably have a successful day-care center, but it wouldn't really serve this community. Now what we have are sixteen day-care homes. We've taken what was already being done in this community, improved its quality, improved its reliability, and . . ." he pauses (that grin again), "the next step for those women is to become a political force."

He goes on to describe how the centers fund themselves in part by signing up for the federal food and nutrition program, thus improving the bodies as well as the minds of neighborhood children. Over the next months, many of the women will be certified in early childhood education, enabling them to begin training other neighborhood women. "So they go from being babysitters two years ago to now being providers, teachers. They are moving from being consumers of public assistance to being entrepreneurs." What he does not say explicitly is that the project beautifully demonstrates two of his own central convictions about fighting poverty: first, build community, and second, keep the resources in the neighborhood.

Reena Crowne is one of those resources. "It's like one big, gigantic family," she is saying as we walk around a capsized shopping cart on the sidewalk in front of her new home, a modest but neat row house in Fremont. "I mean, these people from F.N.I. don't just put you in a nice home and leave you. They stay there. They follow you. They stick by you. And if anything messes up, they help you get back on your feet so you can go further. People like Joyce. I mean Joyce is like a sister to me. I can always depend on her. I wouldn't ever have got this day-care center started if it hadn't been for her."

The day-care center Reena Crowne is referring to is her own; she runs it in a house rehabbed by F.N.I. The center has been going now for two years, and she is about to be approved for an upgrade from eight to ten children. Not only does she now provide a valuable service, but she can support herself as well. "The way I look at it," she tells us, "when God gives you the strength and the know-how, you can either run with it for yourself, or you can take it and share it with somebody else. And if you share it, it's going to come back to you." And she goes on to explain how on the basis of the business that Joyce had helped her start, she had been able to put money down on a nearby house for her own family. Fremont Neighborhood Investments had not only provided her with business training, but had extended a low-interest sweat-equity loan and trained her to purchase and fix up the abandoned house that had now become her own home. "The whole idea behind it," she continues, "is to help people to get the skills they need to build themselves and the community up at the same time." How did she happen to get involved in all this, we ask? A soft smile spreads across her face as she shakes her head, reminiscing.

With two young children, she and her husband were among the first African-Americans to arrive in the neighborhood ten years ago. The rent was affordable for the young family, and the reason soon became apparent. Their landlord, who lived in the city, skimmed off his slim profits by providing almost no up-keep. "We used to have to wear sweaters all day inside, it was so cold," she says, "and the roof leaked and no one would do anything about it."

But one early Fall weekend, F.N.I. sponsored its first "Winter Warm-up," a mass call for volunteer help to winterize homes in the area, and over nine hundred people descended on the neighborhood, weatherstripping doors, tightening windows, "caulking everything in sight." It was part of a larger strategy to involve the whole Evansburg community, to reknit the ravelled parts of the city and incidentally, North acknowledges, "to begin to build a constituency that understands poverty by bringing in people who otherwise would never come near the place." During the course of the day, they discovered homes with no furnaces at all, and later were able to use the sweat equity of the volunteers to qualify for state matching funds to purchase and install ten fuel-efficient furnaces.

At the picnic afterwards, Todd mentioned to someone that it would be nice to harness the energy of all these volunteers in a more sustained way, perhaps as tutors. The following Tuesday, his phone rang. It was Reena Crowne. "I hear you're going to arrange for tutors to come into the neighborhood," she said. "Well, my son Marty is in second grade and needs help."

"Umm, yes, well . . . I was thinking of two or three years from now," Todd stammered. "We don't have a program in place, we don't have the money . . ."

"But," came the reply, "Marty needs a tutor now!"

North asked for her phone number and went home to talk to his wife, Krista, a financial analyst and former Peace Corps volunteer.

"I'm the one he talks to," Krista tells us. "It helps him think through problems. For instance, "Winter Warm-up" really grew out of a conversation between us when I had said, 'It's not true that people don't want to give, because they really do. It's just that so many of them don't know how to. You have to give them something concrete to do, and then they'll do it.' He remembered that for a long time."

She values being able to discuss work with Todd, but now the kids are in school, she has taken on full-time work, and they have less time than they used to for "just talk." She misses this, yet the work she is now doing is also important to her. "In fact, I'm consulting with a friend, Kevin McDonough, who runs the health clinic, right now on the new health care program. It feels good to have a professional relationship with him, and not just be 'Todd's wife.' I used to feel sort of an extension of Todd. But with this new work, that's not an issue."

Krista is the executive director of a regional health planning agency for the low income community. Her position requires long hours, often out of the community. But the work is exciting, and she knows that it makes a difference for people who are otherwise locked out of access to health care. Over dinner one evening, we ask how she came to be doing this sort of work.

"I grew up with a real commitment to having a sense of meaning in your life's work," she tells us. Her mother was a religious educator and her father a professor and minister. There was "a constant stream" of travellers through the house, and she treasures the memory of the day when she was five years old, holding hands with a line of people singing "We Shall Overcome" at a rally where Martin Luther King, Jr. spoke. Her high school years were oriented around a Young Presbyterian group and she loved the opportunity to travel and meet other young people from around the country. Indeed, she explains, what drew her to the group was really the relationships and responsibility rather than the religious doctrine; perhaps because her parents had encouraged her to think for herself, she could never bring herself to believe that only Christians were "saved."

One of her closest friends during her senior year was a German exchange student who was staying with her family, and, after graduation, she spent six months in Europe with her. "She had a real strong interest in China; mine was Latin America. But we shared a common interest in people. We'd sit in my room after homework and talk about social problems and meaning—that kind of stuff. We'd solve all the world's problems."

At Stanford, her interest in other cultures steered her toward Anthropology and International Relations, where she came to see that "you have to have multidimensional ways of looking at things." This took her to Washington after graduation where she interned for a Congressional representative, and later drew on her youth group contacts for a position with the Presbyterian mission office. From there it was only a short step into the Peace Corps, and a year later Krista found herself in a village in Guatemala training schoolteachers to increase egg production from their chicken projects. "The Peace Corps experience taught me that what finally matters is human contacts, getting people together to work on their own problems. The people who are going to be affected need to be involved in the decisions."

Krista also learned that she liked things to be neat. She liked numbers, enjoyed seeing things come out even. So upon her return, she took an M.B.A. and moved to Evansburg to work for OmniCare, a medical supply manufacturer. Before long, in search of new friends, she had begun to attend a church she heard about where people were down-to-earth and said "hello," the songs were reminiscent of her childhood, and where the pastor, an Asian fellow, knew your name. He also happened to chair the board of an economic development corporation and would she like to come along to their annual picnic? "Why not?," she thought. That afternoon, in the annual whiffle ball game, the new director of F.N.I. ("I thought he was kind of good looking") hit a high pop fly. Krista, who had thrown the pitch, caught it—and it was a whole new ballgame. She and Todd were married six months later.

The day after Reena approached him about a tutor for Marty, Todd called back and told her that he and Krista would do it themselves. The partnership stuck; Marty's grades began to improve. Reena took the cue, and within a year she had completed her G.E.D. and begun work at Headstart. There she met Sibahn Grady, a lifelong resident and member of the F.N.I. Board, with whom she collaborated on the effort to rehab and provide day care in neighborhood homes, receiving in the bargain, a full training course from F.N.I. The rest was easy.

"The neighborhood is really coming up," Reena says, looking around approvingly. "It's a lot better than what it used to be." Then after a moment, she adds, "But it all boils down to Todd. You know, you wouldn't expect it from a man like him. When I first saw him, I wasn't too impressed, to be honest. He seemed too quiet, not a go-getter if you know what I mean. But the more I got to meet him and talk with him . . . I mean if you get a crowd together and you look around, you'll see him here and next thing you'll see him there, and next thing he's over there—he's all the way around! That's Todd: wherever he's needed, that's where he's at."

The "Renegade House" story made good copy. Swarms of reporters came to take pictures of the Mayor of Evansburg knocking down the concrete "fortress fence" around the porch with a sledgehammer, "cleaning up the city," as the news story had it.

Not long afterward, however, one of the reporters returned to write a story about the Fremont community itself, sketching its poverty in stark terms, describing "the squalor" of the area and clothing the inhabitants in what he chose to call "hand-me-downs from Good Will." Sibahn Grady was not amused. "Sure you can still see that sort of thing," she says, her eyes growing hard, "but that's not what this neighborhood is about." And she goes on to talk about how important it is for a community not to lose its memory. Having spent all of her fifty-seven years in the neighborhood, Sibahn has perspective that some of the younger folks and newcomers lack.

"When I was a girl, the doctor used to do home births. So my mother would take care of the other kids, and I used to help her. People would take care of each other that way. Whole streets and blocks were just like family."

Her friends' parents were active in neighborhood affairs, one a president of the PTA, another a Scout leader. "So they were real connected with the schools and the kids and each other. Everybody pitched in, and that's just the way that neighborhood had always been."

But when the mid-century prosperity passed the neighborhood by, the community fabric began to unravel. "The property just started going down and down and the neighborhood just gradually changed to where it was very, very bad—it was really bad."

As so often happens, the economic decline leveraged an equivalent rise in domestic violence, and Sibahn's own daughter became a victim. To help her, Sibahn helped start an innovative shelter program called "Casa Nueva." With the help of a crew of young people trained for that purpose, several houses were rehabbed and turned into "safe apartments" for women and children escaping abusive situations.

At about this time, Sibahn accepted an invitation to serve on the F.N.I. board, where her sense of the history of the neighborhood brought a special perspective to meetings. The neighborhood is Sibahn's passion. "When you know how it used to be," she says, "you know it doesn't have to be the way that it is."

But she is leery of the quick fix and the carpetbagger. When Paul Chen first came to her parish fifteen years earlier, Sibahn Grady looked him in the eye and said in her quiet, incontrovertible way, "I was in this community before you came, and I will be here long after you are gone." Her eyes smile mischievously as she tells us the story. "Have you met Paul Chen yet?" Without waiting for an answer, she continues. "You've got a treat in store."

At first glance, the weary brick walls and steepleless profile of the Fremont Methodist Church more closely resemble an abandoned city school than a place of worship. Not sure we have the right address, we tentatively step inside and are greeted by a ten-foot-long banner hanging over the altar of a worn but inviting sanctuary. It reads, *"The Lord delighteth in thee."*

"That banner greets everyone when they first come in. It's a verse from a song. I sent a little Christmas card to one of the members and that was the inscription on it and she took it and made it into a banner."

A small wiry man, Paul Chen carries a power disproportionate to his size. His rapid-fire words take hold, burrow in as he talks.

"People who have been alienated from the church walk in and say 'That banner spoke to me.' It says, 'The Lord delighteth in *me*.' They feel valued. You know the passage in Luke about justice? Opening the eyes of the blind, freeing the prisoners, helping the oppressed? I think that banner picks it up. I mean, that has captured the spirit of this place more than anything else. When we moved that banner to clean it, people asked, 'Where's the banner?' So we knew it was sacred." He chuckles; his eyes dart to the corner. "That, and the coffee pot."

The banner and the coffee pot are central to Chen's concept of congregational life as a healing and transformational community. But these symbols are rooted in his personal history as well. The son of Chinese immigrant parents, Paul grew up learning to survive on the streets of Italian Brooklyn, ducking the taunts of other kids, often fighting back. His father had come to America dreaming of becoming an artist, but was forced to run a laundry instead. His dream shattered, Chen turned to alcohol and became abusive. Paul would have turned to the streets but a youth worker and a schoolteacher encouraged him to stay in school. If nothing else, his father had taught him grit, and he became one of a small core of survivors of a university program designed for minority students but riddled with racist condescension. He entered young adulthood knowing well what it felt like to be excluded. He might have been caught in the backwaters of bitterness, but was inspired by a college chaplain to commit himself to social justice. Later, during his internship at seminary, he met Dick Metcalf, a student of Saul Alinsky. "He was a real mentor. Dick shaped me for what I do," Paul says. "This work is tough. You've got to be disciplined, focused."

Paul married another pastor and spent the seventies with the urban poor in Chicago. The work was demanding. "Constant work—constant, constant," he says, and quotes his mentor: "You gotta keep seeing things whole; you gotta see the big picture." But the long hours and abysmal pay took its toll. In 1978, he moved to Evansburg, a divorced man.

Several years ago, however, Paul remarried. Jessica Basom had also been married before, and brought two children to the marriage. A former VISTA volunteer and trained social worker, Jessica shared Paul's deep commitment to the neighborhood. But their union complicated matters considerably, especially after they decided to have a child of their own.

"Being single for those years," Paul tells us, "I had one loyalty: work, work, and the community. But now my loyalty's split between community and family, and I have to honor my family too." Then, his face softening, he adds, "I don't know too many spouses who would put up with somebody who works such long hours, especially with three kids. Our five-year old is always asking what meeting I'm going to next."

It is important to him that Jessica shares his commitment. "You know, my wife worked 'til three o'clock this morning on her stuff, so we each understand why we do it. We're committed to this. We share a vocation and a passion."

This is not to say that the passion and deep sense of vocation don't get stretched thin. On Paul's desk we notice a small, clay comic figure with the epithet, "God, help me hang in there." The significance of the line grows on us steadily as we hear stories of the tensions and struggles, and begin to see in a more connected way the wider community in which Paul, Jessica, Todd, Krista, Sibahn, Reena, and Marty dwell.

Fremont Methodist Church is linked in a partnership with St. John's Roman Catholic Church several blocks away. It is also yoked in common ministry with another Methodist church across town. "First Methodist" is what clergy sometimes refer to as a "tall steeple church," a classic Gothic building in elegant repair, home to a large, long-established, and affluent congregation. When the effectiveness of the F.N.I. community development network caught the attention of First Methodist, a parishioner proposed linking their resources with the Fremont neighborhood through a partnership with Fremont Methodist Church. Over time, several neighborhood projects were identified, and people from both churches worked in these activities—together applying to First Methodist for financial help. By this means, resources, exported earlier from the community, were returned, at least in small measure, to Fremont.

But the alliance has not been without difficulties. Early on, two women from First Methodist came to help with a teen mothers' program at Paul's church. With the best intentions, they offered to find homes for the babies of several of the young mothers. "The babies didn't need saving, their mothers needed support!" says Paul. "So they had a different perspective," he adds generously. "There was tension on both sides, and we had to educate them, you know: 'This is partnership, not charity.'"

Jessica Basom is president of the Fremont Credit Union, an organization set up by Paul and Todd a dozen years earlier. "We created the credit union because the banks were not helping our community and a lot of people in our neighborhood can't get credit," Paul tells us. Indeed, that particular morning Jessica had been working on a loan application to enable renovations for a set of "Casa Nueva" safehouses.

But it has not always been this way, and the early years of the credit union were difficult. "They tried to close us down twice, but we fought and won," Jessica says, adding, "I can't say I blame them, of course." Bad loans are their most consistent problem, and Jessica worries a lot about their effect, not just on the credit union but on the whole system that it supports. "We do take a lot of risks, and it really hurts when someone you have worked with for years walks away. We have to walk a careful line. But we could go under real quick if we had just five car loans go bad."

Jessica goes on to tell us that they are in the process of a "repo" right now. "She'll come over to the office, tell me how she'll pay up next month, make personal threats. I've heard it all before. But the heartbreak is that without that car she'll lose her job." She looks directly at us—angry—then throws her hands up. "But it's been six months since her last payment. I have the auditors breathing down my neck. Times are tough." She pauses again. "I take these ones home at night."

"How does Paul feel about that?" we ask.

"We might both be accused of being workaholics," Jessica acknowledges, confessing mixed feelings about the time their work takes from the family. "Sometimes I resent the hell out of him being gone to yet another meeting. And I'm sure he feels the same with me at times, too. 'Why is she at the credit union again tonight, balancing those books? Why isn't she home?' People make so many demands that there are times that I feel like our family, our own family, has suffered because there is only so much time and energy to go around.

Part of it is the publicness of it. There are times that I have had great difficulty in dealing with how everyone seems to have a claim on Paul and that everybody would just want a piece of him. It's like, where's the privacy?"

Family time is important to her, and like Krista and Todd, she and Paul worry sometimes about what their commitment may cost their children. She is anxious about rearing her daughter in a neighborhood where violence is so close, noting that her credit union had been robbed three times in the past year. "Is it fair," she asks, "to raise a child in this setting where, instead of waking up in the morning and seeing lots of lovely flowers and beautiful houses and joyful children playing, they may be just as apt to go outside and see someone screaming at their kid and whacking their child? Is it good for your child to see children with no decent shoes or sweaters in winter? Is it good for your child to see people whose only home is a grocery cart?"

When Todd North's father died, the occasion became a time of reflection among several of the parents in the community about what all this meant for their families. "We went through a lot of soul-searching," Jessica says, "about how much time we could legitimately take from our children. I know Todd and Krista feel the same way. How can we balance our lives to make sure our families get the time we need?"

Jessica answers her own question with a long silence. Then she remembers looking out the window on a recent Saturday morning and seeing Paul with Moira, their daughter, helping a homeless man gather and crush cans for refunds. "Then again," she says, relaxing back into her chair, "they benefit from this too—maybe more than we know."

It's almost as though rather than fleeing from the challenge, she leans into it. And despite her occasional qualms, Jessica would not move out of the community. Her friends, the meaning of the work, the deep hope that the children are learning vital lessons are, in the end, what tips the scales. The friends weigh in heavily.

"I feel it's important for people who are really committed to working for anything worthwhile to be networked in a real meaningful way with other people, to keep them going. Not everybody needs to be married to somebody, but you've got to have that support somewhere from other people; otherwise I don't know how you do it."

Yet part of her loves the work at the credit union just for itself—the detailed accounting coupled with the sense of satisfaction she gets from making a contribution. Just that Saturday night, she and Paul had been dancing at a neighborhood block party where there were several clients, people she knew as both friends and customers. "One woman, we were dancing together, laughing, talking about our kids. She's two payments overdue, but we never said a word about it. I know she'll pay."

The office where Jessica's friend drops her payments is nestled in the corner of the "Comprehensive Service Center," a heavy, bustling building on Rindge Avenue, the commercial artery of the neighborhood. At the other end of the building, in a cafeteria-sized room on the ground level, a dozen or so elderly people move about slowly or sit in small groups playing cards. In addition to the credit union, the Center runs a program for the elderly, a fuel-assistance program, an office for the physically challenged, and a teenage drop-in center. Founded in the early seventies, it is run by Hank Deutsch, a close friend of the Norths and Chens. Hank first came to the neighborhood in 1969 as a summer intern with a local service club, and now serves on both the F.N.I. and the Credit Union boards. He and Paul had a painful run-in over investment priorities recently, and the friendship was strained. But Jessica admires him as a man who "has steadily shown his commitment to the neighborhood, for longer than almost anyone I know." A compact man with the playful eyes of a ten-year-old, Deutsch speaks warmly of Sibahn Grady with whom he serves on the F.N.I. board. "She's what this community is all about. It's people like her who have kept this place alive, especially for the next generation who have kids now."

One of that generation is a young mother of three who moved across the city seven years earlier. For years unable to further her own education because of an ailing mother, Edie Gannon seemed headed, she says sardonically, "for a career in front of the TV." But as she watched the neighborhood decline, and shrank under the scorn of her former friends ("Why would you want to live over there?"), she began to realize that "if I didn't do something, no one would."

One day, she noticed with horror two children on her street playing with a discarded syringe. She organized a neighborhood clean-up campaign, even inviting a city councilman to come to kick it off. It poured rain, and he never came, but dozens of people did. "We were out there in our T-shirts and our little brown hats, and we shovelled leaves and cleaned up gutters and front yards. Kids came by the bundles, and everybody had a great time!"

At the event, she met Hank Deutsch, who encouraged her to return to school. "He really showed he cared," she says. "He gives time that just isn't there," adding that he had even attended her graduation. Today she is a full-time teacher's aide, yet she still finds time to volunteer for the Community Association. "I'm just one little person," she says, "but if we can just all get together, we can really do a lot."

We ask her why she thinks her small contribution matters, and she replies, "It's all a community chain link, we all connect in one way or another. The credit union connects to the Community Association, F.N.I. connects with the Health Clinic, the Community Association connects with Urban Network of Evansburg—we all kind of work together. So even though it seems like the world's going to pot and nobody cares anymore, we know there are people out there who care."

Two blocks from the Community Association is the Fremont Health Clinic, housed in what looks like an abandoned A & P. Kevin McDonough, the director, walks us through the waiting room. A mother with a sniffling infant on her lap looks up deferentially as she moves her toddler out of our path; a shockingly thin man stares past us at the wall; an old woman follows us with birds' eyes.

"Over half our patients are uninsured, so these prevention programs are essential," McDonough says as we pass a door reading "Mammography." "We try to integrate social service and health programs as much as we can—we house WIC, for instance."

His board supports such innovations. Jessica Basom is the chair, and Hank Deutsch is an old friend and mentor. "He's my hero," Kevin says with a grin. "Hank was here when I first came twenty years ago. He's very politically astute and he really cares about Fremont. I don't see him much these days, but whenever I do, it's 'How ya doin?' or 'I've got this great idea I want to talk with you about.' I've learned a lot from him."

Kevin first arrived in the early seventies and stayed in St. John's rectory with a group of other students. With the help of the local priest, Fr. John Burke, who was working with Paul Chen to create F.N.I., they formed a singing group, and many of them have remained.

Father Burke, that lean Spencer Tracy on the plaque beside Paul's, likes to talk about how he was responsible for bringing Kevin together with Natalie, a bright youth worker who was writing grants for him at the time. "Burke is that kind of man," Kevin jokes. "Always putting people together to see what will happen." Burke married them, and with F.N.I.'s help they took out a low-interest loan to buy and rehab an abandoned house not far from where Todd and Krista live, eventually filling it with four kids, one of whom we had met earlier when she was baby-sitting for the Norths.

Not long afterward, Fr. Burke put Natalie in touch with Paul Chen, who was chair of the F.N.I. Board at the time, to help develop a collaborative housing effort between his Roman Catholic parish and Chen's Methodist one. It took, and within several months she found herself working part-time for North and doing market consulting with the Credit Union. When her church began to develop its own credit union, she brought Jessica Basom in as a consultant for them. "Do you see how it works?" Natalie exclaims. "Those things happen all the time!"

There are times, she acknowledges, when as much as she believes in the work, she does burn down, if not out. People she counts on fail to deliver, grant proposals are turned down, state and federal funding is cut, and it sometimes seems that "the system" is just too complex, too rigid, too hard to budge. At such times, it would be easier just to forget it, to move out of the area to a safer neighborhood where she and Kevin would not have to work sixty-hour weeks, and where the kids could go to a better school. But finally what keeps her going is the people. "I just get a lot of energy from being with these people and talking things through with them. We know what we've taken on, and I know that what I am doing matters. That's what keeps me going—the people and the work."

confession

The Struggle with Fallibility

"It Doesn't Have to Be This Way"

It is another dusty, tropical day as the knot of townspeople moves along the side of the road under the flat Philippine sun. Gaily painted trucks and motorcycles with sidecars stampede past, streaming fumes through the heavy air along the line of storefronts curiously reminiscent of an American frontier town. Near the front of the crowd walks a young woman, draped in black. Two men on her left are carrying a small casket between them. On her right walks a young American man about her age. Working in her barrio for several months, he has learned to respect her fibre; today he is learning about her vulnerability. In the casket is the body of her three-month-old daughter who has just died of dysentery.

"This is the way life is," she is saying. "Life is hard, that's the way it is. What can you do? It is in God's hands."

He listens in silence as they walk. Surrounding him, the relatives converse almost as though they were on their way to market rather than to the cemetery. His own feelings are a tangle of anger, compassion, grief, guilt, awkwardness, and confusion. "It's such a litany," he thinks angrily. "This damned fatalism. That child did not have to die. It doesn't have to be this way!"

Yet he knows that in the face of such loss, one must lean on something. He knows too that the medicine that could have saved her child is available to millions of other children at the touch of a telephone. Her pain and the sting of the injustice cut deep. The crowd carries him wordless up the hill.

Completing his Peace Corps tour, young David Bradley returned home, married a fellow returned volunteer, and took a job with an international relief agency. But readjustment was rough, the work entailed considerable travel, and his marriage tore apart. Eventually he went into business for himself, starting an independent news agency to provide background material and alternative analysis of international development to mainstream news media which he felt rarely saw the world from the perspective of Third World people. Interviewing eyewitnesses of government-sponsored murders, contradicting official underreporting of land mines, and exposing election fraud, David often put his life in danger.

Now, years later, he seeks to explain what that moment meant to him. "When I go to the Philippines and see the brutality and injustice of that system, I cannot *not* feel that woman's sadness and resignation," he says. "I can't be silent—that's The Work. How can I be silent?"

The distance between the worlds of those two young people could scarcely have been greater. Raised in the suburbs, he had never known what it was to live in such poverty or so close to death; nor had he yet become a parent, much less lost a child. Yet something caught fire in him that still burns. What was the tinder that her suffering helped to ignite and transform into a lifetime of commitment?

Despite what some might view as a privileged upbringing, David had known pain in his youth: frequent family moves during childhood, alienation at private school, and a father too blinded by his own suffering to recognize his son.

During the first twelve years of his life, David's family moved seven times. "Constantly in flux. I never had any roots, never had any community that I belonged to because every time I had it, I lost it. You know, as a kid, it's pretty wrenching, it's a sense of loss, it's not a sense of gain or excitement." It was difficult for him to form steady friendships during these years; he felt always an outsider. Living on the edge felt at once normal and painful.

When David was fourteen, at considerable sacrifice, his parents sent him and his brother to private school. But he was not happy there. He felt put down by the wealthier boys because he wore hand-me-down clothes and was unable to join them in Jamaica or Bermuda during Spring breaks. He felt a deep rage at the injustice of this class difference, a rage galled by being once again on the edge, marginalized at this exclusive preserve, feeling "what it's like to be an outsider in this class-dominated society." Sardonically, he notes, "It was a very important part of my education."

David's father wanted him "to be a good WASP, a successful middle-class businessman" like himself. "The full catastrophe," he grins, echoing Zorba with gentle irony. All his life the older Bradley had worked to buy happiness, yet he died miserable. A salesman, he was often away, and when he did come home, drank too much. When David decided to cut his own pathway, and founded his independent news service, his father would ask him over and over what it was that he did. "I was pained by his disappointment in me, just as I was pained by his inability to get it, to understand what my life was about." Along with the emotional absence, the fundamental contradiction of his father's life cut his son deeply. "In his heart of hearts," says David, "he was not doing what he wanted to do. Yet that's what he wanted for me? He was angry all the time, and as a child I picked that up. I mean you couldn't not. When I'd look at him, I'd feel the failure in his eyes. I always carried a piece of his failure inside me."

Upon graduation from college with a degree in political science, David joined the Peace Corps and was assigned to the Philippines, where he helped to develop local marketing cooperatives. He grew close to several families in his area, and that was how, ten months and a half a world out of upstate New York, David found himself walking beside a grieving mother under a hot sun, struggling with a tangle of feelings about a child who did not have to die.

Saints, Martyrs, and Hypocrites

"These people sound almost Gandhian," said a consultant to our study in a tone that mixed awe and disdain in almost equal amounts. "Are they for real?" The question is a good one, for when we encounter the stories of committed lives, many of us feel uneasy. On the one hand, we want to believe that commitment to the common good is possible, even normal. We want to believe that people can make a difference. On the other hand, it threatens our complacency. We have all struck our bargains with life, and people who appear to have demanded more make us uncomfortable. Better to question their authenticity.

In a certain sense, our reluctance to see committed people as normal human beings is to be expected. Relentlessly, our culture teaches us that "normal" human nature is at bottom merely self-interested. The triumph of the ideology of egocentric individualism has led us to define the human being as ultimately incapable of the good except in the service of the self, narrowly conceived. Thus commitment to the commons can only exist as a virtue against the backdrop of assumed human greed. Caught in this assumption, when we encounter people who sustain a demonstrable goodness toward others, we may perceive them as exceptional "saints," neurotic "martyrs," or duplicitous "hypocrites."

Most often, we canonize committed people, telling ourselves they have an altruistic gene, or are morally gifted—Mother Teresas whom we can admire from afar. While we may honor, even prize what we choose to call their "idealism," we tell ourselves that for most of us, living in the real world is another matter. In this way, we wall the two worlds apart, placing those who might stretch us into a richer imagination of our own potential on one side, and ourselves safely on the other. Dorothy Day, founder of the *Catholic Worker*, used to say that she did not want to be called a saint because she didn't wish to be dismissed so easily.

A second distancing device is to regard a committed person as a martyr—Joan of Arc who gives all for the cause and then burns out or dies young. Such people, we tell ourselves, live out their own needs at the expense of everyone else, generally doing more harm than good. Acting chiefly out of their own pain, they assume that their own suffering gives them insight and license to impose their values on the rest of us. Led by their own bleeding hearts, they conclude that caring until they drop will exorcise the demons from both themselves and others. If such people would just attend to their wounds in private instead of subjecting everyone to their righteousness, we would all be better off.

A third tactic is to charge them with hypocrisy—Elmer Gantrys who profess a holy mission but are finally only out for themselves. Professing compassion, they really crave power; talking charity, they actually covet wealth; asserting justice, they will step on anyone in the way of their cause. The world is a muddy place and one had best not attempt to clear the waters unless one is pure of heart—and no one is.

In fact, there is a germ of truth in each of these caricatures. There are people who radiate extraordinary spiritual strength, and we need such people to serve as exemplars.[1] Surely many people who work for the larger public good are wounded in ways that both fuel and limit their efficacy; and all human beings harbor mixed motives that at times might be construed from the outside as hypocrisy. But beyond the ambivalence, beneath the understandable resistance, lies a sober, sometimes anxious, and thoroughly legitimate question: "What *are* the costs of living this way?"

Costs

The people we interviewed never emphasized the costs of their commitments, and typically minimized those they did experience. As a group they are living satisfying, sometimes even comfortable lives, but many would acknowledge that in the eyes of others they had paid a price for their choices. All choices bring costs as well as benefits, and committed lives are no different.

Most obviously, though most are professionally salaried, few receive the income they might—given their intellect, diligence, and credentials—had they taken other paths in our present economy. And although some have achieved significant status and acknowledgment, as a group they remain underrecognized by the society at large. Because of their choices, some experience high stress, and a few are misunderstood by friends and family. Sometimes, when the work involved challenging the status quo or living under difficult physical conditions, there was tangible danger. There is also the cost of having to bid farewell to naivete, of bearing what the poet David Whyte calls "the bitter, unwanted passion of your sure defeat"[2] without reverting to the luxury of cynicism.

Relationships

For those who were parents, the area that, if any, was most apt to evoke hesitation and doubt was the actual or potential cost to their children.[3] Like the "Evansburg" parents, they registered concern that their work sometimes kept them away from home when their children needed them. Yet we saw little evidence that the people we interviewed spent less time with their children than most hard-working parents, and it was clear that some were notably thoughtful parents, obviously choosing to be committed to their children in a primary way. Those who explained to their kids that their absences at board meetings or conferences were a part of the way they cared for them, felt that their children essentially understood and appreciated their commitments; many have apparently followed in their parents' footsteps.

After concern about children, we heard some concern for spouses. Some marriages were undoubtedly stressed because of the intensity of one or the other's commitments. When commitments were shared, however, the costs were clearly more acceptable and the marriage more nourishing.

Still others had, to varying degrees, been betrayed, let down, or called unrealistic. "Sometimes, if you rattle too many cages, the establishment turns against you," said one person. Whether these were inevitable consequences of commitment or matters of inadequate strategy, they did exact a price.

Health

Ulcers, back pain, burnout. "Oh yeah," said a sixty-year-old man, "I've got ulcers from aggravation, frustration, and just downright determination to make things happen." While we did not include burned-out, joyless folk in our sample, we did include human beings, and the commons can be a stressful place. Some had burned out at an earlier time but had subsequently found ways to hold their commitments more deftly. Others were continually learning from their mistakes—about how many promises they could make, what the core of their commitment was, how much their body and spirit could handle. But for the most part, they appeared notably healthy and buoyant as they aged.

There was one disturbing exception, however. The people of color in our sample, particularly the African-Americans, revealed a significant measure of ill health. A follow-up survey showed that a disproportionate number had suffered early stroke, cancer, and death since the interview. Because our sample is small, we cannot draw any definitive conclusions, but having listened to the accounts of their lives, and informed by other studies, we can speculate that their commitment often comes at a greater price than it does for others. Being part of a disadvantaged minority, some may have suffered less adequate health care. Moreover, serving as bridges between two worlds, they experience what Katie Cannon calls "the 'loneliness' and pain of 'endless and constant' translation." It is harder to find places where they can be "at home" in the same way that others can, and the choice to forgive one's oppressors bears a cost.[4]

Finances

Our sample spans a broad range of the economic spectrum. A very few have substantial wealth, a few live at the edge of poverty, most are located in the middle class. As professionals, even those from Third World countries are a part of the "Global North." But whatever their economic status, typically they acknowledged the need for adequate income and its role in vocational choice. None made a virtue of involuntary poverty, and all recognized the impact of economic inequality on their field.[5]

At the same time, they rarely mentioned personal financial costs without prompting. If they did, it was typically in regard to their children's educations or their own retirement. A few felt pressure from spouses, and the long-term drag of never quite having enough for the extras—nicer furniture, a chance to travel, a better car. And those on the margins understandably worried. Said one, "If I were to receive a million dollars, I would go on doing exactly what I am doing—but I wouldn't have to worry so much."

More frequently we heard concern from managers about fundraising. Georgina Smith has been working for years to establish clinics in African-American communities. Money is a constant worry, even though her work is well received. "We're having to chase the almighty dollar constantly," she complains. She usually finds what she needs, but prays that next time she will get it "earlier than forty-five minutes before."

On the other hand, some were relatively free of financial worries. Several women in traditional marriages, for example, began public work after their children were grown, and have sustained the work over several decades. One man, who received an inheritance in his early twenties, told us that the financial cushion was a significant factor in the formation of his commitment, which he has maintained long after the inheritance has run out.

Our interviewees' basic attitudes about wealth are an important feature of their financial landscape. Those who had early models of charitable giving tend to see life as a "mutuality of gifts" and savor the satisfactions of generosity. "My cup of life is more than half full and that's always with me," says a social worker who works with street kids while living in a fifth-floor walk-up and not owning a car. Those who grew up poor tend to feel that they want to give back, "to lift as they climb" and not accumulate more than they need. They are all aware of paths not taken, but those paths do not seriously tempt them. As a group, they are essentially comfortable with the financial choices they have made.[6]

Busyness and Limited Recognition

Like the rest of us, these folks know the contemporary disease of busyness—a flawed hallmark of the new commons—and some know they work too hard. While some exemplify a good sense of perspective, humor, and ways of taking "time off," several spoke with a certain wistfulness of a desire to play more, seeking a better balance between their own needs for renewal and the commitments that claim them.

A deeper cost may lie in subtle assaults to one's self-esteem. Society does not always celebrate their professional choices, and sometimes their own institutions are ambivalent about their commitments and accomplishments. Without these conventional supports, they can find themselves dependent upon more tenuous forms of affirmation.

Again, however, although the ambiguities are real, they do not appear to be rationalizing choices that would be unbearable or tragic seen through another lens. Most feel that their lives are working well. Along with the sense that they are making a difference, the work itself clearly compensates for the downside. They seem to lean into some broader reality which they may not see clearly, but which casts the shadows of their own lives in a larger light. We will discuss the nature of that larger light in Chapter 7. But first, we need to look more closely at those shadows.

Taboo Motivations and Alternatives to Sainthood

Listening to the Shadow

"The dividing line between good and evil cuts through the heart of every human being," Solzhenitsyn observes.[7] Every life is a complex blend of strength and fallibility. Few people have escaped some measure of pain and suffering in their lives, and human motivations are invariably mixed.

"I think our shadow always motivates us," said a youth worker, "and sometimes the greatest things we achieve are because we're struggling to come to grips with our own inconsistencies and our own contradictions." From the beginning, we suspected that committed people work out of both the light and the shadow of their lives. But how were we to catch that shadow?

As we prepared our interview questions, we knew that it could be hard for many to talk about motivations such as anger, jealousy, need to please, ambition, or power. Even with a methodology like ours, centered in confidential and reflective conversation, we knew that people might quite appropriately limit what they chose to share, and we did not want to be intrusive, presumptuous, or manipulative. Still, we felt that this material was important to a full portrayal of the formation of commitment. After some experimentation, we devised a method for exploring this topic with the measure of specificity and depth we were seeking.

Knowing that a capacity to trust and a sense of agency were fundamental to healthy development, we composed two lists. One represented distortions of a sense of agency: such "taboo motivations" as *ambition, pride, anger, need to please,* and *fear.* The other represented violations of trust: "wounds" like *injustice, abuse, betrayal, oppression,* or *vulnerability.*

These were not exhaustive lists, but they did provide stepping stones into further discussion of what we refer to as "shadow material," those feelings and motivations that tend to be shielded from the public eye and sometimes even from one's own awareness. Given the limits of our methodology, people were very generous and we learned a good deal.

Taboo Motivations

Known and loved by many for his songs of nonviolence and world peace, Pete Seeger used to jolt his audiences by telling them that inside his guitar case, he kept a rock. He would then explain: "I get real angry sometimes when I see what's going on in the world, and I like to wrap my fingers around that rock and hold it for a while before I put it back." Then, pausing for effect, he would add, "But someday if the music stops working, I might have to use that rock."[8] Seeger understood that love, anger, even the threat of force can all dwell together in important, perhaps necessary ways.

David Bradley's guitar case also carries a rock or two. His story suggests that anger plays a significant part for him — as do fear, pride, and the need to please his father. Clearly, a part of understanding why people make the commitments they do requires recognizing what we have called "taboo motivations," by which we mean *those motivating emotions that one is either uncomfortable with or which others regard as suspect — particularly if one aspires to work on behalf of others*. Of the motives we listed, those most frequently acknowledged were *ambition, anger,* and *the need to please,* followed by *pride or ego, fear, perfectionism,* and *the need for control*.

Recognizing their mixed motives, our interviewees typically focused on one or two central ones, sometimes also acknowledging struggles or regrets. A few tried to convey more fully the depth of their vulnerability, the limits on their generosity, or the sobering persistence of their own capacity for hurting others. But for the most part, while they were keenly alert to at least some of their inner realities and limitations, they were not preoccupied with them. Rather, they included these as an inevitable, though not debilitating, part of the landscape. Citizens who are able to sustain long-term work on behalf of the whole human family, it would seem, are full participants in the drama of human potential — and fallibility.

Anger

Anger is a curious problem in the research on altruism because of the mythology of sainthood. How can good people be angry? And how can angry people be good? Surely anger drives some more than it ought to, and when it does, the "cause," whatever it may be, is ill served.[9] Most of those who mentioned anger as a motivation, however, saw it as a source of passion, and would agree with William Sloane Coffin:

> A capacity for anger is very important because if you don't have anger, you will begin to tolerate the intolerable. . . . If you are not angry, you are probably a cynic. And if you lower your quotient of anger at oppression, you lower your quotient of compassion for the oppressed. I see anger and love as very related.[10]

Almost none disclaimed their anger. "I don't think anger is negative," said one. "Anger's my strength," said another.

But while anger may motivate, they know it can also destroy. Clara Kennedy was on the way home from grade school when a small knot of neighborhood kids began taunting her younger sister, a victim of Down's Syndrome. Clara flew at her sister's tormentors and, she reports matter-of-factly, "I beat them up." Years later, after long engagement with education in Latin American and North American inner cities, she quietly reflects that "the rest of my life has been a search for ways to address injustice without beating people up."

Nearly without exception, anger appears in our participants' lives as something to be reckoned with but not feared. It is not anger *per se* but unacknowledged anger that can be dangerous. "I know there's a rage," said one, "and I have to be conscious of that so it's not destructive."

In his autobiography, Myles Horton, the founder of the Highlander Center, which trained dozens of the nation's most influential civil rights workers, offers a useful metaphor. "I had to turn my anger into a slow-burning fire, instead of a consuming fire. You don't want the fire to go out—you never let it go out—and if it ever gets weak, you stoke it. But you don't want it to burn you up. It keeps you going, but you subdue it because you don't want to be destroyed by it."[11]

By keeping the anger banked, they are able to transform its heat to empower their work. Rosalyn Williams, whom we met earlier, told us,

> You ride it like a horse. It fuels the place where your blood rises—your determination—and it keeps you from becoming cynical. Cynicism is a luxury if you are a person of privilege, but you can't afford it if you are a survivor. If you can mobilize the energy that comes from your anger rather than letting it control you, it gives you energizing fire.

Consistently, it appeared that anger appropriately rises up when rights are violated, when wholeness is threatened, when dignity of spirit is assaulted. In these instances, rage is the response of life, affirming and protecting itself. The trick is learning how to bank the anger so it energizes rather than destroys.

Power

Power is integral to "making a difference." Many of the people we interviewed held positions of formal authority; others exercised substantial informal power. Thus, most were familiar with power, and some with the ambition required to achieve it. As such, they were subject to the charge that they were "just in it for the power." When we mentioned this possibility to our respondents, they generally recognized the issue. "I think power is always problematic," one man told us. "I am always struggling to be honest with myself about it." An influential ethicist was quite direct. "I like having power. I really like the fact that my books are read and that I'm invited to speak. It's been a tension, because at one point my motive was more the recognition than the real work for justice and transformation." Meg Powell, a physician and director of her hospital unit, echoed her. "I like being in charge of things," she said. "But I think there is a good context to power and a bad context." While power enables her to further the work of the unit, she has to be careful not to use it simply for control. We heard this often: provided it does not oppress others, power in the service of the work is important.

In our time, many are prone to believe that the only way to gain or exercise power is through position or wealth. Yet Rosalyn Williams describes another kind of power. Recalling "the way loveless power gets undercut by powerless love," she recalls how she learned about that kind of moral power. "People learned during the days of the civil rights struggle what solidarity meant in the face of great odds. I'll never forget what it was like to stand arm-in-arm, and stare these guys with billy clubs down—to have this sense of moral power. Once you've experienced that, it's really hard to settle for anything less."

Moreover, some pointed out that when the power is shared rather than concentrated, it is less likely to corrupt. "Power is attractive, but it's also real important," said a leader in ethical business practices. "And socialized power is about inclusion. If you're really going to use power for the good of other people instead of self-aggrandizement, you've got to be inclusive at a very big level."

Need for control

The exercise of power may express a need for control. Some people acknowledged this, but then tempered it with a willingness to recognize the inevitable interdependence they share with others.[12] The director of a community agency expresses the struggle of conflicting voices.

> I also wrestle with the question of control. There are people who would say that I am bossy—you think you know what should happen when and how. One of the real struggles of my life is to work in partnership and to let go of some of my own control needs so that in the midst of the unknown, something new can happen.

Ambition

Ambition was the most frequently mentioned taboo motivation. As with power, our interviewees noted ambition's dangers, but emphasized the importance of its purpose. As a founder of a major international relief agency observed, one may be ambitious about a number of very different things. "I was ambitious to get things done. But I wasn't ambitious to be a millionaire." Still, the temptation is always there. Dhan Kumar Basnayat, who heads a development project among impoverished people in Nepal, acknowledged this. "I would have liked—and had the opportunity at times—to be a powerful, influential man with visible status. That was attractive to me. But it wasn't the whole purpose of my life. The purpose of my life is a far more long-term, meaningful thing."

In effect, what seems to hold ambition and the unbridled desire for power or control in check is some sense of a larger context of life, a recognition that something greater than the self is at stake in how one chooses to spend and be spent. Sometimes it is the deeper purpose of work, or sometimes simply an intuition of greater meaning. Within this larger context, the inner voices speaking on behalf of one's own surely consequential but parochial interests are not silenced but rather are counterbalanced by other voices, other perspectives. The self has grown large enough to recognize and mediate diverse voices.

Need to Please or to Be Needed

The need to please turned up often, but was substantially more evident in the comparison group.[13] This is not surprising. "Feeling good" as a result of meeting people's needs is the most frequently cited reason for doing volunteer work.[14] But while people committed to the common good did not deny feeling good about their work, most considered good feelings to be an effect, not a cause of their commitment. Moreover, they tended to see the need for approval as a remnant of an earlier time, recalling moments when they would strive to please a mother or an uncle, but then noting that authority derived from success in the work itself was increasingly more important than approbation. Ken Krasner, an author and fundraiser for AIDS research told us, "I constantly have to remind myself, 'Ken, you are an authority here, and people view you as an authority, so get off it!' But part of me is still waiting for acknowledgment."

Fear

Perhaps because it rests deeper in the psyche than other motivations, fear was mentioned somewhat less frequently. Some, however, did acknowledge the fear of failing or of not living up to their own potential in the face of the world's needs. "I am afraid that I may not be doing enough," an advocate for black enterprise told us. "I don't want to take anything to the grave with me. When they put me down under, man, I don't want them to say, 'Damn, man! That cat! Was that sponge ever wet?'"

Others feared for the nation or planet. Speaking of the decline of our cities, a prominent women's health advocate said, "I'm really afraid for us as a nation. We don't seem to have the political will, the common sense to do the right thing. It is frightening."

But as with anger, power, and the need for control, most would agree with the woman who emphasized that it was essential to "be in touch with your fear side." She spoke of how it had made her both more cautious because she feared her political organizing work could get her killed, and more effective because she knew that others who opposed her were also afraid, and this knowledge of shared fear helped her to work with greater wisdom.

Guilt

Although very few mentioned guilt as a significant motivator, citizens who work on behalf of the underprivileged are often suspected of "acting out of guilt." The assumption is that the presence of guilt somehow tarnishes one's efforts. It is not our perception, however, that the complete absence of guilt marks psychological health. Human beings, however well-intentioned, do contribute to the harm of others, and a capacity for guilt is an acknowledgment of human responsibility. The problem is not guilt *per se*, but *appropriate* guilt grounded in a recognition of mutual interdependence. Notably, those who spoke about it tended to reflect on its transformation rather than its elimination.

A woman who has worked for many years with world hunger organizations recalls that when she was younger, "I was one of those people who asked every day when I got up, 'Am I morally justified to be on this planet?'" Acknowledging that such guilt probably played an important part in her early commitment, she says with a certain relief that as she has become more effective and recognized in her work, the feeling has diminished. Like others in our sample, she used to feel guilty that her work was taking too much time from her children, but now in their early twenties, they are happy, caring young people who, she smiles, help her to "lighten up." She adds, "I really think I have done something important in my first forty-six years, and I am much happier now than before; I don't have to prove myself every day."

Perfectionism

Most of those who mentioned perfectionism were people of color who felt they had to be far more diligent than others. Luisandra Hernandez, a high-ranking public health official, told us that she still feels the pressure to be "perfect." She spoke for many when she said, "We are still in a society where, if I should fail, it would not just be 'You, Luisandra Hernandez, who have failed,' but rather, 'Women cannot be leaders, and Hispanics should not be given the opportunity to succeed.' I always feel the world judging me."

Yet they also noted how it strengthened them. Fear of failure, for instance, spurred them toward excellence. Knowing that they were being judged by stiffer standards, they would prepare especially carefully for meetings, take pains to dress appropriately, and spend additional hours polishing work. All of this intensified their determination to eradicate the double standard that had plagued them.

By definition, shadow motivations of the sort discussed here are not readily accessible. It was beyond the scope of our methodology to conduct the sort of depth analysis that might provide further psychological explanation of what motivates people to work for the larger good.[15] What matters here is that the people we studied readily acknowledge the presence of "taboo motivations" and thus are not simply ruled by them. Rather, they seem to transform them over time in the service of the work. In this way, even the shadow contributes to compassion and commitment. Indeed, it has been said that compassion is the energy spawned by life's longing to right itself. If so, then can even the violation of trust and the consequent experience of suffering sometimes engender compassion?

The Experience of Suffering and
Alternatives to Martyrdom

We interview Elmira Frank at a United Nations conference on the environment where she has just delivered a moving speech about the topic she knows best—women in Third World development—bringing tears to the eyes of delegates long hardened by encounters with global poverty. At the age of fifty-three, she is still trying to understand the power that adversity and anger have had in her life. Describing her father to us, she says,

"He was the traditional male head of the family, who said little girls will be seen and not heard, who was bigoted and narrow in his view of everything—his own life, his children's lives, his wife's life, the world."

Perhaps because her mother was "the exact opposite," Elmira had the strength to resist, fiercely refusing to become what he expected of her. But the struggle left her with a deep anger—anger at being told that some children were not good enough for her to play with, anger at being ridiculed for her love of books and good music, anger at losing friendships because of having to move, anger at seeing her mother dominated, anger at his ridicule of her aspiration to become a veterinarian, and, finally, anger at being told she could not take her sophomore year of college in France. At that point, something snapped. Elmira went anyway and did not return for seventeen years.

She has very mixed feelings about the consequences of all that anger. She is quite clear that the battles with her father toughened her and made her a more effective advocate on behalf of herself and others. "Adversity," she says, "can be power."

"But," she goes on, "it's very hurtful, very painful," and she begins to speak of the tender underside of what motivates her: women's and children's pain. She recalls the poverty and degradation of women and children in the village where she lived in Algeria. "I am outraged that anyone is suffering." Her voice breaks. "And so my work is that work." She pauses for a long time, regaining composure. "But I don't know. I'm blessed—or cursed—with this enormous all-encompassing concern for helping other people who are helpless." She is silent. Then, "It's some monster that consumes me." But softly, she adds, "Or maybe it's an angel."

Just as the strengths of trust and agency walk hand in hand, so also do the vulnerabilities of taboo motivations and suffering dwell together in ways that leave us in the ambiguous company of monstrous angels. As we have begun to see, people like Elmira seem able to recognize the Janus-like quality of their afflictions—an ability that opens the way for transforming their monsters into angels.

We need not have experienced unusual suffering to become committed to the common good. Yet as theologian Dorothee Soelle reminds us, "It is impossible to remove oneself totally from suffering unless one removes oneself from life itself, no longer enters into relationships, makes oneself invulnerable."[16] The people we interviewed are not invulnerable. As a group, all had experienced elements of suffering, and at some point in their lives almost half had suffered some significant physical limitation or emotional injury. Such physical incapacities as impaired vision, polio, bodily injury, stuttering, or obesity were frequently accompanied by feelings of differentness and loneliness.

Some suffered severely in their families, whether it was the early death of a mother, or a painful relationship with a father or sibling, or instances of abuse or neglect due to mental illness or alcoholism. Others, while not directly wounded themselves, vicariously felt the pain in a family member's life. Still others described wounds inflicted by the effects of larger, systemic injustice such as racism, classism, or sexism.

In Chapter 3 we suggested that the suffering in a person's life may resonate with the suffering of others and move one to action. This is very clear to Marsha Longstreth, a school administrator. Acknowledging the fear and pain kindled by her own early years in poverty, she told us, "It would be very misguided of me to sit here and not keep those memories real sharp in my mind and have that as a part of the compulsion to make a difference." In effect, it is impossible to ignore the role that the experience of suffering—their own or that of those close to them—plays in the lives of many who choose to commit themselves to work on behalf of the common good.

The findings of other investigators also reflect this. Recounting the stories of a number of people who risked their lives to save others, Michael Lesy concludes that they were motivated out of a desire for "self-reclamation." Each had been wounded at some point in their early years, and their acts of generosity helped to heal the wounds.[17] Deepening our understanding of this dynamic, psychologist Gina O'Connell Higgins notes that "setting things straight for others can help you make your peace." She studied people who had undergone dramatic suffering in their childhood yet who were able to "love well" in adulthood. They had developed "an uncommon sense of efficacy . . . by helping to repair daunting, defeating, or nearly devastating lives for others when [they] could not do the same for [their] families when [they] were children. . . . In this way, they recreate a more ideal version of some essential love that they received only partially, erratically, or fleetingly as children."[18]

There are important differences between these studies and ours. Few of the people we studied had performed the kind of dramatic rescues that Lesy describes, and they are typically not the victims of extraordinarily harsh abuse whom Higgins studied. Yet in both cases, a key feature of their motivation was an ability to feel another's pain. It seems self-evident that one is apt to do that most readily when one has recognized, at least to some degree, one's own pain.

Recalling the effects of his immigrant father's pain on his own life, Paul Chen reflected, "There's not a day that I'm not reminded of human connectedness because of the pain I share because of my background—and because of the pain of many of our neighbors making it day by day, wondering if they're going to survive, seeing the signs of lost hope as my father did, paralyzed by the poverty around them."

Many of the people we interviewed were able to acknowledge and name some aspect of their suffering and, for the most part, could also place that suffering in a larger context, setting it in dialogue with their awareness of the suffering of others.

Transforming the Wound

Since none of us can escape at least some pain in our lives, the question is not whether one is hurt, but what one does with the pain. Some people absorb it, understand it partially, and spend their lives a safe distance from others' suffering. Others bury it so deeply that they scarcely know it is there. So armored that they are unable to love well or make good friends, they drift through life without focus, severed from any deep sense of love or purpose. What we now know of post-traumatic stress syndrome attests to the power of trauma to disconnect and immobilize people. Unaddressed wounds can fester and become destructive; when this happens, there is a measure of truth in the old saw that "you have to heal yourself before you can care for others."

The people we interviewed who described substantial childhood trauma or other forms of wounding, however, had avoided falling into these traps. Somehow, they allowed the pain to touch them, but did not become lost in it. Rather, they healed in such a way that they became neither immobilized or self-absorbed on the one hand nor anesthetized on the other. They were able to choose healing work rather than be merely driven to it, and thus served both others and themselves simultaneously. How did this happen?

Healing Guides

Recall the story about David Bradley that opened this chapter. He described three areas in which he had sustained wounds as a child—lack of affirmation from his father, loss of childhood friends, and alienation at school. He also vicariously felt his father's unhappiness, and at some level perhaps feared the same for himself. But David was not alone. A series of ameliorating factors provided a crucible within which his pain could be transformed.

Though his older brother followed his father into business, David was never able to feel close to his dad. In his very human longing for understanding and connection, David turned toward his mother, a journalist with a local newspaper, whom he saw as the more open, creative and "moral" of his two parents. In contrast to his father's resignation, David's mother embodied the idea that almost anything was possible, and in aligning himself with her he "chose a path of optimism rather than surrender." Her life was an affirmation that "It doesn't have to be this way," and it is not surprising that he ultimately followed her vocational choice rather than his father's. Journalism became a source of healing for him.

As he entered puberty, and as his "father wound" grew more painful, there appeared "a light of a man" in the form of Father Wilder, the local church rector under whose urging David became an acolyte and youth group officer. In Wilder, David saw a gentle older man who reflected both an openness and "a kind of pathos." Trapped in a painful marriage with an alcoholic wife, Wilder carried "a sense of both tragedy and light." In that light David received the nourishment he needed, and a model of the capacity to acknowledge and live gracefully with one's brokenness.

His early years were scored with the pain of frequent moves, but when he was twelve his family moved to upstate New York, to a home grounded deep in his family's past. The Oneida Community is best known today for silverware by that name. But the community was originally founded in the mid-nineteenth century by John Humphrey Noyes, a visionary social reformer. David recalls visiting his grandmother in the Mansion House, the community center where she lived for most of her life. Thus, in a kind of compensation for so disrupted a childhood, David came to know himself also as part of a deeply rooted community with a historical tradition of social innovation and commitment.

Moreover, though David was then sent to the boarding school where he felt so alienated, a special teacher, Jonas Windsor, took a personal interest in him and challenged him to develop his own ideas and to see the world in new ways.

David recalls Windsor pointing to a map on the classroom wall and asking why the United States was in the center of it. He never saw world maps the same way again, and notes the irony that while his parents sent him to prep school with the intention of straightening him out, in fact, he ended up discovering "how much more there was than just my parents' existence."

In her study of abuse victims, Gina O'Connell Higgins found that in almost all cases, a grandparent, neighbor, or teacher—some "caring adult" in the home or community—served to assure the young person that the chaotic and fearful world they knew was not the only world, that there was another way.[19] Bradley's story is similar. The wound matters less than the form of healing, for the way in which the surrounding social fabric holds us affects the meaning that we make of our suffering—as inconsequential or significant, our own fault or the result of larger forces, a burden to bear alone or one that others may help us to carry.

Healing Work

The people we studied seem to have healed, not only because there were important adults who gave them alternatives, but also because in many cases they chose to work with people whose suffering echoed their own. It was not unusual, for instance, for someone who had suffered severe illness as a child to undertake work in the health field, or for a woman who had felt the sting of discrimination as a girl to work for women's equality.

Ken Krasner's mother died when he was a toddler, and he lived with his father until he left for college. But shortly after he arrived there, his father died. In the midst of his grief, he saw a poster advertising a summer volunteer opportunity in India and decided to go. The experience of being in a strange land with a community of other young people was a perfect antidote for his loneliness, and working close to the lives of people who knew misery and death intimately, he was able to see his own pain within a larger fabric of shared humanity. He returned, finished college, and joined VISTA with a new and more mature recognition that if he were to relieve the distress with which he resonated, he would have to address the systemic injustice that lay at its source.

By choosing work that spoke to their particular concern in this way, people like Ken found themselves with colleagues who shared similar purposes, creating a healing environment in which the conversation was always relevant to the source of common suffering. In such work, there was an implicit promise: as we heal others, we will heal ourselves.

Systemic Perspective as Healing Agent

A systemic perspective is crucial to the transformation by which one's own pain is recognized as part of a larger community of suffering and hope. Recall Roy Matthews from the first Interlude. Beginning with his mother's shame and hurt on being hit by a rock-laden snowball thrown by a white boy, Roy Matthews' awareness of racism evolved from the personal to the communal as he experienced growing up in segregated Raleigh, to the national as he felt the barbs of discrimination at college, to the international as he traveled to South Africa. At each new horizon, he was able to recognize larger causes of his own pain, as the "self" who suffered in an earlier era was relativized and a new context challenged him to recompose his understanding of the work in a way that cast his suffering into a broader frame. Matthews's experience suggests that in addition to deepening one's capacity for empathy, perhaps intense suffering also spurs important reflection, provoking us to ask "why?" in the profound and far-reaching ways that foster the development of the habits of mind discussed in Chapter 4.

Living the Struggles Well

Each of us carries a unique mix of clarity, confusion, self-awareness and determined ignorance. Most of us have been hurt in some ways, and we all share at least some motivations that friends who know us well would have to forgive. But what characterizes the people in our study is that, just as they can accept and work with the complexity and ambiguity of the new commons, they can likewise work to accept and manage the complexity and ambiguity of their own hearts. Rather than seal off their shadows, their habits of mind enable them to engage productively with that mix. Rob Carroll, a priest who works in San Francisco's "Tenderloin," understands what one might call "the practice of fallibility" when he says, "None of us is perfect. We're not saints. We're all struggling with our relationships, with our own personal problems. And there's got to be a willingness on all our parts not to erase our struggle, but to live those struggles well."

By paying attention to a cast of inner voices which contradict and balance the tug of the shadow, Rob and others in our sample host an interior dialogue that lends them a kind of grace and elegance as they steer through the sometimes turbid waters of the contemporary world. They know that life is in motion, and that the challenge of uncertainty is to be met not by fortifying oneself, but by moving with clear purpose in the dynamic flow of interbeing. Rather than naively martyring themselves, they choose a kind of prudent openness over armor.

Two practices seem to be pivotal: an ability to acknowledge, reflect upon, and give voice to all parts of one's inner conversation, and a capacity to forgive.

Giving Voice to the Inner Conversation

Essential to the free flow of all of one's tributary inner voices is the capacity to see and reflect upon one's own inner world. If the metaphor for one's inner voices is that of a committee, then the capacity for reflection and choice constitutes the chair of the committee.[20] A good inner chair provides hospitality and ensures that a range of voices is welcome, even (perhaps especially) those deprecated by other committee members. This ability provides a kind of protection to all of the members from dictatorship by any one of them, and ensures that the shadow (a form of "otherness") is welcomed in as well as the light. Here, a woman describes the necessity of doing this. "We busy ourselves so much with the little issues or the ego issues or the power issues that we do not take enough time to go deep enough to center ourselves, to keep questioning our own motives and our own purity as we work. I don't think that is ever a completed process."

Central to that capacity is the ability to listen to the internalized voices of others without coming to premature closure. This requires treating them (including the voices we have come to call "taboo motivations") in much the same way that one does external voices—with patience and respect. That is, our participants seem to be relatively willing to acknowledge the truth of their own hurts and needs, their own particular tuning.[21] Such hospitality to the voice of "the other," both without and within, appears crucial to the maintenance of a balanced inner conversation and the capacity to hear one's complex polyphony.[22] It is this ability that enables the taboo voices, the voices of suffering, and the voices of responsibility within to be heard.

Indeed, it is our perception that when the ability to entertain internal counterpoint is poorly developed or wanes for whatever reason, when some voices are suppressed and others amplified, burnout or destructive behavior is most likely to occur. When all are heard, none can hold full sway.

We were struck by the relative lightness with which many of our people held their own introspective capacity. They seem appropriately cautious about the

danger of becoming paralyzed by self-absorption, and seek a sense of right proportion, neither discounting nor becoming preoccupied with either their
vulnerabilities and deficiencies or their strengths. They work to cultivate a
stance of conscious awareness of life which makes it possible to discover deeper
truths. This discipline of mind and heart enables them to maintain their perspective, to discern the links between the momentous and the minor, and thus
to keep sorting the important from the trivial.

Forgiveness of Oneself as well as Others

Forgiveness and generosity of spirit are terms not often heard in the literature
of social science. More often such sympathies are grouped under something
like "tolerance of ambiguity." Yet it appears that much of the staying power of
committed citizens resides in their capacity for "confession," a willingness to
acknowledge one's limitations to oneself and others, to receive acceptance
and forgiveness.

Time alone may not be enough to heal all wounds; it may simply drape the
wound with forgetfulness. Beneath the layers of scar tissue the wound may continue to fester. True healing demands a recognition of the wound, a coming to
terms, a forgiveness.[23] Awareness of these elements of soul develops gradually; often
it was most evident in those who were older and further along the path of dialogue
with their shadow. One mid-life woman, now aware of the role her father's alcoholism played in her life, told us that she had entered the convent in part "to make
everything right." "But," she added, "I couldn't have told you that until only a
few years ago." This discovery contributed to a sharp reordering of her professional
commitments. Struggling with her feelings about betrayal, she went on to say,

> We experience pain and think it's abnormal when in fact it's normal. Part of our sin is that
> we think we are responsible for it. I entered religious life because it was the way I could
> pay God back so my father would stop drinking. But he drank because he was an
> artist who couldn't do work. So I carried his darkness. I had to forgive God the father.

Another told us,

> Faithfulness has to be learning how to accept that people will go as far as they can, and
> when they can't go any further then you have to figure out what to do. Elsewise, I would
> just give up. I think that's one of the reasons why we burn out and why black people
> don't talk to white people anymore and why women are getting more and more angry
> at men—that we haven't really worked out a theology of betrayal and forgiveness.

[191]

Often people burn out because they cannot relinquish what is beyond their control. Many of those we interviewed, however, seemed able to let go of old insults with a flexibility born, perhaps, of readiness to interpret individuals and societies through forgiving rather than suspicious eyes. Displaying a kind of hospitality to the shadow, an ability to recognize the inseparability of private hurt and public pain, they thus honored the interdependence of both personal and systemic reality.

But this is not cheap grace. There is a toughness here as well, a fierce will to look the beast in the eye and to recognize with Pogo that the enemy is us. As one man said, "I'm not God, I goof. I make mistakes all the time. I'm just doing the best I can, and I come with my own baggage; we all do."

In the ritual of forgiveness, confession comes first. These people acknowledge that they do trip, do become snagged in their own stuff. They know that listening well to all the voices is a hard discipline. They have all felt defeated or helpless at times. And they struggle to find a way through, a possibility on the other side. They know also that they cannot do it alone. Forgiveness is a public as well as a private act, an important consequence of systemic thought, and a feature of the practice of citizenship in the twenty-first century.[24] Committed citizens seem to know that forgiveness and transformation are one and the same, and you can't be about the work of transforming society without a robust capacity to forgive—both yourself and others.

In his important book, *Emotional Intelligence*, which reveals the strength of the emerging body of research on human emotion, Daniel Goleman compellingly draws attention to the ways in which the education of the emotions goes hand in hand with education for character, for moral development, and for citizenship. Awareness of self and others, the capacity for empathy, and the management of anger are key elements in the emotional literacy he describes. His observations and analysis are deeply resonant with the capacities we have observed in committed lives. At the heart of the self-awareness that constitutes emotional health, he contends, is the ability to defer immediate gratification.[25] In committed lives we see this capacity, deepened into the willingness to live with many forms of complexity and paradox both within and without, beginning with the story of Joel Rosen in Chapter 7.

commitment

The Power of the Double Negative

Connected with the World

The middle son of a successful San Francisco family, and graduate of Stanford Law School where he sat on the Law Review, Joel Rosen might have been worth several million dollars when we interviewed him. Instead, he is "between jobs," taking a midlife sabbatical to assess his next step after twenty years in poverty law and as co-founder and director of "The Place," a center for at-risk youth that has achieved international recognition for its creative and comprehensive services.

"Commitment isn't quite the right word," he is saying. "It's like I feel identified with the reality of service. It's become internalized. I'm not interested in the world because somebody said I should or I think I should be. I really have no choice. It's become a part of me. It's what I feel I'm about and what I care about." We ask about his early expectations and how they do or don't coincide with the life he is now living.

"Well," he replies, "there were seeds of this for a long time. I led a pretty ordinary life until I was in my mid-twenties," then adds that his father was quite concerned about public affairs and "was always pointing out what was going on in this or that country." An attorney, his father did a lot of *pro bono* work and "seemed to care about humanity and the well-being of people." Indeed, Joel vividly remembers an incident when his older sister was complaining about not having the latest toy that her friends had. Angrily, his father put her into the car and drove her through a nearby slum area. "That was his orientation—that there were people a lot less fortunate, and our responsibility was to try to make a better world for more people."

In most respects they were a comfortable, conventional Jewish family, nominally religious and essentially following the contours of social expectations. And yet something in Joel hungered for some greater passion for life.

In their mid-twenties, Joel and his new spouse, Sarah, who shared his longing for more spiritually fulfilling work, were drawn increasingly into the antiestablishment currents of the late sixties. After a year's clerkship under a judge with a reputation for tough sentences, he was offered a lucrative job with a law firm but turned instead to a two-year fellowship to study urban poverty law. The experience changed his life.

"I began to practice law and represent poor people and tenant groups and welfare recipients and all kinds of causes. It was an awakening into the tremendous inequality and injustice in our society." He was furious.

> I was angry on two counts. One, at the injustice itself. I was really pained, and couldn't believe it, and worked very hard to bring about change within that system. The other thing that made me equally angry is that the schools I went to—supposedly among the greatest academic institutions in the world—had taught me only part of the truth.

Developing a new set of lenses and commitments in solidarity with other young lawyers, he learned for the first time what it felt like to be, himself, an outsider. "Moving into the counter-culture made me the enemy," he reflects. "It gave me the sense of being 'outside' and disempowered."

"My true effectiveness came when I resolved that anger," he told us. "There came a point when I had to choose to stay angry or to resolve it. That led to a deeper, quieter, more effective stance." Then he adds that paradoxically, "To become marginalized was very powerful."

Sarah, who subsequently became an obstetrician in a major teaching hospital, had much to do with this transformation.

> From the beginning, the relationship has been a major partnership in terms of trying to discover what life is all about, trying to uncover the meaning, venturing out into unknown territory, being willing to challenge systems and our own ways of life. We've pushed each other a lot in that direction, and have a relationship where we challenge

each other's way of life and discoveries, and it's very good. I've always felt she brought a tremendous wisdom to the situation, sometimes reinforcing my own resolve about my own commitment.

But in those early years, his commitment was still tender, and urban poverty was harsh. After several years, he and Sarah began to feel that "the existing culture and society wasn't worth it, and we'd better put our energies into building a new culture, a new society." As they were contemplating a move out of the city to start some sort of community, Bjorn Scoval appeared. He was the founder of an intentional community which valued both spiritual quest and public involvement. "And that was very attractive to me and to Sarah." They joined the community.

Bjorn became an important mentor for Joel. He had a directness about him, "an insight, wisdom, and humanness" that held the small community of a dozen young professionals together enabling them to develop their careers and to create "The Place" over the succeeding years, building it into a model center serving several hundred adolescents each evening with a full range of services, from academics to ballet, first aid to legal aid.

"Being part of a community has been an enormous support for being willing to keep going against what seem like insurmountable odds," Joel says. But the connections of commitment do not stop with their own circle. Committed to what he calls "a transformative process in society and the world," the community also created a global network of concerned professionals, and Joel feels "very connected to that wider work and to others who are working on that, even others I haven't met, people like myself who are not in any way famous, but they're out there. And I just feel there are thousands, tens of thousands of them in every country around the world who I'm connected with."

Grounded Commitment

Having explored and reflected upon how citizens committed to the whole earth community are formed and sustained, we have come to believe that the answer to our two central questions—"How do people become committed to the common good?" and "What sustains them?"—is finally the same. They are sustained by the very processes that have made them who they are. The people we interviewed have learned that they and all others are an integral part of the fundamental interdependence of life. Knowing this, when faced with a violation of what they know to be true, they can*not* *not* act. Their commitment derives from knowing that we are bound to one another and to the planet; it is as untenable to turn away from the world's pain and unrealized potential as to abandon one's child or sever one's hand. As an acorn takes root or a field flourishes in the Spring, they grew into their commitments bit by bit.

And yet, we know it is not that simple either. Not every seed takes root, not every field flourishes. The soil matters, and the wind, and the rain. . . .

Reflecting on "vocation," Frederick Buechner has written, "Neither the hair shirt nor the soft berth will do. The place God calls you to is the place where your deep gladness and the world's deep hunger meet."[1] On the surface, vocation seems a somewhat different notion than commitment. And yet the Latin origins reveal an interesting confluence. Both "vocation" (rooted in *vocare*, to call) and "commitment" (rooted in *cum*, with, and *mittere*, to send) suggest a response to some outside force: being called or sent on a task. Both imply a relationship rather than an individualistic choice. And although the conventional understanding of commitment often connotes a kind of fierce holding on, a determination to see a work through no matter what, we saw something quite different in those we studied—not so much a white-knuckled grip and clenched teeth as an open hand and discerning heart. Thus, like many creative people, they often speak of feeling "drawn out" or "led" as if by some force or truth greater than themselves. On to the art of life, they appear willing to be hooked by some wider reality that asks something of them. As one person told us, "It's not that we sustain a commitment; it's more that people like myself are sustained by the commitment." Or as Buechner might put it, their commitment seems continually reborn at that point where the heart's deep gladness meets the world's deep hunger.

Where the Heart's Deep Gladness . . .

As we have noted elsewhere, we saw very little sense of sacrifice among those we interviewed. On the contrary, most spoke of the "deep gladness" they felt in their work. "It wasn't duty and it wasn't self-sacrifice," said one person. "It was just a deep sense of growth and pride and love." Then, acknowledging the pain and hard work, she also added, "going through that brings joy." And while almost everyone acknowledged occasional ambivalence, most felt solid in their commitment to the larger good, if not always the particular form it was taking at the time. Most would agree with the low-income housing advocate who said, "This is what I love, what my purpose is, what drives me, and makes me happy."

Then, listening more closely beneath the expressions of satisfaction, we heard something quite unexpected. In this culture "freedom of choice" is often regarded as an ultimate value. We are exhorted daily to rejoice in the choices that a free market offers. To limit choice is an act of subversion; to do so willingly seems insane. Yet, in one way or another, many of our people echoed the woman who said, "I would have to tell you there was never a choice about any of it," or the man who said, "It's not something I choose to have. It's there and it's all encompassing." "I just always assumed that's what you do," said another.[2]

Often this was expressed in the form of a double negative:

- "It's as simple as 'you can't *not* do it'."
- "I can't be silent. I can't not act."
- "I couldn't help but act. There was nothing else for me to do."

It is as though some doubting voice is being transcended by another part of the self responsive to something larger. "What keeps me going is belief in something much bigger that we're fighting for, knowing that I could never do anything else." When we asked what it felt like to risk commitment, one person responded, "Risk? The greater risk is in *not* doing it." The given, the ground of identity, has become the imperative to do the work. The ground of commitment is experienced, not as a struggle to do something that one would prefer not to, but rather a response to a call that one ignores at peril to one's soul. In effect, to quit would mean to part company with reality.

. . . Meets the World's Deep Hunger

They often refer to that "something larger" as "the work," and whether manifest in action on behalf of better education, responsible business practices, participatory democracy, or environmental sustainability, at its core we heard a thrumming concern for a future in which life, "the most basic, bottom stuff" could flourish—as though they were responding to some call from Life to realize Itself more fully through them.

- "I feel somehow almost led to do it, by circumstance..."
- "I've just been bitten by a bug that says you must contribute."
- "I have been called from the time I was young to do something about the world."

Not all, but many felt the call as a spiritual imperative.

- "It is such an important part of meaning in my life...I couldn't quit. That would be spiritual death."
- "My spiritual life is going to become the life of the world because the world is in such urgent need right now. The only honorable choice for those with capabilities is to enter the fray."
- "We didn't ask to be born at this time. And yet we are chosen to be born at this time — chosen by history, chosen by the cosmological process. And so to feel we are people of destiny is again a question — not of mere grim survival but of a creative destiny in the face of...(pause)...whatever."

Where the heart's deep gladness and the world's deep hunger meet, commitment is conceived. The self becomes identified with the work to be done, understanding it as integral to the motion of life itself.[3] Thus the work matters everything. "It's the only game in town," said one person. And the work takes on importance for them, not out of some abstract notion of political correctness, but because people are suffering in the here-and-now and they cannot turn their backs on it. Hear the fire in the words of this multi-term Republican legislator.

> It is not acceptable in your town with plenty of people with money to have people starving on your streets. It's not acceptable. And it's not acceptable in the world at large when you have surpluses from our farms not to be concerned with feeding people starving in Africa. It's not acceptable. It's not decent. No decent society should stand by and say, 'Tough. I'm just glad it's not my family and that's not my country.'

Her commitment held throughout her life precisely because she could see and feel the real suffering of real people. The gap between her and those "starving in your streets" was intolerable precisely because we are inextricably linked with one another. It could be bridged only by reaching across on behalf of a larger, common good.

In *The Good Society*, Bellah and his colleagues signal that "democracy means paying attention."[4] This legislator cannot imagine not paying attention. Noticing, attending to the conflicts inherent in suffering and injustice, precedes action. Another told us:

> I've always had a clear sense that there were significant problems with how the world operated — cruelty, injustice, racism. I could see no reason for it to be this way. It was

just mind-boggling to me. And it made me angry, which I think is the response of someone who feels they can do something about it. I think you get depressed if you don't. But I always had a sense of "yes, I can—let's do something about this."

Thus, when we asked "What would be at stake if you quit?" one man looked at us bewildered. "Quit the commitment to the truth of my life? I can't imagine that. That is like impossible. I have no reason whatsoever to do that!" Others echoed him.

- "I don't think I could get to the point of stopping caring about the world. I don't think I can do that."
- "I'm neither romantic nor naive about the barriers that we face, but I'd have to become totally cynical to quit—or else I'd have to become someone else. I just don't know how you can not notice some of the injustices—the wrongs that are in front of you. And if you know them but don't allow yourself to think about them or address them, then you must be a pretty unhappy person."

This conviction that to quit would betray one's most profound sense of self was deeply felt by virtually everyone we spoke with. "It's not even up for grabs anymore. This is who I am," said one woman matter-of-factly. "I am my commitments," said another, "so I would be forsaking myself if I quit. The work that I do is the outward expression of whatever my inner life is." Recall Joel's words, *"I really have no choice. It's become a part of me. It's what I feel I'm about. . . ."*

Ambivalence

But the heart's gladness and the world's hunger do not always rest easily together, and the meeting place is sometimes elusive. We have emphasized the humanity, even vulnerability, of committed citizens, and it would be misleading to suggest that their commitment is invariably rock-solid or that the work is without obstacles. They do encounter significant frustrations: key funding is cut, their institution seems impervious to change, people they relied upon fail, opposition grows vicious, co-workers lack commitment, some problems only worsen, public inertia feels overwhelming. They do experience times of uncertainty, doubt, even despair. They do come to places where the haunting questions flourish: Am I just naive? Is this the right thing to be doing? Am I doing more harm than good? Should I stay in this position? Does any of this really matter—finally? Samantha Reagan, a woman who has spent years struggling to promote a more just society through education, sometimes wonders:

> I sometimes doubt whether at this phase in the history of the earth, the human species will survive. I think we could really blow it; I think that's a real possibility. There is such a tremendous rate and severity of dehumanization in the world. I think as there have been more of us, and as we have more command over the environment in many senses of the word, we become both more wonderful and more horrible. And at this moment we are experiencing profound dehumanization, a really anti-life kind of energy is out there. And I think we could make some irrevocable mistakes that would shatter the life-supporting capacities of the planet.

The questions are real, and they lodge in the hearts of those we interviewed. But they seldom take center stage in the inner dialogue, and when they do, they don't prevail for long. The few in our sample who had burned low for varying periods implicated personal health or family losses, and none was permanently defeated by such doubts.

Rather than relinquish the commitment, people are more likely to question the form of the work or a particular strategy—a social worker feels bogged down and shifts to community organization, a classroom teacher becomes frustrated and develops new curriculum, or a politician gets ahead of his constituents, is voted out, and takes up higher education reform. In cases like this—which were not unusual—people were able to come to terms with their own limitations, re-examine their deepest purposes, and then move on. The commitment itself did not go stale, only the form in which it was being lived out. "Success is not the measure of a human being," said one legislator, "effort is." Then she adds, "always tempered by humility before truth and the search for justice."

Hearing people speak of the importance of "letting go" of the results of their work, it is tempting to see them as enlightened souls who somehow have come to "renounce attachment to the fruits of their labor."[5] But it may be more accurate to suggest that they have a mixed attitude in which results matter a great deal, but because they are sufficiently anchored in their larger commitment, they can be flexible, reframe the situation, and let go of those "fruits" that have failed to mature or grown overripe. Viewed this way, the "double negatives" we heard take on fresh meaning: they have both voices, but the deeper commitment undercuts the voice of doubt and enables them to move ahead on a different and often more powerful path. As Samantha Reagan says when we ask her what vision sustains her in the face of her fears,

> I don't bring it up before me like an icon, and say, "This is what it is." I would not be able to describe it. But it would be an image of the future in which the interconnectedness of life was so assumed in the thinking of people and so evident in relationships that violence would be a real aberration, it would be an illness, and we would deal with it as an illness.

For her, the immediate messages of despair are less persuasive than a conviction that we have simply digressed from the deep truth of the incontrovertible interdependence of life.

The Connected Imagination

The Interdependent Conviction

Although committed people imagine a more adequate way of being human and hold what some call ideals about how things might be here on earth, they are deeply realistic. Indeed, it is their fierce refusal to deny reality that fires their commitment. What is unreal for them is the belief that so often animates the "real world"—that each of us is alone in the world, an independent, autonomous being, carving out our scrap of fate at the necessary expense of others. For the people we studied, the really real world is fundamentally more variegated, complex, and wondrous than a "survival of the fittest" philosophy can account for. It has "a terrible beauty," which we apprehend but do not fully comprehend. For them, the radical interdependence of all life is not just the way it could be, but the way things really are.

One woman told us, "I have this image of a net, because in a web any communication gets felt by everybody. So it seems to me that if it is a net, everybody has the potential for being in communication. It is a process that's among equals, full of dialogue."

"And without that, something is lost?" we ask.

"Something's endangered," she replies, "something precious, like survival of the world."

Similarly, Adam Curle, a wise colleague, who set aside a successful academic career in Third World development to mediate disputes in Biafra,

Northern Ireland, Sri Lanka and other trouble spots, told us that he keeps himself from becoming discouraged by trying not to become too attached to the outcomes of his work. But, he emphasized, his highest value, what keeps him connected, is compassion. "How do you hold those two together," we asked, "detachment and compassion?" He responded by describing "Indira's web," an image central to Hinduism. The ultimate reality is that the universe is a web in which each node is a living being. Each one is influenced by everything else in the universe.[6]

Although the metaphors may differ, we heard some form of this from many people.

- "There's not a day I'm not reminded of our connectedness."
- "We have a responsibility to live like we are all connected."
- "I am you and you are me and we're all in this together."
- "Nobody's free unless everybody's free."

To be sure, not everyone articulates their sense of the world in specifically these terms any more than we necessarily reflect upon or fully understand why our arm swings back as we step forward. The body just does things that way. But those we studied do live their lives in a manner that reflects an ingrained sense of interdependent life.

This bone-deep knowing that the sometimes overwhelmingly interdependent complexity of contemporary life is but a manifestation of the interrelated nature of all life grows out of the responsible imagination we discussed in Chapter 5. In their responsiveness to the tug of life, these committed citizens have not only experienced the complexity of the contemporary commons, they have been able also to practice an imagination that continually builds bridges across boundaries between tribes, makes connections through the gaps between competing ideologies, dismantles the fortifications around alienated constituencies, forges bonds beneath cynical interpretations, and repeatedly reframes a more adequate embrace of the whole so as to recast prejudice, stereotypes, and inadequate assumptions into forms that are more truthful because they take more into account.

Committed lives can be recognized, therefore, by their faithfulness to the conviction that because all of life is deeply interconnected, everybody counts. As William Sloane Coffin has put it, "Human unity is not something we are called on to create, only to recognize and then make manifest."[7] Thus every new and additional perspective, though perhaps initially irritating, has the potential to inform, revise, and create a new conviction of possibility.

Yet the responsible imagination does not indiscriminately stir everything into a single stewpot. Respect for fitting connections requires one to make important distinctions that honor the integrity of the particular, and typically the people we interviewed do this well. But they can also hold the particular within and accountable to the whole. They separate to distinguish, but never to divide.

This is not to say that the responsible, connected imagination finds the continual ebb and flow in the composing of commitment always easy. It is only to say, once again, that people who live committed lives know they *can't not* engage with life. They know they not only see possibilities to which they are committed, but they steward an awareness, a consciousness, essential for the survival of our species. As one expressed it, "I think that those moments of humanity and those moments of connectedness between humans are the silent medicine for our planet."

In this reality, the ego is relativised but not obliterated, for the world is too much with these folks for them to subscribe to ascetic detachment. The self has simply found its place in the ecology of the commons as a whole.

A Paradoxical Sense of Time and Place

Recall that Rosalyn Williams commented that "one of the gifts of blackness is being connected to a sense of history, so that one's life isn't just for today but it's for the hundreds of years that went before and the hundreds of years that come after." This recognition that the work spans more than one's own lifetime showed up frequently, not only among African-Americans but across the whole sample.

The work of the connected, responsible imagination takes time, and they know that effective strategies may require a keen sense of timing, pacing, and waiting. But the stance is steady, enabling a kind of daily "hanging-in" that reflects the buoyancy of spirit and larger sense of time that arises from an awareness of the interdependent nature of reality.

A physician working with babies whose mothers are addicted to crack tries to imagine what these children will be like as adults. She knows that the conditions that lead to the tragedy that surrounds her daily will not change overnight. She is sustained by the image of glaciers, of "the sense of flow and change and something happening over a long period of time—not necessarily needing to have it happen in your lifetime." Likewise, a woman working to reduce public violence acknowledged, "I won't see peace in my time; you've got to be realistic about that."

Perhaps this is because they see things as larger wholes, as complex systems, and they know that systemic change takes time. Perhaps it is because they know that the deeper changes that must occur are both cultural and personal, are political, economic, religious and philosophical. Perhaps it is because they know that pervasive change cannot be coerced but must be learned over time as the myriad threads in society are rewoven into new, more harmonious and appropriate patterns.

For all their long-term perspective, however, these are not people who can lean back and just leave the work to the next generation or others. Their sense of time is not only larger but more immediate than what many take for granted. While the changes they seek may not come to pass for generations, they feel what one person called "a holy urgency" about the work, a sense that "I must engage here and now." They carry a sense that though their work may not come to fruition during their lives, if they don't do what they can now, others will go through their whole lifetimes never knowing justice, or peace, or health and well-being. That sense of urgency was mentioned twice as often by those in our sample as by those in the comparison group.

Just as time for them is both vast and immediate, so is their sense of their own importance a poignant mix of hubris and humility. "I think about the beach," a relief worker told us. "I am a grain of sand on that beach." Then after a moment, he added, "But it's the billions of grains of sand that make the beach; without my grain, it would not be the same beach, so the work that I do is both inconsequential and the most important work in the world right now. That duality is critical in sustaining my commitment." Another described himself as "a flea on the tail of a dog," then quipped, "but at least I'm on the dog biting strategically!" Said another, "It's a short life. I'm a minor little speck in a huge, huge universe." Then, like so many others, she added, "but I'm related to that universe in some way." This sense of being connected to a larger force or entity or purpose while doing work of immediate consequence seems to enable them to maintain their equilibrium in the face of setbacks, discouragement, and existential doubt.

This paradoxical sense of place is also apparent in their sense of home. People committed to the common good tend to create a "home base"—a place, people, and way of proceeding to which they make promises. At the same time, their conviction of interdependence fosters a sense that they can be at home in the world. One said, "I have many places where I am at home, and home is something that I carry in my expectations."

[204]

An Emergent Vision

People like those we interviewed are often described as visionaries. But when we asked them to describe their visions, we were initially a little disappointed. Few were able (or willing) to describe clear visions of the future. We came to realize that while most do have a powerful sense of purpose, and often a personal vision, they are not visionaries in the usual sense: people who conjure a compelling image of the future, articulate the goal, and then invite others to follow them. Rather than spell out an explicit vision, or attempt to impose one on others, they instead described a more participatory stance, preferring to establish conditions for shared envisioning, staying closer to shifting circumstances and "proceeding as the way opens." They seemed more responsive, in short, to the context.

Asked to define her vision, Sue Drucker, the global educator, said, "If you abandon yourself to a vision, you can't do the concreteness that's in front of you, or you don't choose to do it well." And another educational leader replied that it was more important to create "public spaces where people can develop visions and flourish, where we can be the best we can be." Another told us, "In a lot of ways my vision of the future is really amorphous; it's more a vision of the present: to be faithful to what I love and value and to have joy."

Yet simply facilitating a process was not enough. A sense of clear purpose *was* essential; it was just that the kinds of complex, shifting circumstances under which most worked called for a more responsive, interactive stance than might be associated with the idea of a "vision." Thus, as one person put it, "You need goals, but you can't paint what the finish line is going to look like."

In part, this reluctance to construct a definitive vision may lie in the belief held by many that no one can possess the whole truth. Indeed, our people showed a marked distrust of particularist visions posing as holism and of grand abstract visions that finally lead to very concrete oppression. For them, the "common good" is an emergent vision best constructed in a fashion respectful of the full diversity of the commons.

A Preference for Collaborative Work

For this reason, we heard a frequent preference for work settings that valued collaboration. Said a woman with long experience in organizational development, "I know that if you live with cooperation and trust and if you don't set things up hierarchically but rather in a more cooperative way, it takes a lot of time. But you sure have more trust, and it's a better way to live." Collaboration did not mean that people had to agree all the time or that all decisions had to made by everyone, but there was a marked confidence in the value of bringing diverse groups of people together in a manner that made it possible for them to focus on common problems. As one person put it, "We try to provide a place where a variety of human concerns can somehow meet and clash and grope toward some kind of companionship with each other." The willingness to invest energy in this way seemed to be fed by a conviction that the effort to bridge traditional boundaries and take into account a variety of perspectives simply results in better decisions and greater long-term effectiveness.

Communities of Comfort and Challenge

Not surprisingly, the recognition of interdependence leads one to place high value on mutually nurturing relationships with others. "You don't make it on your own," a public interest lawyer told us. "And in my experience, people who tried were the people who lost their commitments." Another added, "I don't think you can serve anywhere or anybody until you have worked a fundamental relationship with another person."

All people are dependent upon relationships with others and most learn to value them. For the most part, the need for friends and kin is assumed, regardless of what one believes or does. But the people we interviewed more readily recognize this need than do some others, and relationships nourish them in particular ways.

What these people believe and stand for matters keenly to them; they work often against the odds. Yet we never heard anyone say, "I don't care what others think." What others think does matter. Like all humans, they share a universal need to be recognized. "When you get discouraged, what keeps you going?" we would ask, and this man spoke for most when he replied, "Other people I trust. I keep coming back to that. People whose judgment I trust, whose character I trust, whose intelligence I trust, whose sense of reality I trust, who continue to believe that this is the right thing to do."

Though cast in a wide variety of forms, they depend on communities of confirmation. The love of family and supportive relationships with friends and colleagues means a lot to the people we interviewed and is closely allied to the quality of their commitment to the larger good. But they valued these connections with kindred spirits not just for the comfort they provided but for the challenge as well.

Friends and Kin

Friendships were often brought up in the interviews. They serve as support when people feel stuck or discouraged; they help people stay anchored in their sense of purpose. One person spoke of "wonderful dinners with friends, talking about issues, or telling stories." Another saw them as "an incredible gift because I don't feel alone or isolated." For people who are often doing work that sets them apart from conventional practice, friends and colleagues can be reminders that they are not crazy, that there are others who "really share my vision and are excited about the same things." Beyond this, a deep friendship can be a sort of model for how one might live well in the world. As one person put it, "Friendship is absolutely essential. It serves as a sort of warrant for hope in the world, a proving ground of how we can be worthy of trust so that we can be better for others."

We were surprised to hear how important parents were, even to people in their forties and fifties and beyond. Says one woman well past midlife, "When I look back, what has sustained me are very deep love relationships, including increasingly, my dad." And a man in his seventies told us with tears in his eyes how toward the end of a stormy lifetime together his more conventional father had told him that "he thought that I'd lived the way that was right and that he wished he'd been able to live more that way himself." Parental approval may, indeed, be all the more valued by the many in our sample who followed a drumbeat that often took them far from their parents' lives and expectations.

Children

For many, the family had a special power, serving as a "laboratory in being faithful," as one person put it. Many people, particularly men, spoke of how much their children have "humanized" them, reminding them of their own tenderness. "Having a family has made me more sensitive to children and families and vulnerability," one man said. And a woman added, "Having kids around sort of serves as a laboratory to test your stuff out on and gives you a whole different set of eyes to see the world with."

Indeed, a decision to bring children into the world and rear them is one of the most intense commitments one can make, and the people we interviewed were keenly aware of this. "Children have a very large stake in the world," said one person; and another reflected that when she looked at her little daughter, she felt, "if I don't have hope in the future, then it was very irresponsible of me having her." And of her grandchildren, a world health advocate says, "You do not want to see your grandchildren fall into the terrible conditions that you see through so much of the world." Children ground one's commitment in a most concrete and immediate way.

Even when they do not have children of their own, many people find children a powerful source of motivation. A pediatrician told us, "The hope of our own families, our communities, and our world is in our children. If you don't really have hope for the future, then you don't value your children." And when we asked an environmentalist in his eighties, "What is the driving force behind your work?" he replied, "The greatest single thing is the children. I cannot bear leaving to the children a world—a planet—any more damaged than I can help."

Networks

Human connection consistently served to nourish committed people. Again and again they told us that what sustained them was the knowledge that there were others like themselves—some with whom they worked regularly, some whom they saw occasionally, and some whom they had never known but whose mere existence was a model and a comfort. A thick bed of research confirms this finding.[8] Conversely, a study of angry and burned-out environmentalists found that most felt abandoned by others and "everyone described a deep sense of loneliness."[9]

Knowing that one is among friends and colleagues who share a common purpose can remind the weary of their own commitments and help to create a kind of synergy that both gives and receives new strength and reorders one's perspective. In a supportive community, people can feel safe to let down their guard and talk about their disasters as well as their successes.

"There are moments when I get tremendously upset and discouraged, disheartened. When I'm just me, myself, that's when I get down," said one person. "But I've been so blessed because I was surrounded by people who all felt strongly the way I did. Having other people who feel strongly, that's the answer. You feel so much stronger. You feel like you can do anything if you have a group of people around you who are supportive and who say, 'So you lose on this one.'"

This sense of being a part of a network may go far beyond face-to-face contacts, and, like Joel Rosen, others also took courage from knowing that there were many whom they have never met—living and dead—with whom they have a sense of solidarity and shared commitment.

Like friends and kin, networks provide not only support but also challenge.

"We all need to have our feet kept to the fire and to be held accountable for the hope that's in us," Rosalyn Williams told us, "and to be challenged about our strategies from a variety of perspectives." Like a number of others, she finds the interchange of points of view stimulating. It keeps her from growing smug.

Further, the crossfire of perspectives in a vibrant community can mimic the larger world and enable people to deal more effectively with complex challenges. Several people spoke of convening round tables to explore pressing problems from different political and disciplinary viewpoints before taking the discussion into a larger public forum.

Deep Currents
As the chapters in this book have unfolded, the reader has perhaps begun to sense the deep currents shaping committed lives. Over and over again people committed to the whole earth community have responded to the movement of their lives in a manner that has made possible a *connection with otherness*, giving rise to *compassion* (the capacity to suffer with). Taking the perspective of the other and bringing it under the aegis of critical and systemic habits of mind, has, in these lives, given rise to *convictions of possibility*. These convictions of possibility are grasped and held by metaphors, which give form to a more adequate and faithful reality that grounds the *courage to risk*, which in the committed life is simply an act in tune with the interconnected reality that we are. This stance enables them to regularly *confess* the fallibility of their own understanding, to forgive themselves and others, and thus to sustain the practice of responsible imagination that we call *commitment*.

Sustainable Commitment

The last thing he needed was to rock the boat. As a young white pastor in Kalamazoo in 1962, Don Butyne had enough to do just to keep his congregation afloat. But racial tensions in the city were rising and as a means of heading off violence, a civil rights march was planned to address issues of fairness in employment and housing. Annie Brown, a widely respected black woman in church circles and a close friend of the Butyne family, was asked to represent black women in the community and walk directly behind the color guard at the head of the march. She wanted to go, she told him, but she was afraid. "Will you come with me?" she asked.

"We couldn't say no to Annie," Butyne reported years later, after he and the churches he served had become leaders in the struggle for racial equality and human dignity. A prominent member of his church had called the day before the march, threatening Butyne personally in an effort to deter him. But to this day, the image of his foot stepping off the curb into the street marks for Butyne the beginning of his commitment to social transformation.

Partway through our study, one person, reflecting on some of our early findings, asked an intriguing question: "When these people became committed, was it a close call or was it inevitable?" Did the kind of commitment Butyne represents begin only when his foot hit the street? If Annie Brown had not come along would he have remained on the curb for a lifetime? Or were the conditions set years before, so that if it had not been Annie, it may well have been someone else?

At the time, we were not sure how to respond. But as we continued to hear more and more stories, and as the patterns we have described grew increasingly salient, the answer came into sharper focus. The people we studied were formed little by little, step by step to become the kind of citizens they are. Their commitment was not skin deep, nor were the daily choices they made impulsive. They had grown that way over the years. "We couldn't say no to Annie," he said. That double negative again. Annie and what she stood for had become an interdependent feature of his sense of himself, his world, who and what counts. He could not say no. In some way, who he was and who she was had become linked long before she asked her compelling question.

It is clear from other studies of the formation of commitment,[10] as well as our own, that although it may appear this way to people, it is probably "quite rare in life that there is a Rubicon to cross."[11] We would wager that when Butyne stepped off that curb he had been walking toward it for much of his life.

Moreover, commitment snowballs. "The moment one definitely commits oneself, then Providence moves too," said Goethe. And so it seems. Each step builds on the prior one and prepares for the next. As one of the interviewees put it, "We are only asked to take one step that makes another step possible."

But simply recognizing that our lives may have a certain coherence is no argument that they will inevitably bear us toward compassion or wisdom. In his memoirs, German war minister Albert Speer describes in jarring detail how each move bound him ever more tightly to the Nazi party.[12] What distinguishes the lives that we studied is that rather than the extreme tribalism that characterized the Nazi mentality, we found a propensity to cross tribal boundaries, to make personal connections with the other, and to engage in work explicitly on behalf of a larger imagination of what it means to be human.

From early in life, the people we interviewed had engaged in some compassionate way with people different from themselves, learning again and again to cross, and thus to redraw, the boundaries between "self" and "other." Over time, the sense of who "we" are grew larger, more encompassing, as they participated in and grew through communities that both formed and nourished them. As their understanding of community expanded, so did their own awareness of who they were in the wider life of the commons.

Along with this growth in awareness, the stories, images, and symbols that invigorated those communities came to take on richer meaning, igniting the fire of a common imagination, and moving them toward responsible action. At the same time, the very dialogue of their lives—with both their inner and outer worlds—was marked by a quality of confession that enabled them to keep their balance in the midst of the world's complexity, their despair, and their own fallibility. Over the years their hearts' deep gladness became so integrated with the world's deep hunger that they found a home in that "sweet spot" where everything connects and were finally unable to turn away from its claim on them. They could not "just say 'no.'" Beneath the double negative, embedded in their most adamantine sense of truth, was a profound "yes." Almost without their noticing, their roots had taken a fierce and luxuriant hold in the soil of the world, and they had become dedicated spirits, the people we need.

epilogue

Compass Points: The Power of
Location and Direction

When the way to proceed is uncertain and vision hampered, a compass can provide orientation and direction. In the context of the new global commons, it is useful to reassess our particular location, the deepest purposes that beckon us, and the directions in which we want to move to prepare ourselves for citizenship in the twenty-first century. Paying attention to the conditions in which we now find ourselves, assessing how we came to be where we are, and reflecting upon possible paths ahead, is one way of creating a "compass" to orient us as we move into the future.[1]

In this epilogue, we focus on twelve sectors of our society, located, as it were, around the commons. Each sector represents a critical feature of our common life, a particular set of perspectives, responsibilities, and opportunities; each sector can make a strategic contribution to the formation of a shared moral compass, helping us to get our bearings as together we work to create a positive future. The sectors are households (children, youth and family); schools; higher education; the professions and professional education; religion; arts and media; public policy; business; nonprofit organizations; the health and therapeutic community; foundations and philanthropy; and you, the reader. While our choice of sectors is somewhat arbitrary, we have selected them because they are primary institutional forms that can foster the learning now needed, and they have the power to encourage ways of living that directly serve the well-being of the commons.

[213]

Taken individually, the sectors we have identified suggest distinctions that are somewhat artificial in the interdependent reality of the commons. For example, we have identified as separate sectors schools, higher education, and professional education. Yet education also needs to be seen whole—from the time of earliest family life to kindergarten through professional studies and beyond. More, we learn in both formal and informal settings. Likewise, though public policy, business, and non-profit sectors may be usefully distinguished from each other, they are intimately related in the complexity of the new commons. On the other hand, there are facets of our society that we have subsumed within these twelve sectors that might have been distinguished: for example, architecture, science, or the military.

We briefly identify the essential purpose each sector serves—recognizing the power of its location in our common life—and then we suggest a few key directions in which those directly engaged in this sector may want to move in order to contribute to the formation of the kind of citizenship now needed. The directions we suggest are neither original or exhaustive. They are, however, congruent with the findings and implications of this study, and they have been informed also by focus groups of people representing each sector.

Those working within a particular sector may be keenly aware of additional directions to pursue. We encourage all readers to imagine directions that may be equally or more vital. These are intended only to invite dialogue and ongoing revision as conditions continue to change and new priorities and strategies emerge.

We begin with four primary directions which we believe provide key points of orientation for all sectors.

Four Primary Directions

Create Time to Pause, Reflect, and Assess

Biologists tell us that when confronted with a changing environment, the first response of most organisms is to do what they have always done, only faster. As our human environment faces significant adaptive challenges, we find ourselves plagued by busyness and cumber. Creating time for reflection, learning, and reorientation can be a significant act of citizenship. This may begin with simply claiming deep, restorative rest that renews the energies of mind and spirit. But the pause that is now needed also clears the path toward a courageous, informed, and creative assessment of our "mattering map," a term coined by the novelist Rebecca Goldstein. What is located at the center of your mattering map? What do our personal and organizational mattering maps reveal about the topography of our sense of meaning, purpose, and commitment? Where does your mattering map take you? Does our shared mattering map help us make our way in the new global commons?

"Stopping" in a world gone busy—whether as individuals or as organizations—is not easy; but contemplation in "pause time" can be productive in unexpected, vital, and strategic ways. The life of the new commons and its future depends, in part, upon the renewal of "sabbath" practices that reorient our sense of purpose and direction in a complex age (see Chapters 1, 5, and 7).

Cultivate the Strengths of Living Both Within and Beyond "Tribe"

We all need a "tribe"—a network of belonging that provides security and encourages our finest aspirations. In the complexity of contemporary life, many of us belong in varying degrees to multiple "tribes." It is useful to recognize our patterns of belonging and to assess how these patterns of affiliation do and do not nourish our capacity for citizenship in the twenty-first century. Over time we may need to shed some associations and to deepen and enlarge others to garner the strength to live well both within and beyond "tribe."

As we live and work in an increasingly diverse world, it is significant that we found *constructive engagements with otherness* to be the single most critical element undergirding commitment to the common good in the lives of those we studied. There is a vital need in every sector of the commons to encourage meeting and dialogue across the divides of culture, race and ethnicity, religion, generations, economic class, and political persuasion. While this is particularly important for young people in their formative years, it remains essential for all of us. Superficial encounters with those who are different can often lead to stereotyping and fortressing, but encounters which evoke empathic recognition of a shared humanity and will-to-life foster a generous commitment, not simply to me and mine but to the common good upon which we all depend (see Chapter 3).

Develop and Practice a Consciousness of Connection

We have much to learn about how to recognize the interdependent fabric of our common life. Steeped in the virtues of individualism, we are vulnerable to assuming we have autonomy, control, and individual responsibility when we do not, taking for granted many relationships on which we, in fact, depend.

Practicing a consciousness of connection—whether with our families, colleagues, neighbors, the natural world, or people, places, and problems far away—can be a critical first step in learning to see how apparently diverse people, issues, and things are related. This may mean choosing to serve as a "threshold person" by supporting a child next door who needs our personal presence, or paying attention to young adults in our sphere of influence who are waiting for mentorship; it may mean supporting local schools or placing one's organization in partnership with a sister organization to make a more effective contribution to the commons; or it may mean developing networks, creating rituals of recognition and appreciation, or courageously contending with violations of mutual respect. We might ask the "why" and "how" questions that can yield a deeper awareness of the complex connections among things: Why do we have a growing gap between the Global North and the Global South? How do the policies of international, federal, state, and local government interdependently shape our common life? Why do committed lives both inspire and unsettle us? Why did I choose the work I'm doing? How does "choice" happen? (See chapters 1, 3, 4, and 6.)

Attend to the Character and Use of Language

"Language," broadly understood, is critical in creating the assumptions, emotional climate, and behavioral norms that define people, their environment, and what is and is not possible within it. The new commons is characterized, in part, by shifting patterns in our forms of communication. We are an increasingly video-dominated society; new technologies offer us new forms of connection and community along with new forms of the temptation to distort truth and exclude those who should also belong; we are facing the unprecedented challenge of the "transfixed mind" and the entertained society on a global scale. As we move into the new commons, paying attention to the character and use of images, symbols, stories, and songs is essential. Each person and organization can play a role in cultivating and choosing the images we feed our young as we prepare them for the future. We can choose language which works not to obscure and manipulate, but rather to uncover, reveal, and name the realities of life in the new commons—its promise and its perils. The nature of our own discourse and the behavior we display and encourage as we move through an average day conspire to encourage commitment to the common good or to erode it—in children, youth, and adults (see Chapter 5).

The Reader

Every person is a part of the new global commons. As a part of that interdependence, by intention or default, each person participates in shaping our common life. In the patterns revealed in this study, some readers will recognize much that resonates with their own story and experience of commitment to the common good. Others may find encouragement to renew their energies on behalf of the new commons. If so, a number of steps can be taken to move more deeply into commitments already felt, however dimly or keenly.

Take the First Steps

Healthy commitment nourishes itself. Committed people agree that we can only take one step at a time, but each step can make another step possible. First steps include paying attention to the contradictions, dissonance, or needs that attract and stir *your* conscience (see Chapter 5). Create time to pause and listen to the prompting at the deep center of your life. Reflect upon your particular location in the new commons and the opportunities that attend it—then pitch in. For example, if you are working in a company, consider the nature of the products or services you help to provide, their meaning in our common life, and in what ways you may be able to enhance their contribution. If you are a parent, consider ways in which you can nourish your child's imagination about what it means to be a good citizen. (See Chapter 2.)

If you are in your early twenties and longing for a sense of direction, be patient. Let people into your life who share your aspirations and are addressing the challenges that you think are important. Seek mentors. If you are older, remember that some people make their most significant contributions later in life (see Chapter 2).

Link with Others Who Share Your Aspirations for Practical Action

This study indicates, and other research confirms, that people who try to go it alone are rarely able to sustain their commitment. Committed people need to know that there are others like themselves striving to live lives committed to the common good. Be one of those people. Find good friends you can rely upon and invest time in those relationships so that they can be sustained for the long haul. Find or form a group in your workplace or elsewhere who meet regularly for study, discussion, mutual challenge and support, and exploration of ways to serve the life of the commons more strategically and effectively (see Chapters 2, 6, and 7). Identify people and organizations, known and obscure, who can serve as models, guides, and inspiration—and who are responsive to your gifts and energies. If you have not had constructive encounters with people significantly different from yourself, seek out people, organizations, and travel that can help you do that (see Chapter 3).

Take Care of Yourself

The people in our study emphasized the importance of caring for oneself as well as the world. Cultivate a sense of proportion. Know when enough is enough. Develop strategies that work without burning you out (see Chapter 6). Reclaim the practice of "sabbath"—at least one day in seven when you can rest, gain perspective, and nourish your spirit. Enlarge your mind and heart through reading and travel; maintain a sense of humor; spend time in the natural world (see Chapter 5).

Celebrate your victories and mourn your defeats. When you have reached a goal—or achieved a small step—congratulate yourself and your co-workers. When you are defeated, share your grief with others, and grieve deeply so you will be able to restore energy and hope. Find ways to forgive yourself and others (see Chapter 6).

Spend Time with Young People

Be aware of your importance as a model for younger people. Your influence reaches farther than you may think. Find people with particular needs or promise and take time with them, affirm their compassion for others, say "yes" to their best aspirations. Be particularly aware of children who need someone to protect and affirm them, teenagers who need to participate in adult conversation and work, young adults seeking mentoring wisdom. Attend also to older adults in transition who are ready to re-formulate and deepen their commitment (see Chapter 2).

Households: Children, Youth, and Adults

Crafted in the bonds of kinship, covenant, and hospitality, the household constitutes the mini-commons in which children and youth learn the essential features of committed citizenship: trust and agency, belonging and responsibility, confession and forgiveness (see Chapters 2 and 6). For adults too, the everyday claims of the household—in whatever form—serve to inform the meaning and practice of commitment. Households can be centers of love where we are able to learn essential skills. More, one of the chief benefits of the house is that it "protects the dreamer," serving as a base from which we can cultivate and sustain imagination, perspective and proportion.[2] From "homeplaces" we learn how to be at home in the world (see Chapter 2).[3]

Although many in our sample grew up when the traditional family was still predominant and a few recall idyllic childhoods, then as now, some kind of suffering marked most people's experience of family and homeplace. Nevertheless, in most cases family life was "good enough" and made key contributions to the capacity to care for the common good. It is important to recognize the positive power of the household in the following ways.

Strengthen the Family Household as the Ground of Commitment

However defined, the family household can provide four fundamental elements:

- A *safe environment* that provides reliable shelter and nourishment;
- At least one *trustworthy adult* who sees the child, adolescent, or young adult as precious, unique, lovable, capable, and worthy of respect;
- Opportunities to learn that one can *make a positive difference*, first in small ways, later in larger ways;
- *Time and space to express and heal* the inevitable pain and hurt of life—including rage and bereftness—in a way that strengthens the spirit and deepens the capacity for compassion toward both oneself and others (see Chapter 6).

In the absence of these elements, people may develop various forms of emotional armor which numb them to the wider life of the commons.

Households can foster the conviction that "everyone counts" through practices of dialogue and explicit perspective-taking among its members; in rituals of fairness and forgiveness, recognition and celebration; and through storytelling that encourages the development of positive family lore. These practices counter the "default setting" that increasingly dictates the norms of family life: diverging schedules, meals eaten individually and on the run, TV and other entertainment replacing presence and conversation, minimal expectations of care for the physical and emotional environment, and unresolved hostility or isolation.

Recognize That "Home" Extends beyond Domicile

Only in relatively recent history has the word "home" come to connote an individual domicile rather than town or region. Households and families are most apt to flourish when they are woven into the fabric of a viable community. Cultivate connections with individuals and institutions that strengthen and enlarge the family circle. Carefully tend your relationships with relatives, teachers, colleagues, people who share your faith and traditions. Form partnerships with those who can become additional adults for the young and who can help to sustain the energies of adult commitments (see Chapters 2 and 7).

Welcome the World into the Home

The practice of hospitality has a powerful function in the formation of commitment. Through the rituals of hosting and being a guest, the home can serve as a safe gathering place where we enter each other's worlds and recognize our interdependence. Hospitality to the wider world may also be practiced—with care—through media such as books, newspapers, television, video, the Internet, the telephone. These experiences are most positive in their effects when they are shared and discussed with others.

Most of the participants in our study were avid readers. Reading widely clearly enriches one's awareness of the world beyond the home, but more, it encourages identification with those different from oneself. One of the simplest and most effective things parents can do is to encourage their children to read or create their own artful play instead of only watching television.

Encourage an Ethic of Family Service

Many people recalled at least one "public parent" who actively cared for the wider world or took public stands on issues of justice. Some remembered joining with family and others to work on projects that served the larger community. As adolescents and young adults seek their own ways to meaningfully contribute to the adult world, family lore can teach that commitments to the common good are part of their heritage and identity. The family household can provide a place of reflection and encouragement as they weigh the choices before them (see Chapter 2).

Schools

Schools paradoxically hold both the past and future of the culture. Effective schools work collaboratively with the traditional and emerging sources of wisdom in the culture to discern and teach the knowledge, skills, and attitudes that the next generation will need as citizens. When schools function well, they prepare the ground for the habits of mind and heart required for the confident and humane participation now needed in both the local and global community (see Chapter 4). The transitional stress that schools are undergoing in this multicultural and technological age may become more productive if it can be oriented in the following directions.

Develop a Whole School Environment That Models the Values and Cultivates the Knowledge Needed in the New Commons

Evidence suggests that the whole school environment contributes to what students learn. Small schools that exemplify positive community are particularly effective in promoting commitment to the common good. Ways of being, disciplines, and dialogue that promote democratic values of inclusion, respect, accountability, fairness, and compassion can play a significant role in enabling children and young people to learn that "this is how we do things."[4] Learning multiple habits of attention and interpretation, cultivating an active imagination of a positive future, and discovering the rewards of becoming comfortable with what was initially unfamiliar in both the natural and social worlds can provide deep and lasting lessons about how we can dwell together well (see Chapters 3 and 4).[5]

If you are a teacher, staff person, coach, or administrator, remember that your efforts to recognize students as particular people can have lifelong influence. Creating a climate of common work and high expectations can encourage the development of trust and agency so foundational to commitment in a complex world (see Chapter 2).[6]

Content matters. Children and adolescents need to learn from a well-conceived curriculum as well as from what is already important to them. Learning is most powerful when students are given experiential opportunities to integrate new information about the world into their existing frameworks in ways that lead to fresh insights and new habits of mind (see Chapter 4).

How history is interpreted and what stories are created, told, read, and viewed can be significant. Whether fictional or biographical, good stories raise moral questions. Linking morally stimulating stories to students' lives through discussion of their own real-life dilemmas fosters understanding and compassion (see Chapters 2 and 5).

Design Ways to Learn About and with Others Who Are Different

Global curricula in geography and cross-cultural studies are important. But so are experiences that enable young people to learn to know those who are significantly different from themselves as real people who live in a world both similar to and legitimately different from their own—especially those in their own community. School should be a safe place for shared dialogue, not simply discussions about "them." This is particularly important for majority students. Sharing a project or meaningful purpose with those who are "other" has a particular power to expand tribal boundaries for children and youth. Diversity in a student body is more a strength to celebrate than a problem to solve. (See Chapters 2, 3, and 4.)

Break the Classroom Routine by Varying Location, Schedule, and Activity

Bedridden as children or teens, a number of people in the study apparently benefitted from having time out from the lock-step pattern of schooling. While day-to-day consistency is important for some forms of learning, breaks can create a fertile pause. Solitude is vital for learning how to wonder, read, and reflect. Time in the natural world as well as the classroom, special projects and trips, and good vacation time (without homework) all may awaken new perspectives (see Chapter 5).

Claim a Partnership with the Community for the Life of the School

Schools cannot flourish without engaged and fiscally accountable communities. A school's effectiveness is dependent upon citizens—particularly parents but also other individuals, institutions, and sectors—who recognize the critical role of the school in the life of the commons. Citizens can also link schools with the wider world by encouraging programs that take students into the community to make use of local and global resources that bring talent and challenges from the surrounding environment into the schools.

Higher Education

Two and four-year colleges and universities serve as communities of inquiry and imagination on behalf of society. They are charged with teaching critical reflection and practicing research that informs knowledge and inspires vision. They steward intellectual and material resources vital to the life of the commons.

At their best, colleges provide space and stimulus for a process of transformation through which students move from modes of understanding that are relatively dependent upon conventional assumptions to more critical, systemic thinking that can take many perspectives into account, make discernments among them, and envision new possibilities.[7] The deep purpose of higher education is to steward this transformation so that students and faculty together continually move from naivete through skepticism to commitment rather than becoming trapped in mere relativism and cynicism. This movement toward a mature capacity to hold firm convictions in a world which is both legitimately tentative and irreducibly interdependent is vitally important to the formation of citizens in a complex and changing world. It can be encouraged in the following ways.

Assess the Institution's Capacity—Actual and Potential— to Contribute to the Life of the New Commons

Work to establish mutually beneficial partnerships among administration, faculty, students, and the wider community. Through the active development of participation in neighborhoods, enterprise zones, and international networks and projects, colleges and universities—often in collaboration with other sectors such as business, health, religion, and the arts—can bring their influence, insight, and resources to the work of the commons, both local and global. This may include but need not be limited to consulting activities and internships (see Chapter 1).

Develop the Institution as a Mentoring Environment

"Texts" joined in dialogue among the members of the college or university community constitute the complex ecology of higher education as a mentoring environment that can provide challenge, support, and inspiration for both students and younger faculty. Individual or group conversations with faculty, administrators, college chaplains, and visiting speakers were pivotal influences in the lives of several of the people we interviewed. Residence hall programming, study abroad, internships, service opportunities, and intensive summer programs, along with opportunities for leadership in the course of campus life, can be vital, especially when combined with study content and discussion that casts such experiences in a larger frame (see Chapters 3 and 4).

Whatever the area of study, consistently extending hospitality to questions about the relationship between the academic discipline and one's vocation in the world, plays a decisive role in the formation of citizenship and needs in every way to be encouraged (see Chapter 7).

There is a critical need for student loan structures that make higher education more available and encourage career choices that serve the common good. There is a comparable need to vigorously strengthen student and alumni placement services to facilitate access to career opportunities in the public sector and other sectors that encourage commitment (see Chapters 1 and 4).

Cultivate Habits of Mind Leading to Practical Wisdom

Critical, systemic thinking is recognized as vital to the life of the academy, but without comparable attention to the development of holistic thought higher education may foster only narrow expertise inattentive to the complexities of our wider life. Colleges and universities can become models for how very different perspectives, disciplines, issues, and people come together in a more adequate synthesis, developing prototypes of what can be done (see Chapter 4).

Critical, systemic thought becomes most positive in the formation of commitment when the "text," the content of study, gives explicit attention to contemporary and complex challenges and retains a human face. Good literature, drama, films, and direct engagement with critical social and intellectual challenges can add a crucial affective element to the educational mix.

Create Opportunities for Constructive
Engagements with Otherness

Race and ethnicity, class, and gender are critical forms of diversity on campus; there are, however, more subtle forms of difference such as differing disciplinary lenses or contrasting career goals that are just as real. From both kinds of diversity students and faculty can gain a sharper recognition of their own particularity, a broader understanding of their location in the larger commons and a greater ability to carry on effective dialogue across tribal boundaries. But, one college president warned, "Expect conflict; diversity is not tidy."

Learning to understand one another despite important differences does not happen simply by physical proximity. It takes time and the opportunity for significant dialogue. These require conscious design and sustained attention to the general social milieu of the implicit and explicit curriculum.

This kind of learning happens in the classroom when particular traditions that have shaped culture in profound ways—such as the Western or Asian tradition—are worked through in a rigorous and coherent manner that takes present conditions into account and opens to a deeper dialogue and appreciation of other traditions. This approach is most successful when hospitality is extended to voices previously marginal in the life of the university, cultivating a multitribal dialogue around a common hearth in which all participate and are held mutually accountable (see Chapters 2, 3, 4, and 5).

The Professions and Professional Education

To have a profession is to have a particular stance—a way of perceiving and practicing that is held in common with and accountable to a community of others who bear like responsibility. It provides a privileged doorway into the life of the commons, in which the professions play a pivotal role in nearly everyone's life.

Professional education is an initiation into the purpose, knowledge, and skills of a profession. It encourages ongoing re-framing of professional insight and competency. Professional education typically facilitates socioeconomic mobility, creating access to goods, services, and economic, political, social, and spiritual power. The challenges and opportunities of the new commons encourage movement in the following directions.

Reclaim the Most Profound Purposes of the Profession
As They Affect the Well-Being of the Commons
A clear sense of worthy purpose is essential to the formation of leadership, particularly in an age when every profession is being reordered by the development of global communications and economies, when multicultural societies challenge the ethical assumptions of past eras, and when cynical interpretations of professional motivations abound (see Chapter 1). It is vital to reclaim, boldly articulate, and practice the deep purposes of the professions in a manner that recognizes both their private and public duties in the complex opportuni-

ties of contemporary professional life. Clarity of worthy purpose can attract and inspire sustained commitment that serves the common good.[8]

Design a Mentoring Environment That Corresponds to Professional Purpose and Best Practice

It has been said that education, particularly professional education, is preparing people for a world that isn't going to be there. Several of the professionals we interviewed expressed deep frustration and concern about the limited capacity of professional guilds and professional education to prepare them and others to become citizens in the new commons.

A professional school can, however, appropriately initiate young and older adults into the norms and standards of a profession by meeting naive assumptions, idealism, and cynicism—all in a manner that fosters more rigorous and comprehensive analysis without blunting the potential for meaningful commitment. Professional education must cultivate expertise, yet must also reveal that professional practice is as much art as formula—an art that can be mastered only across a lifetime.

The implicit and explicit curriculum needs to be attentive to the fundamental character and content of its learning model. If it is characterized by humiliation and erosion of self-esteem, it is likely to foster obedience and conformity and build up armor rather than maximizing competence and creativity. In contrast, a curriculum that fosters the excellence that is now needed informs, challenges, supports, inspires, and encourages the balance of hubris and humility that we see in committed lives.

The design of the mentoring environment needs to account for the reality that norms of professional life are learned through the interdependent experiences of both formal professional education and the "first job." Institutions such as law firms, corporations, and religious organizations share a critical and evolving partnership with professional education in the life of the new commons.

Develop an Appropriate "Mattering Map"

Potential contributions to the commons are significantly shaped by what does and doesn't get put on the "mattering map" in the course of professional education.[9] For example, if the systemic reach of every professional transaction is recognized, ethics can be emancipated from the margins of curricular interest and find its place on the "mattering map"—at the core of professional identity and education.[10] This can foster attention to "swamp issues"—important, complex and messy problems that resist technical analysis more amenable to "high, hard ground" where problems are also real but less important to both individuals and the wider society.[11]

Foster Interdependent and Holistic Thought

Physicians have to think about allocation issues, lawyers have to take the bottom line into account, educators need to take their full place in dialogue with regulators, and military officers cannot be indifferent to matters of social and political import. Escape into a role-based morality in which it is assumed that "if I just do my job and everyone else does theirs, somehow it will all come out all right" offers no reasonable alternative.

Professional education often encourages critical, systemic thought, but when holistic thought is also sponsored, professionals learn to work with individuals and communities with multiple issues lived out not in discrete entities but as an integrated whole. Multiple perspectives and "out-of-the-box" thinking rather than narrow expertise or disembodied economic models are essential in the new commons where all professionals work interdependently with professions other than their own.

Religion

It has been observed that "where there is no vital community to hold up precious ethical and religious ideals, there can be no coming to a moral commitment."[12] Through practices that nourish a posture of awe and gratitude, a desire for truth, and ethical participation, religion at its best inspires and fosters a response to life by which a community may learn to live as a faithful, loving, just, and whole people. By moving in the following directions, religion can encourage discerning and contemporary responses to the ancient question, "How are we to live?"

Create Inclusive Communities That Practice
Love, Justice, and Mercy

Honoring the integrity of its own memory and hope, a community of faith develops a distinctive identity, serving as a center of belonging and care essential to human flourishing. In the diversity, complexity, and ambiguity of the new commons, churches, meeting houses, mosques, temples, synagogues, and their related institutions can be both vital centers of belonging and public space, fostering trust in life and active care for others.[13] A religious congregation that practices an ethic of hospitality and dialogue can encourage constructive encounters with otherness, developing compassion, insight, and the courage to risk "revising our boundaries outward" (see Chapters 2, 3, 4, and 5).

Pay Attention to the Strengths and Limits of Symbols, Stories, and Songs

Religion bears responsibility for cultivating symbols, stories, and songs that can orient the soul of a people to the cosmos. Religious tradition, however, is filled with both treasure and treachery. Many of the interviewees who described themselves as "spiritual but not religious" felt alienated from religious symbols and religious communities in a variety of ways. Religious communities are being asked to do the good and hard work of both reclaiming and creating stories of cosmology and covenant, harmony and hope, confession and forgiveness in a changing, multicultural, and scientifically informed world in which both injustice and hope abound. As people move from more provincial understandings of reality into the new commons, we need metaphors of an interdependent wholeness that enable us to move faithfully into the future.

This kind of religious leadership is essential as society wrestles in new ways with the power of symbols and language. The pervasive influence of contemporary media—particularly film and global telecommunications—has no precedent in human experience. They have become primary sources of the imagination by which human faith and the imagination of the commons are being recomposed, placing us all on new moral and ethical frontiers (see Chapter 5).[14]

Foster Habits of Mind Which Enable People to See Life As It Is

Any expression of human faith—any belief, theory, interpretation, or idea— is inevitably partial, yet in the complexity of the new commons religious faith cannot be "simple." That is, mature faith shuns the simplicity on this side of complexity, yet invests its full strength in seeking the "simplicity on the other side of complexity." When political tensions polarize on the global commons, religious communities can make a critical contribution by practicing fidelity to truth and reconciliation; by encouraging dialogue; perspective-taking, critical, systemic, and holistic thought; and by offering opportunities for confession and forgiveness so essential to the practice of citizenship (see Chapters 4 and 6).

Foster a Sense of Vocation

Finding a meaningful place in the scheme of things and having a sense of purpose in a large and interdependent world is manifest in a sense of vocation. Young people depend upon faithful communities of discernment and confirmation to provide developmentally appropriate experiences as they seek that place where their ambitions and aspirations meet the hungers and hopes of the new commons. Adults also need periods of reflection, invitation, challenge, and renewal that reorient their lives to that place where the heart's deep gladness meets the world's deep hunger.[15]

Bring Religious Insight and Search to Dialogue in the Commons

Though the dominance of the scientific-technological paradigm and the emergence of a global market culture appear to have marginalized much of mainstream religion, many of the people we studied affirmed the integration of religious commitment with public life. The voice of responsible religion in dialogue with the various professions is needed to enable people to see the connections between religion and public life, to infuse trans-market values into political and economic discourse, and to foster a public imagination that maximizes the health and welfare of the whole commons.[16]

Art and Media

The moral life of a community is determined, in part, by the images available to it for the formation of the imagination by which it lives. Artists and what we now call "the media" are primary providers of those images in the contemporary world. The vocation of the artist in whatever medium is to reveal the truth of the human condition and to enlarge our imagination of life, through the exploration of the beautiful and the sublime, the ordinary and the degraded. It has been said that artists serve a prophetic function in society, not because they can see into a crystal ball, but rather because they are so attentive to what is happening in the present when others are looking through the spectacles of yesterday. The word "art" is rooted in the act of connection, fitting things together. Art is an act of the imagination which pushes things up against each other—sound and silence, love and rage, self and world—seeking to discover and reveal the truthful relationships among them. One of the artists we interviewed described how doing art was a way of getting inside the "circuitry of life."

Artists are sometimes defined, even dismissed, as merely alienated or disruptive individuals who do art only for "art's sake." But historically, the artist as a citizen has made vital contributions to the common good, creating images of truth and possibility that can awaken and help us to see and understand. Art that serves the common good emerges from faithfulness to that place where the truth discovered in inner "solitarity" meets the truth emerging from simultaneous "solidarity."[17] One's location and what is learned there in the give and take with "otherness" can have moral, orienting power.

In the new commons art finds itself in partnership and competition with the media of mass communication—film, other recording technologies, radio, television, and computers—all of which intensify our interdependence in the new commons. They connect us in new ways, reorder the nature of our interaction, and dramatically affect how we understand our world and each other.

A distinguishing feature of modern media is their power of amplification. What once may have held a modest place at the edge of the commons can now be amplified into the heart and hearts of the commons—and thereby prevail in the formation of the human imagination. This study suggests that art and media might move in the following directions in the service of the common good.

Increase Participation in the Arts to Cultivate the Habits of Mind That Are Now Needed

The creative process engenders engagement with mystery and tolerance for ambiguity. It also fosters a process orientation and patience with practice. One said, "Painting has been for me a mind-blowing experience because not only do you not get it right the first time, but you aren't supposed to." The artistic process encourages and expands multiple forms of perception and expression, thus enhancing the ability to see and hold larger truths.

Foster Encounters with Otherness

Artistic expression can open some people to their own suffering and aspirations, awakening them to similar experience in others, giving rise to compassion and action. Many in our sample came to a greater understanding of themselves and others through poetry, theatre, fiction, biography, film, radio, newstories, and photojournalism. "World Music," signifying the power of music to stand as a metaphor for the harmonious ecology of a multitude of voices, has become a new category only in very recent decades (see Chapters 2, 3, 4, and 5).

Develop Meaningful Ethical Norms

Since the electronic "media" are a new and powerful technology without precedent in human experience, there is no body of traditional wisdom by which we can understand and assess their effects on the formation of people, communities, democracies—or a global commons. As this kind of wisdom begins to emerge, we need to pay attention to the difference between art that can inspire or journalism that can inform and entertainment created primarily to serve commercial interests. A promising step is to examine media that make their appeal to children and youth during the years when citizenship is taking form and when images that will shape or distort a sense of trust and agency are being planted at the heart's core. The human community has long since affirmed the importance of giving free expression to the artist. We are now being invited to move into a deepening understanding of what "freedom" means in the arrangements of public and private-commercial support of the arts, as we seek a new ethic by which to live in the new commons.

Public Policy

In a democracy, a central purpose of government is to create and maintain a vital arena in which common concerns may be aired; constructive dialogue among competing claims, perspectives, and philosophies may be practiced; and public choices may be freely and responsibly made. This grows increasingly important as mounting complexity and tribalism make it more difficult to craft and carry out successful policies that enjoy broad support. Yet social health is dependent upon an ecology of effective policies developed at local, state, or provincial, national, and international levels of government. To that end, public policy needs to proceed in the following directions.

Develop Policies Which Foster Both Trust and Agency

In whatever domain—commerce, health care, the budget, the environment—the commons is well served when public policies foster a trustworthy sense of inclusion and support and simultaneously encourage an appropriate and confident sense of agency—freedom, choice, responsibility, the opportunity to make a difference. When public policy fosters both trust and agency, a balance of support and incentives is created which enhances the possibility of committed participation in the commons.

[231]

Support Families and Communities as Cradles of Commitment

The capacity for trust and agency so foundational to commitment is initially nurtured in the context of family households. In order for public policies to foster the economic well-being of families, employment policies must enable both professionals and hourly wage earners to be good family members, and health policies must encourage the development of physical and emotional health, particularly in children.

But as individual development is hampered without family, so also is family life impaired without a sustaining community. We need policies that strengthen the institutions that constitute healthy neighborhoods—businesses, schools, hospitals and clinics, museums, libraries, parks, religious communities, and voluntary organizations—while simultaneously honoring their necessary interdependence. Particular encouragement needs to be given to organizations which bring people together and foster a positive experience of the commons—community orchestras, athletic leagues, theater workshops and productions, youth events, and regional environmental projects.

Strengthen Public Education, Especially for Youth

It will be increasingly difficult to function effectively in the new commons without adequate education. Strong and focused energy should be invested in improving public education. This needs to include a re-evaluation of the kind of knowledge and skills that are now needed, an assessment of the ways in which families and schools necessarily collaborate in the cultivation of emotional well-being, and the development of the capacity for constructive dialogue in the midst of change, complexity, and diversity.

Much of the violence in our cities and across the globe is perpetrated by young males between the ages of fifteen and thirty. Traditionally integrated into their cultures in ways that channeled their energies as we have described (see Chapter 2), this group is becoming increasingly marginalized as environments deteriorate, populations migrate, and technology becomes more complex and dangerous. The cost of this neglect is evident in human waste, destruction, and growing fear across the global commons.[18] We need social and economic policies that foster positive learning environments for all young people, including adult-guided and experiential learning programs for adolescents; recreational opportunities that encourage skill and character development; and internships and service opportunities such as the Peace Corps—particularly those that enable young people to provide a service in exchange for college tuition.

Cultivate More Adequate Patterns of Interdependent Policies at All Levels

Policy-makers need to recognize that local, state, national, and international policies are inevitably interdependent in their effects. As much power as possible needs to be vested at the level of people's daily lives, while maintaining vital national standards which ensure that local powers are not abused and that states or provinces are able to work collaboratively when appropriate. Just as we need policies to strengthen the local organizations that foster practical engagement with the common good, so also do we need vigorous attention to the development of policies at global levels, so that the new global commons may function successfully in all dimensions. This includes a reassessment of our relationship to the natural world, the effect of unharnessed market forces on the global migration of labor and capital, the consequences of unrestricted media saturation of all societies and age groups, and the growing tendency toward isolation and fortification at all levels.

Model Critical Habits of Mind

The role of public policy-makers is not simply to determine what people say they want and give it to them. Responsible leaders encourage reflection and dialogue among all members of the society, are able to take multiple perspectives, work responsibly with image and symbol, and provide leadership in creating "alternative visions of what is desirable and possible . . . [to] broaden the range of potential responses and deepen society's understanding of itself."[19] At all levels of governance, leadership that encourages the habits of mind which can encourage constructive conflict and seek "common ground," is to be prized and supported.

Business

At its best, business creates and manages dynamics and organizations that sustain livelihoods, provide goods and services, and foster fulfilling work on behalf of the well-being of society. At the heart of economic life, business is a primary force in the formation of the global commons. One of our interviewees commented, "I think that business is the most powerful tool for social change in this society. Traditionally people concerned about progressive social change have shied away from business. But the reality is that business is a tool, and you can use it either to oppress or to free. You can use it to destroy the planet or you can use it to save the planet." How business is done will profoundly affect the fate of the new commons. Business leaders can and are making a difference by moving in the following directions.

Assess the Strengths and Limits of an Ideology of Individualism and Market Logic

In an interdependent world, the modern market can function as an extraordinary achievement of civilization and a powerful tool. It is a poor master. An economic faith based on the assumption that the market simply consists of individual consumers making individual choices, thus perfectly ensuring that the well-being of society will be realized, fails to take into account the profound interdependence of life and important values which the market has the capacity to destroy but not discern—nor does it take into account the billions spent to manipulate consumer choice. As the realities of the new global commons places everyone on an unprecedented ethical frontier, business people are needed who can work both competitively and collaboratively, be informed by market indicators and cognizant of market limitations, and exercise understanding, judgment, imagination, and commitment in a manner that maximizes the effectiveness of the market and also brings trans-market values to corporate decision making.

The complexity of this task requires the capacity to build alliances across traditional tribal boundaries of business and government, management and labor and to practice critical, systemic, holistic, and paradoxical thinking (see Chapters 3 and 4). A successful entrepreneur working to integrate business practice with the common good draws on the tradition of the "Middle Way" as the practical path between values that seem incompatible:

> The Middle Way is not balance, nor is it a kind of compromise. It's a course that keeps in view competing aims: . . . making money versus being kind; having a kick-ass attitude versus having patience. The Middle Way is not "this way" or "that way," either-or; it's *one way that integrates both* . . . implementing paradoxes on a day-to-day basis. . . . Like a boatman navigating a swirling river, [you] steer between analysis and intuition, goals of profit and social responsibility, hardball and softball."[20]

Build a Workplace Characterized by Respect for Difference and Commitment to the Well-Being of All

One of the primary environments where people do and should encounter others who are significantly different from themselves is in business—in interactions with colleagues, employees, clients, customers, and suppliers. In the confusion and discomfort of a changing sociality, people need time and support to learn to work together.[21]

Moreover, the business context is a primary mentoring environment for the great majority of workers. More than just a job or career, business can be a vocation (see Chapters 2 and 7). The way that business leaders define "success" significantly determines the aspirations and ambitions of young people entering careers in business and affects their sense of participation in the common good (see Chapter 2). They are well served when loyalty to self and the organization can be practiced as features of a larger loyalty to the commons.

The power of business metaphors commands particular attention. The many metaphors drawn from "game" and "war" typically fail to convey in the way that is now needed the reality of what is at stake in business practice and the outcomes that will best serve the new commons (see Chapter 5).

Support Commitments to the Common Good

When colleagues, employees, or clients seek integrity between their work and their sense of commitment in the wider world, welcome their perspectives, suggestions, and decisions. Encourage the development of management vision, labor organization, environmental consciousness, and company and regulatory policy that can enable all who are a part of the global commons to flourish. Create policies and practices that support people who are taking steps to live more vibrant lives by seeking a balance between home and work, career and family, financial success and other values (see Chapters 2 and 6). Prepare retirees for ongoing service to the commons.

Nonprofit Organizations

Prime avenues for citizen concern, voluntary work, and philanthropic activity, nonprofits exist by definition to serve some aspect of our common life.[22] They range from young, grassroots enterprises energized by direct, immediate concern and passion, to "corporate nonprofits" such as long-established schools, hospitals, institutes, charities. They may be local, national, or international. They include enterprise zones, community development organizations, religious institutions, and agencies of all sorts.

Many of our interviewees work in nonprofit organizations. A number trace the seeds of their adult commitments to nonprofit institutions such as public libraries and museums, or youth organizations such as the "Y" and scouting. Some found avenues toward commitment in a first job or internship in a nonprofit organization. With almost half of the nation's people volunteering their time, nonprofits are key settings in which commitments to the common good can ferment and mature. There are, however, important directions in which nonprofits now need to move.

Build Commitment to the Larger Whole As Part of Your Mission

As nonprofits carry out their specific missions and work to build and sustain supportive constituencies, the urgency of their tasks and the press of limited resources may obscure their crucial role as cultures in which long-term commitment to the common good may be nurtured. Nonprofits that create opportunities to mentor both younger and older people into the skills, values, and purposes of their work and its relationship to the larger ecology of the society, are making an investment either directly in their own organization or in the commons at large that will yield returns many times over in the future. We found that the first year of the initial job or internship often proved formative for a whole life's work. Staff, especially supervisors who most often work with new arrivals, should keep mentoring in mind. This important work should also feature prominently in their job descriptions and evaluations (see Chapter 2 and 7).

Develop Dialogue Among Staff and Board Members

Nonprofits also serve as a locus of commitment for their own employees and board members. In this regard, dialogue among colleagues is critical to sustaining commitment. Time out from the regular press of work for more reflection on the sources and meaning of basic commitments and the challenges of living them out can be of value for newcomers to hear and veterans to revisit (see Chapters 4 and 6). Decision-makers can create opportunities at retreats and conferences, or when a new project is being launched, or work well done is being celebrated, for staff and board members to enter into reflective dialogue with other committed professionals or paraprofessionals (see Chapter 4).

Appropriate dialogue can also help staff members transform difficult or painful experiences in their own lives into a deeper capacity for resilience, empathy, and other sustaining habits of mind, thus strengthening them over the long haul (see Chapter 6).

See the Work through in Hard Times

Particularly when resources are short, the capacity for collaborative reframing of strategy becomes a virtue. Involving staff in reframing can help them renew their personal commitments, particularly when the process includes reconnecting with the deepest purposes of the organization and the people who serve it. When drawing heavily on staff and volunteers in hard times, remember that families and others also play a key role in sustaining commitments. Whenever possible, resist overtaxing those free sources of sustenance (see Chapter 6).

Lay the Ground for Commitment Among Your Clientele

As the commitment builds, staff and trustees can together examine how programs might extend the positive participation of clients in the wider life of the commons. By examining the relationships among the organization, clients, and the public, it may be possible to include clientele as partners in the larger work and to expand their participation in public life.

Health and Therapeutic Community

Health is most comprehensively understood as the capacity to maintain a sense of well-being, coherence, and the ability to function in the face of changes.[23] Healing entails addressing sources of health, stress, and disease in a manner that can restore wholeness and develop the capacity to maintain one's equilibrium amidst shifting forces. In the context of the new commons, therefore, the deep purpose of healing is to manifest wholeness in the largest sense—the wholeness of spirit, body, society, and the entire earth community.

The new commons brings complex challenges to the health and therapeutic community. Old distinctions between body and mind, the individual and the society, prevention and cure are breaking down. At the same time, socioeconomic disparities and cultural diversity are creating immense stress and new opportunities. We are beginning to understand the ways that systemic forces both hurt and heal. These are some of the directions that may lead toward the promise of a healthier commons for all.

Strengthen the Capacity to Work Effectively under Stress

Many of the people we studied endured high levels of stress. One way they did this was to recognize in themselves a variety of different voices, an "inner committee" with effective leadership. As health professionals cope with significant stress both in their own lives and in the lives of those who seek them out for healing, hospitality to deep and "reorienting" dialogue can make a critical contribution. This entails recognizing "taboo motivations" such as anger, ambition, the need to please, and fear—including their possible sources in personal suffering (see Chapter 6). For most, it also entails seeking colleagues and friends with whom they can work effectively, speak frankly, and gain perspective (see Chapters 2 and 7).

The people we studied were clear about why they were doing the work; they did not yield to cynical denigration of their own or others' best motives. As new technologies often distance the patient from the healer, and as a maze of economic opportunities and constraints threaten to swamp a sense of calling and conscience, it becomes important in new ways to "stalk one's calling,"[24] reconnecting with one's original sense of vocation. Find ways to build communities and organizations that confirm the deep purposes that brought you into therapeutic work (see Chapter 7).

Recognize Your Importance as a Model in the Lives of People in Crisis or Long-Term Illness, Particularly Children

Several of our interviewees were bedridden as children. The adults who cared for them during those periods modeled lives guided by compassion and care, often opening pathways for their future commitments. They fondly recalled meaningful conversations with healers who gave them focused, concentrated attention.

Welcome New People into the Profession

Health professionals in our sample found their vocation was significantly shaped by the mentoring they received in their first job or internship. Devote time to newcomers, conveying the grounding purpose that animates your profession. Expand their vision of their role in the commons while they are learning new knowledge and skills (see Chapter 2).

Urge Clients to Be of Service to Others as a Path to Their Own Healing

There was little support among our interviewees for a reified belief that "you must heal yourself before you can heal others." Frequently, their own suffering was relativized as they recognized the suffering of others; the work and the healing went hand in hand (see Chapter 6). We have heard of therapists who ask their clients to incorporate service into their healing process. Exercised with discretion, this practice enables people to recognize their lives as a part of a larger whole, move through grief and loss, and find healing (see Chapter 4).

Teach That on the New Commons the Health of Each Depends on the Health of All

Respect for the interdependence of life suggests that if the new commons is to be a healthy place, we will need an institutional and economic imagination that values the provision of basic health care for all. To achieve this will require people who can contend with the complexity and ambiguity that pervades these issues.

Foundations and Philanthropies

The deep purpose of philanthropy is to cultivate a generosity of spirit throughout the society and enhance the welfare of all the inhabitants of the commons. Historically, philanthropy has made strategic contributions to our common life, particularly in times of profound cultural transition. One thinks, for instance, of the effect of patronage during the Renaissance or the contributions of an Andrew Carnegie.

Many of the foundations that are now a part of the new commons were established in an earlier era and are guided by charters written before the development of the conditions that are now at hand. Philanthropic leadership is, therefore, now being called upon to interpret and sometimes reframe earlier visions and commitments in the light of unanticipated realities and to enable their institutions and publics to adapt in appropriate ways. Foundations, old and new, have extraordinary opportunities to encourage investments of money, time, intellect, heart, and spirit in a future in which a vital commons anchors an enhanced quality of life for all.

Invest in the Development and Practice of the New Commons

Philanthropy can empower voices and ideas that help us re-frame our common problems and aspirations. This represents a special responsibility at a time when many are tempted to retreat from contemporary complexity—stockpiling private resources in more fortified forms, often believing that government should do the same (see Chapter 1).[25]

By providing financial support and other incentives, philanthropy can nourish the sense of common space, fostering conversations and forms of collaboration among both recipients and donors that clarify important issues, establish priorities, develop strategies, and engender hope amidst the numbing complexity of the emerging global reality. Philanthropy plays a key role in supporting those whose imagination and skill are committed to the commons but whose work, either in direct service or basic research, is unlikely to be otherwise adequately supported. Foundations have a critical role to play in strategic advocacy on behalf of the poor. These strategies can encourage an awareness of the interdependencies among issues, institutions, and initiatives, and alleviate suffering.

Invest Strategically in People to Enable Them to Become Committed to the Common Good

Virtually everyone we studied had experienced a constructive engagement with people who were significantly different from themselves. The philanthropic sector can encourage such encounters by sponsoring initiatives that bring diverse individuals and groups together encouraging dialogue across projects, issues, and sectors (see Chapter 3 and 4).

Just as philanthropic foundations play a strategic role in supporting education and the arts, they can make a powerful contribution by giving particular attention to media likely to be present in the homeplace, or to any form of media which shape our imagination of life in the new commons. A new ethic of media technology is particularly needed (see Chapter 5).

There was clear evidence in our study that those who had grown up in economically and culturally disadvantaged settings had benefitted significantly from personal recognition and support. They had responded in turn by investing their lives on behalf of others. In establishing funding priorities and developing strategy, philanthropy can play a vital role in the more equitable distribution of life-bearing resources.

Practice Essential Habits of Mind

Hearing the patterns that emerged in this study, the president of a foundation asked, "What would it mean for a foundation to function like a person committed to the common good?" In partial response to that question, this study suggests that the foundation would foster and practice habits of mind that enable the foundation to become at home in the world—in the new commons. This includes perspective-taking; critical, systemic, and holistic thought; flexible framing; tolerance of ambiguity; and long-term vision coupled with focused passion. As a consequence, the foundation would, on the one hand, design flexibility among funding categories as external conditions shift, yet at the same time work to renew and deepen its own vocation and commitment.

The awareness and practice of dialogue with otherness is key. When we look broadly at philanthropy in relation to the new commons, it is evident that philanthropic investment tends to be tribal. Fostering a more adequate response to diversity may invite foundation officials themselves, along with the resources they steward, to cross tribal boundaries more readily—inviting partnership both with other individuals and institutions, and bringing diversity to boards and staffs. Networking, attention to contradictions, the search for right images, reflection, and renewal are keys to good practice. As is the practice of some foundations already, such renewal necessarily includes periods of time set aside, in some cases daily, to pause and to contemplate the deepest purposes of philanthropy, the changing conditions of the work, and paths toward life-bearing investments. This quality of contemplation needs to be matched by its most authentic fruit—a quality of consequent action which eschews mere abstractions and transforms suffering and despair.

Conclusion

Becoming the people we need is a great work, dependent upon each and all of us throughout every sector of the new global commons. The people we interviewed found the pathways of commitment to the common good because people and institutions that collectively constituted a common moral compass recognized the agency and promise of their lives, provided trustworthy colleagueship and leadership, and established policies and structures and ways-of-being-in-relation that encouraged commitment. In contrast, those who were least able to face global complexity effectively were significantly more isolated.

We have become convinced that whenever young people are sponsored or mentored into a compelling imagination of future possibility, and older people are challenged and affirmed in ways that nourish and steady their commitments, our common strength is enhanced. Whenever individuals or organizations can make the connections step by step that help us to see more accurately the conditions and opportunities we all share, and whenever they practice ways of life that are congruent with those realities, citizenship for the twenty-first century is being composed.

The way ahead is vexed by unprecedented conditions and enormous ambiguity. The promise of our future lies in paying attention to the wonderful and terrible Mystery in which we all participate, which gives rise to the passion and compassion that kindle the common fire of commitment.

appendix

The power of any insight or understanding depends, in part, on the weight of the data in which it is anchored. Here we convey to the reader the nature of our study—what can and cannot be claimed, and with what degree of confidence. In general, the precision of any answer varies inversely with the size of the question, and we asked a very big question. Thus, we view the conclusions presented here as tentative and perhaps provocative. But we believe them to have great power and promise.

There are many ways to study human motivation and behavior, each of which has its own particular power to illuminate and obscure. We believe that the method one chooses ought to be appropriate to the phenomenon one is studying. We are studying a particular form of consciousness, how people achieve it, and its implications for our common life. For that reason, we have chosen what is best described as a "modified phenomenological" model. That is, we attempt to approach our subject with open minds, and at the same time we recognize that what we are able to see is affected by what we already know. The search for understanding is necessarily a mix of previous conviction and new discovery, systematic rigor and accommodation of the unexpected.[1]

We also know that the stories people tell about themselves may vary according to the listener, the moment in the life of the storyteller, and how close to Friday it is. Drawing conclusions from stories that people have recomposed from their experience of an earlier place and time is fraught with risk. But where lies risk, lies adventure, and each interview became a field of rich possibilities as we followed unanticipated avenues, deepening both their reflection and our understanding. Thus, while any single account must be handled cautiously, taken together, patterns can be reliably discerned that may suggest something important about human behavior and potential. Moreover, conclusions do not rest on this data alone; they were set in dialogue with several bodies of related research that sometimes corroborated, sometimes contradicted the patterns we found.

Every methodology has its limitations. The limits of retrospective work, for example, have been well documented.[2] Our stance is far more probabilistic than deterministic.[3] We walk the line between demonstrable correlation and tentative inferences of causality with caution.[4] We are not attempting to prove hypotheses. We have, however, generated some fertile insights which we believe are sufficiently strong to serve as a basis for action and further research.

Choosing the Sample

We selected the sample by what is known as "multiple-entry snowball" method. That is, on the basis of our criteria, we identified an interviewee. At the end of an interview, we would ask him or her to identity others whom we might interview. Each interview led on to the next. Since we were four interviewers, however, there were four "entry points." Moreover, since this was not a random sample, we sought people who met certain demographic criteria as well. Gender, ethnicity, and sexual preference roughly match U.S. patterns. We also attempted to achieve an appropriate age distribution and a reasonable spread of professions and fields of endeavor, geographic region, economic class of origin, and religion.

Beyond demographic representation, however, we were building a sample of a particular kind of person, one capable of sustaining commitment to the common good in the face of global complexity. To do this, we screened according to several "contingent criteria." These are elaborated in Chapter 1, but in outline they are:

Commitment to the common good. There is evidence that they have a particular work and perceive it as serving the well-being of the society as a whole, and that other reasonable people would concur.

Perseverance and resilience. They have sustained their commitment for a minimum of seven years without burning out, or have subsequently learned to work without burning out.

Ethical congruence between life and work. The quality of their personal life is congruent with the work. They appear to function as "reasonably decent human beings."

Engagement with diversity and complexity. They are aware of the global and cultural complexity that characterizes contemporary life, see the systemic implications of their work, and have a critical perspective on their own culture.

Who Is in the Sample

In order to produce a "core group" of 100 representing a reasonable demographic profile, we interviewed a total of 145 people. Of these, 20 were found not to meet the "contingent" criteria and were placed in a "comparison group." The core group are as follows.

Gender	F	M	Both
	50	50	100

Ethnicity	F	M	Both
White	31	35	66
Black	9	6	15
Hispanic	4	2	6
Asian	1	1	2
Native American	—	1	1
International	5	5	10

Age	F	M	Both
30–40	7	9	16
40–50	16	12	28
50–60	12	13	25
60–70	8	8	16
70–80	5	7	12
80+	2	1	3

(Average age = 53)

Socioeconomic Status of Family of Origin	F	M	Both
Poor	7	7	14
Working class	6	15	21
Middle class	19	18	37
Upper middle class	12	7	19

Family Origin (con't.)	F	M	Both
Economically elite	5	3	8
Changed in childhood	6	2	8

Geographic Origin	F	M	Both
Northeast	17	14	31
Mid-Atlantic	12	9	21
Southeast	4	2	6
Midwest	5	10	15
West	2	9	11
Puerto Rico	2	1	3
International	8	5	13
	50	50	100

The Interviews

The interviews, in the semiclinical tradition of qualitative research, ranged from one and a half to three hours, were tape recorded, and confidential. In a few cases, we returned to our informants several times. We were seeking to understand certain aspects of their lives, yet we also wanted the respondents to pursue and reveal what they perceived to be important. We established a range of open-ended questions and follow-up "probes" with which to explore their responses, creating an interview that was conversational in character yet guided enough to ensure attention to similar themes across the sample.

After the first twenty interviews, and again at a later point, we held consultations with a small group of interviewees and revised our questions to pursue areas that had emerged as significant.

At the time of the interview, we asked people to fill out a form asking for demographic data, and near the completion of the study, we mailed out a brief questionnaire to secure data on some themes that emerged late in the study.

Analysis

The interviews were taped and transcribed. After the initial twenty interviews, we identified a number of emerging themes. These became the basis for forty-one discrete but overlapping "theme packets," collections of relevant quotes from the interviews for paradigmatic[5] analysis. These were systematically compiled by our research associate, Karen Thorkilsen, who also served as another reader of the interviews. Careful analysis of each packet (in some cases over two-hundred pages of excerpts) enabled us to focus on the most salient elements in the data.

Recognizing that this form of analysis limited our ability to understand how individual lives evolved, we also analyzed each interview as a unit for the presence of 210 separate variables. This "syntagmatic" analysis[6] allowed us to identify other important patterns and is the basis on which many of our generalizations are formed. We have generally not reported percentages relative to the interpretation of data because the methodology does not yield data that reflects the precision implied by numbers. Thus, a reference in the text to "most" people means that the phenomenon appears to hold in over three quarters of the sample; "typically" means more than half; "many" means roughly half; "some" means fewer than half; and "a few" means that a pattern that emerged was not typical but was interesting or might hold an important aspect of something larger.

The Comparison Group

This group of twenty is made up of those that upon analysis did not provide evidence of systemic awareness and a critical perspective, or in some other way did not meet the contingent criteria. By comparing this group with the one hundred "core interviews," we were able to cast some patterns in sharper relief. This comparison group is not to be confused with a "control group," which would be used in another kind of research design requiring a demographic match with the core group.

Further Research

This study is above all an invitation to the reader to test the validity of the patterns described here in his or her own experience and also in further studies that can both correct and deepen these findings.

notes

Chapter 1
Connection and Complexity

1. See Linda E. Olds, *Metaphors of Interrelatedness: Toward a Systems Psychology* (Albany: New York State University Press, 1992), xi.

2. Hazel Henderson has observed that Western society has distinguished between the commons as property and the commons as closed systems accessed collectively by agreed-upon rules. Thus, "the march of industrialism has involved the enclosure of the commons begun by force in 17th-century Britain . . . by the Enclosure Acts." We are now repeating that process with our oceans and air. See Hazel Henderson, "New Markets and New Commons" in *Futures*, 27, 2 (March 1995): 113–123.

3. See Howard Rheingold, *The Virtual Community: Electronic Frontier* (Reading, MA: Adison-Wesley Publishing Co., 1993).

4. Willis Harman, "A System in Decline or Transformation?", *World Business Academy Perspectives* 8, 2 (1994); Robert Kaplan, "The Coming Anarchy," *Atlantic Monthly*, (February 1994): 44–76; Matthew Connelly and Paul Kennedy, "Must It Be the Rest Against the West?", *Atlantic Monthly* (December 1994): 61–91; Richard J. Barnet and John Cavanagh, *Global Dreams: Imperial Corporations and the New World Order* (New York: Simon and Schuster, 1994); Paul Kennedy, *Preparing for the Twenty-First Century* (New York: Random House, 1993).

5. See Ronald A. Heifetz, *Leadership Without Easy Answers* (Cambridge, MA: Harvard University Press, 1994).

6. Bill Berkowitz, *Local Heroes: The Rebirth of Heroism in America* (Lexington, MA: Lexington Books, 1987).

7. Our analysis of the small international sample of five women and five men suggests very few differences with the rest of the core group. If anything, the factors that distinguished our interviewees and led to sustained commitment were more salient in this group, suggesting that there is some applicability of our findings to other countries.

8. See Adrienne Rich, *What Is Found There: Notebooks on Poetry and Politics* (New York: Norton, 1993), 20.

9. There is one exception. In the Interlude, "The Hundreds of Years that Come After," we have with permission quoted Dorothy Height, whom we did interview, because of her own public stature and the recognizability of her association with Mary McCleod Bethune.

10. See David W. Orr, *Earth in Mind: On Education, Environment, and the Human Prospect* (Washington, DC: Island Press, 1994).

11. Colin Greer, "Who Are Americans in Need?" *Parade Magazine* (15 March 1995).

12. See Garrett Hardin, "The Tragedy of the Commons," *Science* 162 (December 1968): 1243–1248; Christopher Lasch, *The Culture of Narcissism* (New York: Norton, 1978); George C. Lodge, *The New American Ideology* (New York: Knopf, 1976); and see also *Managing Globalization in the Age of Interdependence* (San Diego: Pfeiffer & Co., 1995); Robert N. Bellah and others, *Habits of the Heart* (Berkeley, CA: University of California Press, 1984 and 1996); and Amitai Etzioni, *The Spirit of Community: Rights, Responsibilities, and the Communitarian Agenda* (New York: Simon and Schuster, 1994).

Studying levels of civic involvement in the United States over the past decades, Robert Putnam notes a curious fact: "More Americans are bowling today than ever before, but bowling in organized leagues has plummeted." We are disconnecting, following our individual interests instead of the community's. He goes on to document sharp declines in local political participation, public meetings, and membership in such groups as labor unions, the PTA, Scouts, Red Cross, and most service clubs and thus, a loss of social capital. "Bowling Alone Revisited," *The Responsive Community* 5 (Spring 1995): 2, 24.

13. Juliet Schor, *The Overworked American: The Unexpected Decline of Leisure* (New York: Basic Books, 1993).

14. Jeffery C. Goldfarb, *The Cynical Society: The Culture of Politics and the Politics of Culture in American Life* (Chicago: University of Chicago Press, 1991).

15. Donald Kanter and Philip H. Mervis, *The Cynical Americans* (San Francisco, CA: Jossey Bass, 1989).

16. See Peter Block, "Cynics, Victims, and Bystanders" in *Stewardship: Choosing Service Over Self-Interest* (San Francisco: Berrett-Koehler Publishers, 1993), ch. 14.

17. See Jim Wallis, *The Soul of Politics* (Maryknoll, NY: Orbis Books, 1994), and Cornel West, *Race Matters* (Boston: Beacon Press, 1993).

18. Alasdair MacIntyre, *After Virtue* (Notre Dame, IN: University of Notre Dame Press, 1981), see esp. 212–213.

19. See Jonathan Kozol, *Amazing Grace: The Lives of Children and the Conscience of a Nation* (New York: Crown, 1995).

20. T.W. Adorno and others, *The Authoritarian Personality* (New York: Harper & Brothers, 1950) and H. Richard Niebuhr, *Radical Monotheism and Western Culture* (New York: Harper and Row, 1960).

21. We recognize that some readers will find our position on the common good too minimalist and will want a more robust and detailed view, while others will detect too much universalism even in our minimalist approach. Readers are referred to two

sources as starting points for more extensive research: *The Responsive Community: Rights and Responsibilities*, a journal published since 1991 by the Center for Policy Research in Washington, DC, and *Liberals and Communitarians* (Cambridge, MA: Blackwell Publishers, 1992), a review of key literature in this area by the British scholars, Stephen Mulhall and Adam Swift. See also Bruce Jennings, Daniel Callahan, and Susan M. Wolf, "The Professions: Public Interest and the Common Good," A *Hastings Center Report*, Special Supplement, February 1987, 3–11; Roger A. Lohmann, *The Commons: New Perspectives on Nonprofit Organizations and Voluntary Action* (San Francisco: Jossey-Bass, 1992), ch. 10.

Chapter 2
Community

1. Thich Nhat Hanh, *Peace Is Every Step* (New York: Bantam, 1991), 95–96.
2. See Margaret Wheatley, *Leadership and the New Science* (San Francisco: Berrett-Koehler, 1992).
3. There is some evidence for genetic predisposition to empathy. Studies by Batson and his colleagues suggest that we are born, not selfish, but with a capacity for selflessness which can be brought out in a good enough environment. Daniel Batson, "How Social an Animal: The Human Capacity for Caring," *American Psychologist* 45, 3 (March 1990): 336–346. Developmental psychologist Erik Erikson suggested that sociogenetic evolution brings us eventually to the capacity to care, necessarily, for ever-increasing spheres. "Youth: Fidelity and Diversity," in *The Challenge of Youth* (New York: Anchor Books, 1965), 1. At least one study of twins evidences shared empathetic concern. See K.A. Matthews and others, "The Heritability of Empathetic Concern for Others," *Journal of Personality* 49 (1981): 237–247.

   The research on the role of the environment in the development of empathy is particularly compelling. Alfie Cohen's extensive review of the literature on altruism, *The Brighter Side of Human Nature: Altruism and Empathy in Everyday Life* (New York: Basic Books, 1990), 219–220, finds the studies claiming heritability unconvincing in their design and conclusions. In particular, family and home environment have been shown to have a significant influence. In a longitudinal study, compassion for the suffering of others was more likely twenty-seven years later if fathers had participated in childcare, if both parents had used reason instead of physical punishment, and if mothers had been tolerant of the dependence of the child and satisfied with their own role. R. Koestner, C. Franz, and J. Weinberger, "The Family Origins of Empathic Concern: A 26-Year Longitudinal Study," *Journal of Personality and Social Psychology* 58, 4 (1990): 709–717.
4. Erik Erikson, *Childhood and Society* (New York: Norton, 1950), ch. 7.
5. Sam Keen, *The Passionate Life* (New York: Harper & Row, 1983), 36.
6. See Nel Noddings, *Caring: A Feminine Approach to Ethics and Moral Education* (Berkeley: University of California Press, 1984).

7. See Robert Kegan, *The Evolving Self: Problem and Process in Human Development* (Cambridge, MA: Harvard University Press, 1981).

8. See Sharon Parks, *The Critical Years: Young Adults and the Search for Meaning, Faith, and Commitment* (San Francisco: Harper Collins, 1986), ch. 2.

9. See D.W. Winnicott, *The Maturational Processes and the Facilitating Environment* (New York: International Universities Press, 1965), and Kegan, *The Evolving Self*.

10. Growing evidence suggests that "prosocial behavior" is more likely to be fostered in homes characterized by a loving and responsive atmosphere, a preference for reason over force to settle disputes, and a practice of pointing to the consequences of one's behavior for the self and others. See Daniel Goleman, "The Roots of Empathy," *Emotional Intelligence* (New York: Bantam, 1995), 96–110, and E. Staub, "The Origins of Caring, Helping and Nonaggression: Parental Socialization, the Family System, Schools, and Cultural Influence," in Oliner and others, *Embracing the Other* (New York: New York University Press, 1992), 390–412.

11. M. Ainsworth, "The Development of Infant and Mother Attachment," in *Review of Child Development Research*, vol. 3, ed. B.M. Caldwell and H.M. Ricciuti (Chicago: University of Chicago Press, 1973). Three patterns stood out. One group of mothers tended to ignore their babies' efforts to communicate; subsequently these "underattached" children seemed to become isolated and to lack confidence. A second group were attentive, but in accord with their own, rather than their children's needs; these youngsters tended to become "overly attached" and were helpless when left alone. A third group were attentive in accord with their babies' needs, responding appropriately to both the child's need to be held and to be released. "Securely attached," these children were able both to snuggle lovingly and explore independently, a finding resonant with the development of trust and agency.

   For a summary of "attachment theory" on which Ainsworth's work is based, see Goleman, *Emotional Intelligence*, ch. 9.

12. See D.N. Stern, *The Interpersonal World of the Infant: A View from Psychoanalytic and Developmental Psychology* (New York: Basic Books, 1985), and Staub, "Origins of Caring." The centrality of the father's involvement for later empathy was documented in Koestner, "Family Origins."

13. The term "good enough" is used in the literature of child development, referring to an appropriate balance between overanticipating a child's needs and ignoring them. In like manner, we mean simply that no parent is "perfect," yet though the quality of parenting was sometimes marginal, there was at least enough attention and care that a rudimentary trust and confidence could be formed. The two who did not have even this (as far as we can determine), had dramatic, transforming religious experiences later in life which appear to have been instrumental in healing deep wounds and losses from their early years.

14. See also Gina O'Connell Higgins, *Resilient Adults: Overcoming a Cruel Past* (San Francisco: Jossey-Bass, 1994), ch. 3.

15. For research on parental service as a key predictor of teenage service, see Paul Schervish, Virginia Hodgkinson, Margaret Gates and others, *Care and Community in Modern Society* (San Francisco: Jossey-Bass, 1995).

16. See Douglas Huneke, *The Moses of Rovno* (New York: Dodd, Mead and Co., 1985).

17. See Jaques' speech in "As You Like It," II:7, ll. 139–166, and Daniel Levinson and others, *The Seasons of a Man's Life* (New York: Knopf, 1976).

18. See Sharon Daloz Parks, "Home and Pilgrimage: Companion Metaphors for Personal and Social Transformation," *Soundings* 72, 2–3 (Summer/Fall, 1989): 297–315. For additional critique and elaboration of developmental paradigms, see Gil G. Noam, "A Constructivist Approach to Developmental Psychopathology," in E. Nannis and P. Cowan, eds., *Developmental Psychopathology and Its Treatment* (San Francisco: Jossey-Bass, 1988), 91–121.

19. See Jean Piaget, *Six Psychological Studies* (New York: Random House, 1967), 54–60, and Erik Erikson, *Young Man Luther* (New York: Norton, 1962). "Because man needs a disciplined conscience, he thinks he must have a bad one; and he assumes that he has a good conscience when, at times, he has an easy one. The answer to all this does not lie in attempts to avoid or to deny one or the other sense of badness in children altogether; the denial of the unavoidable can only deepen a sense of secret, unmanageable evil. The answer lies in man's capacity to create order which will give his children a disciplined as well as a tolerant conscience, and a world within which to act affirmatively" (263).

20. See Thomas Lickona, *Educating for Character: How Our Schools Can Teach Respect and Responsibility* (New York: Bantam, 1991).

21. Connie Muther has observed and interviewed more than sixty teachers who were highly regarded by colleagues and students. She found that such teachers love teaching, the content they teach, and their students; they bring their personal experience and interest to their teaching; and they have a mission or passion. *ASCE Education Update* (May 1995), 8.

22. See Victor and Mildred Goertzel's classic study of the biographies and autobiographies of four-hundred gifted individuals, one fourth of whom had childhoods marked by illness or handicap. *Cradles of Eminence* (Boston: Little, Brown & Co, 1962), 272–273.

23. Herman E. Daly and John B. Cobb, Jr., *For the Common Good: Redirecting the Economy Toward Community, the Environment, and a Sustainable Future* (Boston: Beacon Press, 1989), 170.

24. Howard Gardner with Emma Laskin, *Leading Minds: An Anatomy of Leadership* (New York: Basic Books, 1995), 287.

25. See James P. Keen, "Pre-College Programs as Communities of Imagination, Exploration, and Foresight," unpublished report, Lilly Endowment, July 1994.

26. Harold Loukes, *Friends and Their Children: A Study in Quaker Education* (London: George G. Harrap, Friends Home Service Committee, 1969), 93.

27. For a discussion of the demonization of teens, except when they are seen as potential consumers in the economic market, see "Ten O'Clock Lock," *Utne Reader*, 69 (May–June, 1995): 27–32.

28. See Cheryl and James Keen, "The Governor's School of New Jersey," *Educational Leadership* (Nov.–Dec. 1990).

29. See Daly and Cobb, *For the Common Good*, 172.

30. See Levinson, *Seasons of a Man's Life,* regarding the "novice adult's" dream. See also, Sharon Daloz Parks, "Young Adults, Mentoring Communities, and the Conditions of Moral Choice," in *Approaches to Moral Development: New Research and Emerging Themes* (New York: Teacher's College Press, 1993), 214–227.

31. Barely half as many in the comparison group recounted this kind of experience.

32. See Laurent A. Daloz, *Effective Teaching and Mentoring: Realizing the Power of Adult Educational Experiences* (San Francisco: Jossey-Bass, 1986).

33. There are a number of institutions—formal and informal—which have served many of the functions we describe here, e.g. salons in the Jewish community and other similar social milieus. See Mary Belenky's forthcoming study of "cultural workers."

34. See Sharon Daloz Parks, "The University as a Mentoring Environment" (Indianapolis: Indiana Office for Campus Ministry, 1992), and "Social Vision and Moral Courage: Mentoring a New Generation of Educators" *Cross Currents* 40, 3 (Fall, 1990): 350–67.

35. See William G. Perry, *Intellectual and Ethical Development in the College Years: A Scheme* (New York: Holt, Rinehart, and Winston, 1967). See also ch. 4, this volume.

36. Erik Erikson, "Fidelity and Diversity," in *The Challenge of Youth* (New York: Anchor Books, 1965).

37. See Derek Bok, *The Cost of Talent* (New York: Free Press, 1993), 20.

38. Phil Brickman's research suggests that gradual commitment lasts longer. *Commitment, Conflict and Caring* (Englewood Cliffs, NJ: Prentice Hall, 1983).

39. Lydia Bronte documents creative commitments continuing on into people's nineties. *The Longevity Factor: The New Reality of Long Careers and How It Can Lead to Richer Lives* (New York: Harper Collins, 1993).

40. See Lillian B. Rubin, *Women of a Certain Age: The Midlife Search for Self* (New York: Harper & Row, 1979); Terri Apter, *Secret Paths: Women in the New Midlife* (New York: Norton, 1995); and Maria Harris, *Jubilee Time: Rituals for Women in the Second Half of Life* (New York: Bantam, 1995).

41. Craig Dykstra, conversation.

42. The women in our comparison sample who had resistant spouses were more likely to have remained married than those in the core group who experienced the same circumstance. The absence of supportive dialogue may make it harder to engage larger complexities and ambiguities.

43. Goleman provides rich evidence for the benefits of partnerships to reduce the costs of stress, *Emotional Intelligence,* esp. ch. 13.

Chapter 3
Compassion

1. Thomas Ogletree, *Hospitality to the Stranger* (Philadelphia: Fortress Press, 1985), 45.

2. See Parks, *The Critical Years,* 61–69, 89–96.

3. See "On the Importance of Being Tribal and the Prospects for Creating Multicultural Community," *Utne Reader* (July/August 1992): 67–95; Harold Isaacs, *Idols of the Tribe* (Cambridge, MA: Harvard University Press, 1989). See also Laurent Daloz, "Beyond Tribalism," *Adult Education Quarterly* (Summer, 1988): 234–41.

4. Erik Erikson used the term "pseudospecies" for this tendency, recognizing its manifestations throughout human history. "Mankind, while one species, has divided itself throughout its history . . . into various groupings that permit their members, at decisive times, to consider themselves more or less consciously and explicitly, the only truly human species, and all others . . . as less than human." In "Reflections on Ethos and War," *Yale Review* 73, 4 (Summer 1984): 481–486. See also Garrett Hardin, "Population Skeletons in the Environmental Closet," *Bulletin of the Atomic Scientists* 28 (June 1972): 39; Robert C. Fuller, *Naming the Antichrist: The History of an American Obsession* (New York: Oxford University Press, 1995); and Ronald Marstin, *Beyond Our Tribal Gods* (Maryknoll, NY: Orbis Press, 1979), 37.

5. Art Levine observes that the two main activities in which college students mixed across tribe were in sports and theater (personal communication). See Arthur Levine and Jana Nidiffer, *Beating the Odds: How the Poor Get to College* (San Francisco: Jossey-Bass, 1996).

6. It appears that particularly for many of the white males in our study it wasn't until they were in their twenties that they had the experience of being part of an "out" group or of otherwise engaging with "otherness." Dominant in our society, they were insulated from certain forms of rebuke and exclusion and were thus less aware of the experiences of others.

7. See Ogletree, *Hospitality to the Stranger*, 4.

8. Mary Watkins, "'In Dreams Begin Responsibilities': Moral Imagination and Action" (paper delivered at the conference, "Facing Apocalypse," Salve Regina College, Newport, R.I., June 1983). See also *Invisible Guests: The Development of Imaginal Dialogues* (Hillsdale, NJ: Analytic Press, 1986).

9. This finding is corroborated again and again in the biographies and autobiographies of people who have contributed to the common good. See, for instance, David Dellinger, *From Yale to Jail* (New York: Pantheon, 1993); Marian Wright Edelman, *The Measure of Our Success* (Boston: Beacon Press, 1992); Nelson Mandela, *Long Walk to Freedom* (New York: Little, Brown & Co, 1994); Holly Near, *Fire in the Rain . . . Singer in the Storm* (New York: William Morrow and Co., 1990); Blanche Wiesen Cook, *Eleanor Roosevelt*, vol. 1 (New York: Viking, 1992); Howard Thurman, *With Head and Heart* (New York: Harcourt, Brace, 1979); and Wallis, *The Soul of Politics*.

10. Eisenberg claims that "empathy predicts altruism." This assumption has been borne out in the research of the Oliners, Huneke, and others on Holocaust rescuers and in other settings. Nancy Eisenberg, *Altruistic Emotion, Cognition, and Behavior* (Hillsdale, NJ: Lawrence Erlbaum, 1986). See also her most recent work, Nancy Eisenberg and Janet Strayer, eds., *Empathy and its Development* (Cambridge: Cambridge University Press, 1990).

11. Samuel P. Oliner and Pearl M. Oliner, *The Altruistic Personality: Rescuers of Jews in Nazi Europe* (New York: Free Press, 1988), 174–175.

12. See John Rawls' discussion of features of the moral sentiments in *Theory of Justice* (Cambridge, MA: Harvard University Press, 1971), 479–485.

13. See Erving Goffman's works, e.g., *The Presentation of Self in Everyday Life* (Garden City, NY: Doubleday, 1959) and *Stigma: Notes on the Management of Spoiled Identity* (Englewood Cliffs, NJ: Prentice Hall, 1963).

14. Anthropologists have long observed that those marginal in their own group or tribe are the first to reach out to strangers. Dr. William Mitchell, personal communication. See H. Russell Bernard, *Research Methods in Cultural Anthropology* (Newbury Park: Sage Publications, 1988). See also Helen Astin and Carole Leland, *Women of Influence, Women of Vision: A Cross-Generational Study of Leaders and Social Change* (San Francisco: Jossey-Bass, 1991), 34.

15. Douglas Huneke, personal communication. See also Huneke, *The Moses of Rovno*. Perry London identified a similar characteristic of rescuers, which he called "social marginality." See "The Rescuers: Motivational Hypotheses About Christians who rescued Jews From the Nazis," in *Altruism and Helping Behavior: Social Psychological Studies of Some Antecedents and Consequences*, L. Macauley and L. Berkowitz, eds. (New York: Academic Press, 1970), 241–245. Eva Fogelman's review of the research and her own extensive study on what motivated rescuers has led her, however, to conclude, with the Oliners and others, that a small percentage of rescuers perceive themselves as being "out of synch" with the social milieu. *Conscience and Courage: Rescuers of Jews During the Holocaust* (New York: Anchor Books, 1994), 259. The Oliners found the rescuers did not differ from the nonrescuers in this characteristic (13 and 14 percent respectively). See Oliner, *The Altruistic Personality*, 306.

    The kind of commitment that calls for a sustained, critical perspective on society and therefore a comfort with separateness and difference, may explain why roughly twice as many of our interviewees (39 percent) describe growing up in a value-based marginality.

16. The uncommon courage and practical compassion of Le Chambon has received considerable attention. In 1979, Philip Hallie told the story in *Lest Innocent Blood Be Shed* (New York: Harper & Row). Subsequently, one of the children of the village, Pierre Sauvage, now grown, returned to make an inspiring film about the village called *Weapons of the Spirit* (1987), which was later the subject of a presentation and interview with Bill Moyers on public television.

17. In what has been viewed as a classic study of altruism, Edwin Hollander says that marginal people become "altruists" because they stand at the edge of their society looking in and thus can judge it more objectively. See "theory of idiosyncratic credit" in Edwin P. Hollander, *Principles and Methods of Social Psychology* (New York: Oxford University Press, 1981).

18. Cornel West, *Race Matters* (Boston: Beacon Press, 1993).

19. Adrienne Rich, *What is Found There: Notebooks on Poetry and Politics*, 6. The Oliners come in *Embracing the Other* to a similar conclusion: "It is not sufficient that people view others as part of a universal humankind; they must learn to prize others for their distinctiveness", 383. See also Rosabeth Moss Kantor and Barry Stein, *A Tale of "O"* (Cambridge, MA: Goodmeasure, 1993).

20. Mandela, *Long Walk to Freedom*, 544.

Chapter 4
Conviction

1. Perry, *Intellectual and Ethical Development*, 41–42.
2. Haan characterizes the distortions of reality that keep people from acting as denial, repression, and projection. See *Coping and Defending: Processes of Self-Environment Organization* (New York: Academic Press, 1977).
3. Vygotsky was among the first to point to the way in which outer speech becomes inner speech. Lev Vygotsky, *Thought & Language* (Cambridge, MA: M.I.T. Press, 1962).
4. Significantly, although dialogue is often thought to entail give and take between only two parties, in fact, it is better understood as a conversation among numerous voices in accord with the Greek, "to speak through."
5. Some of these fathers became depressed when their daughters were about thirteen, and a flatness overtook family talk, depriving them of rigorous, lively dialogue at a crucial time in their development. The comparison group, recall, are doing good work, but find it difficult to feel at ease with complex, global problems and often struggle with burnout. Perhaps when the dialogue with the world gets too challenging, they find they lack early models for staying in the discussion.
6. D. Finkelhor, *Sexually Victimized Children* (New York: Free Press, 1979), cited in M. Belenky, B. Clinchy, N. Goldberger, and J. Tarule, *Women's Ways of Knowing* (New York: Basic Books, 1986), 164.
7. Robert Selman, *The Growth of Interpersonal Understanding* (New York: Academic Press, 1980).
8. Huneke, *Moses of Rovno*, 7.
9. Howard Thurman, "Mysticism and the Experience of Love," Pendle Hill Pamphlet #115 (Wallingford, PA: Pendle Hill Publications, 1961), 18.
10. Belenky and others, *Women's Ways of Knowing*, 121. See also Noddings, *Caring*, and Carol Gilligan, Nona P. Lyons, and Trudy J. Hammer, *Making Connections: The Relational Worlds of Adolescent Girls at Emma Willard School* (Cambridge, MA: Harvard Univ. Press, 1990).
11. Robert Kegan, *In Over Our Heads* (Cambridge, MA: Harvard University Press, 1994), 92ff. See also Peter Senge, *The Fifth Discipline* (New York: Doubleday, 1990).
12. Martin Seligman's research suggests that the power to change things derives from the learned habit of optimism. *Learned Optimism* (New York: Pocket Books, 1990).
13. See Milton Bennett, "Towards Ethnorelativism: A Developmental Model of Intercultural Sensitivity," in *Cross Cultural Orientation*, ed. Michael Paige (Landam, MD: University Press, 1986).
14. See Gil G. Noam, "'Normative Vulnerabilities' of Self and Their Transformations in Moral Action," in *Building a New Paradigm* (San Francisco: Jossey-Bass, 1993).
15. Michael Basseches, "Dialectical Thinking as a Metasystemic Form of Cognitive Organization," in *Beyond Formal Operations*, ed. M.L. Commons and others (New

York: Praeger, 1984); J.M. Rybach, W.J. Hoyer, and P. A. Roodin, *Adult Cognition and Aging* (New York, Praeger, 1986); Mihaly Csikszentmihalyi, *Flow* (New York: Harper and Row, 1990) and M. Mitchell Waldrop, *Complexity: The Emerging Science at the Edge of Order and Chaos* (New York: Simon and Schuster, 1992).

16. Armon's longitudinal research found that no one under age twenty-six could do dialectical thinking. This is interesting in light of our finding, referred to in Chapter 2, that it wasn't generally until twenty-six that our interviewees found a clear sense of their work amidst the complexity of the issues that concerned them. C. Armon, "Ideals of the Good Life and Moral Judgement: Ethical Reasoning Across the Lifespan," in M.H. Commons, *Beyond Formal Operations*.

17. James Adams, *Conceptual Blockbusting* (New York: Addison-Wesley, 1986), 24–31.

18. "What is demanded of man is not, as some existential philosophers teach, to endure the meaninglessness of life, but rather to bear his incapacity to grasp [life's] unconditional meaningfulness in rational terms." See Viktor Frankl, *Man's Search for Meaning*, trans. Isle Lasch (Boston: Beacon Press, 1959), 122.

19. James Fowler, *Stages of Faith* (San Francisco: Harper & Row, 1981), 198.

Chapter 5
Courage

1. See Romans 8, "the spirit is groaning with us in travail."

2. See Anne Colby and William Damon, *Some Do Care: Contemporary Lives of Moral Commitment* (New York: Free Press, 1992), 71.

3. See Aletha C. Huston and others, *Big World, Small Screen: The Role of Television in American Society* (Lincoln, NB: University of Nebraska Press, 1992). See also Nancy Carlsson-Paige and Diane Levin, *Who's Calling the Shots?: How to Respond Effectively to Children's Fascination with War Play and War Toys* (Philadelphia: New Society Press, 1990). See also J. Bryan Hehir, *God in the Newsroom* (Cambridge, MA: Nieman Reports, 1993).

4. See George C. Lodge, *Managing Globally in the Age of Interdependence* (San Diego: Pfeiffer & Co., 1995).

5. See Suzanne Langer, *Philosophy in a New Key: A Study in the Symbolism of Reason, Rite, and Art* (Cambridge, MA: Harvard University Press, 1942), 42.

6. See Samuel Taylor Coleridge, *The Friend*, vol. 1, ed. B. Rooke (Princeton: Princeton University Press, 1969), vol. 1, 177.

7. William F. Lynch, *Images of Faith: An Exploration of the Ironic Imagination* (Notre Dame, IN: Univ. of Notre Dame Press, 1973), 63. See also Sharon Parks, *The Critical Years*, ch. 6.

8. Here we are indebted to conversation with Karen Thorkilsen. See Karen Thorkilsen, "The Edge of Knowing," in *In Context: A Quarterly of Humane Sustainable Culture* 5 (Spring 1984): 4–5.

9. See James Loder, *The Logic of the Spirit* (Jossey-Bass, forthcoming). See also Craig Dykstra, *Vision and Character: A Christian Educator's Alternative to Kohlberg* (New York: Paulist Press, 1981), 81–87, and Parks, *The Critical Years*, ch. 6.

10. For this insight we are indebted to conversation with Anita Landa.
11. Gaston Bachelard, *The Poetics of Space*, trans. M. Jolas (Boston: Beacon Press, 1969), xviii.
12. See Langer, *Philosophy in a New Key*, 55.
13. H. Richard Niebuhr, *The Meaning of Revelation* (New York: MacMillan, 1952), 172.
14. Kevin Carter was awarded a Pulitzer Prize for this photograph a few weeks before he committed suicide. *Time Magazine* (Sept. 12, 1994), 70–73.
15. The Independent Sector's recent survey of predecessors of volunteerism among teens suggests that seeing an admired family member or adult help others increased the likelihood of volunteering. Paul Schervish, *Care and Community in Modern Society*.
16. See Walter Brueggemann, *The Prophetic Imagination* (Philadelphia: Fortress Press, 1978).
17. Eighty percent of the exemplars studied by Colby and Damon attributed their "core value commitments" to their religious faith. *Some Do Care*, 78.
18. See Wilfred Cantwell Smith, *Faith and Belief* (Princeton: Princeton University Press, 1979), 11–15, 42f. See also William F. Lynch, *Images of Faith*.
19. Douglas Steere, *Dimensions of Prayer* (General Board of Global Ministries, United Methodist Church, 1982). See also E. Glenn Hinson, ed., *Spirituality in Ecumenical Perspective* (Louisville: Westminster/John Knox Press, 1993).
20. See Diana L. Eck, *Encountering God: A Spiritual Journey from Bozeman to Banaras* (Boston: Beacon Press, 1993), and George Rupp, *Commitment and Community* (Minneapolis: Fortress Press, 1989).
21. See Diana L. Eck, *Encountering God*, ch. 4.
22. See Linda E. Olds, *Metaphors of Interrelatedness* (Albany: SUNY Press, 1992).
23. See Craig Dykstra's editorial on the power of stories in *Initiatives in Religion: A Newsletter of Lilly Endowment Inc.*, 2, 2 (Spring 1993): 2, where he also cites Martha Nussbaum's observation of Aristotle's insight that literature encourages moral inquiry because it "searches for patterns of possibility—of choice, and circumstance, and the interaction between choice and circumstance—that turn up in human lives with such a persistence that they must be regarded as *our* possibilities." See also Thomas H. Groome, *Sharing Faith: The Way of Shared Praxis* (San Francisco: Harper Collins, 1991), chs. 4 and 8.
24. Biography, autobiography, and letters gave people access to lives of moral purpose and perseverance. Among these we note *Lives of the Saints* and biographies of Lincoln, Gandhi, Eleanor Roosevelt, Mandela, Vaclav Havel, and Quaker women. References to influential fiction included *A Tree Grows in Brooklyn*, *The Grapes of Wrath*, *Exodus*, *Little Women*. Alice Walker, Richard Wright, and Charles Dickens were cited as authors who inspired action. Poets and playwrights included Samuel Beckett, Gerard Manley Hopkins, Shakespeare, Les Brown, Emily Dickinson, and Wallace Stevens. Wisdom literature—including Buddhist, Hebrew, and Christian texts, along with Thoreau and Emerson—was cited. Nonfiction included *The Silent Spring*, *The Federalist Papers*, *The Cantonsville Nine*, and *The Phenomenon of Man*. References to film included *Dead Poets Society* and *Chariots of Fire*. Folk, popular,

and classical music was mentioned, ranging from spirituals to symphonies to lyrics set by the Grateful Dead. Newspapers and magazines, including *National Geographic*, were cited as having memorable headlines and photos.

25. See Gary Nabhan and Stephen Trimble, *The Geography of Childhood: Why Children Need Wild Places* (Boston, MA: Beacon Press, 1994).

26. See Huston, *Big World, Small Screen*, esp. chs. 1 and 2.

27. See also Olds, *Metaphors of Interrelatedness*, 55f.

28. James P. Keen, "Cultivating Vision: Inviting Talented Young People to Care for the World," in *Aspects of Hope* (New York: ICIS Center for A Science of Hope, 1993), 149–158.

29. H. Richard Niebuhr, *The Responsible Self: An Essay In Christian Moral Philosophy* (New York: Harper & Row, 1963), 55–57.

30. Robert Morneau, Roman Catholic Bishop of Green Bay, Wisconsin, seminar discussion, Ecumenical Institute of Spirituality, 1992.

Chapter 6
Confession

1. While traditional notions of sainthood no longer prevail today, we need contemporary models of possibility and responsible goodness. Numerous awards and other forms of recognition for good citizenship, and perhaps the existence of books like this, are evidence of this impulse in our time. Conversation with Sandra Schneiders, Washington D.C., November 1993.

2. David Whyte, "Self-portrait," in *Fire in the Earth* (Langley, WA: Many Rivers Press, 1993), 10.

3. The same finding emerged from Colby and Damon's study of moral exemplars. *Some Do Care*, 68.

4. See Katie Cannon, "The Fruit of My Labor," in Sara Lawrence-Lightfoot, *I've Known Rivers: Lives of Loss and Liberation* (Reading, MA: Addison-Wesley, 1994), 81. Strong evidence links health problems among African-Americans to high stress. See Richette Haywood, "Why Black Americans Suffer with More High Blood Pressure than Whites," *Jet* (1991), 87, 5, and Harold Freeman and Linda Villarosa, "Emergency: The Crisis in our Health Care," *Essence* (September 1991).

5. See Bok, *The Cost of Talent*.

6. For related findings, see David Myers, *The Pursuit of Happiness* (New York: William Morrow, 1992).

7. Aleksandr Solzhenitsyn, *The Gulag Archipelago* (New York: Harper & Row, 1973), 168.

8. For this account we are indebted to Arthur Levine, who heard Seeger speak.

9. David Adam's reading of ten activists' biographies discovered that the most common difficulty was in integrating anger, leading to derailment, breakdowns, or sectarianism. See David Adams, *Psychology for Peace Activists: A New Psychology for the Generation who can Abolish War* (New Haven, CT: The Advocate Press, 1987). Paul Loeb's journalistic study found that activists who were angry at the system and at colleagues who "betrayed" them lost their effectiveness. See Loeb, *Hope in Hard Times* (Lexington,

MA: Lexington Books, 1987). Colby and Damon also found that in three of their twenty-three interviews (all three being nonreligious people) an "inability to forget those who betrayed them" was an important theme. *Some Do Care*, 277.

10. William Sloane Coffin, *Alive Now!* (May–June, 1993), 37.

11. Myles Horton, *The Long Haul* (New York: Doubleday, 1990), 80.

12. In *A Feminist Ethic of Risk* (Minneapolis: Fortress Press, 1990), Sharon Welch distinguishes between an "ethic of control" and an "ethic of risk." The former embodies "power over" and the latter, "power with."

13. While a third of the core group mentioned "need to please" as a motivation, two-thirds of the comparison group did so.

14. See Allan Luks with Peggy Payne, *The Healing Power of Doing Good* (New York: Fawcett Columbine, 1991), and Robert Wuthnow, *Acts of Compassion: Caring for Others and Helping Ourselves* (Princeton, NJ: Princeton University Press, 1991).

15. See Adams, *Psychology for Peace Activists*, and J.A. Piliavin and H. Charng, "Altruism: A Review of Recent Theory and Research," *Annual Review of Sociology*, vol. 16, ed. W.R. Scott and J. Blake (Palo Alto, CA: Annual Reviews Inc., 1990)

16. Dorothee Soelle, *Suffering* (Philadelphia: Fortress Press, 1975), 88.

17. M. Lesy, *Rescues: The Lives of Heroes* (New York: Farrar, Straus and Giroux, 1991).

18. Higgins, *Resilient Adults*, 235, 239.

19. *Ibid.*, ch. 3.

20. Our view of the self's inner ecology is that of a self-organizing organic system, which means that the committee and its chair are internally organized out of the counterpoint of internal and external experience as the self develops and that both committee and chair are mutable according to context and function.

21. Heifetz, *Leadership Without Easy Answers*, 271.

22. Polyphony is the composed, meaningful interaction of a number of voices held within the self. James Keen, unpublished manuscript. For further discussion see H. Hermans Kempen and J. van Loon, "The Dialogical Self: Beyond Individualism and Rationalism," *American Psychologist* 47, 1 (1992): 23–33. See also John Dewey, *Human Nature and Conduct* (New York: Modern Library, 1957), 288.

23. See Gina O'Connell Higgins, *Resilient Adults*, 299–310. She makes helpful distinctions between the healing power of genuine forgiveness and "the folly of forgiving hastily and unreflectively" without recognition, remorse, and reparation.

24. Donald Shriver, *An Ethic for Enemies* (New York: Oxford University Press, 1995).

25. Goleman, *Emotional Intelligence*, 80–83, 286.

Chapter 7
Commitment

1. Frederick Buechner, *Wishful Thinking: A Theological ABC* (New York: Harper & Row, 1973).

2. See Hallie, *Lest Innocent Blood Be Shed*.

3. See Jill Ker Conway, *True North* (New York: Knopf, 1994), 60.

4. Robert Bellah and others, *The Good Society* (New York: Knopf, 1991), 254 ff.

5. "Renounce attachment to the fruits . . . When your intellect has cleared itself of its delusions, you will become indifferent to the results of all action." *The Bhagavad-Gita*, trans. Swami Prabhananda and Christopher Isherwood (New York: New American Library, 1951), 40–41.
6. See also Olds, *Metaphors of Interrelatedness*, 113 ff.
7. Coffin, *Alive Now*, 34.
8. See Kenneth Keniston, *Young Radicals* (New York: Harcourt, Brace & World, 1965); Loeb, *Hope in Hard Times*; Colby and Damon, *Some Do Care*, and Astin and Leland, *Women of Influence*.
9. James Thornton, presentation at *Commonweal*, Salinas, CA, October 1993.
10. Colby and Damon, *Some Do Care*. See especially their central construct, "goal transformation," 167–199.
11. Brickman, *Commitment*, 166.
12. A. Speer, *Inside the Third Reich*, trans. R. Winston and C. Winston (New York: Macmillan, 1970).

Epilogue

1. Francis Moore Lappé and Paul Martin DuBois, *The Quickening of America: Rebuilding Our Nation, Remaking Our Lives* (San Francisco: Jossey-Bass, 1994).
2. See Gaston Bachelard, *The Poetics of Space*, 6.
3. See Sara Lawrence-Lightfoot, *I've Known Rivers*, 1–7.
4. See *Standing Tall: A K–12 Program that Teaches Kids the 3 C's—Courage, Caring, Community* (Langley, WA: The Giraffe Project, 1995).
5. See Mary Catherine Bateson, *Peripheral Visions: Learning Along the Way* (New York: Harper Collins, 1994).
6. See William Damon, *Greater Expectations: Overcoming the Culture of Indulgence in America's Homes and Schools* (New York: The Free Press, 1995). See also Arthur Levine and Jana Nidiffer, *Beating the Odds*, esp. pt. III.
7. See Stephen Brookfield, "Self-directed Learning, Political Clarity, and the Critical Practice of Adult Education," *Adult Education Quarterly*, 43, 4 (1993); Jack Mezirow, *Transformative Dimensions of Adult Learning* (San Francisco: Jossey-Bass, 1990); Zelda Gamson, *Liberating Education* (San Francisco: Jossey-Bass, 1984).
8. See Ronald H. Heifetz, *Leadership Without Easy Answers* (Cambridge, MA: Harvard University Press, 1994), 274–276.
9. Conversation with Professor Martha Minow at Harvard Law School.
10. See Sharon Daloz Parks, "Professional Ethics, Moral Courage, and the Limits of Personal Virtue," in *Can Virtue Be Taught?* ed. Barbara Darling-Smith (Notre Dame, IN: University of Notre Dame Press, 1993), 175–193, and Robert Granfield, *Making Elite Lawyers* (New York: Routledge, 1992).
11. See Donald Schon, *Educating the Reflective Practitioner: Toward a New Design for Teaching and Learning in the Professions* (San Francisco: Jossey-Bass, 1987), and Ellen Schall, "Learning to Love the Swamp: Reshaping Education for Public Service," *Journal of Policy Analysis and Management*, 14, 2: 202.

12. Cornel West, *Race Matters*, 56.
13. See James W. Fowler, *Weaving the New Creation: Stages of Faith and the Public Church* (San Francisco: Harper Collins, 1991), and Larry L. Rasmussen, *Moral Fragments and Moral Community: A Proposal for Church in Society* (Minneapolis: Fortress Press, 1993), and Kenneth J. and Micheal R. Himes, *Fullness of Faith: The Public Significance of Theology* (New York: Paulist Press, 1993); David Hollenbach and R. Bruce Douglass, *Catholicism and Liberalism: Contributions to American Political Philosophy* (New York: Cambridge University Press, 1994).
14. See Margaret R. Miles, *Seeing and Believing: Religion and Values in the Movies* (Boston, MA: Beacon, 1996).
15. Sara S. Lee and Michael Zeldrin, eds., *Touch the Future: Mentoring and the Jewish Professional* (Los Angeles: Jewish Institute of Religion, 1995).
16. Wendall Berry, "Two Economies," *Home Economics* (New York: Farrar, Straus and Giroux, 1987), 54–75.
17. Samella Lewis, *The Art of Elizabeth Catlett*, published in collaboration with the Museum of African American Art, Los Angeles (Claremont, CA: Handcraft Studios, 1984), 93–94, quoted in Adrienne Rich, *What Is Found There*, 50–51.
18. See Geoffrey Canada, *Fist, Stick, Knife, Gun* (Boston: Beacon, 1995).
19. Robert Reich, ed., *The Power of Public Ideas* (Cambridge, MA: Ballinger, 1988), 3–4; Harry C. Boyte, *Commonwealth: A Return to Citizen Politics* (New York: Free Press, 1989).
20. Tom Chappell, *The Soul of a Business: Managing for Profit and the Common Good* (New York: Bantam, 1993), 184–185.
21. See Barbara A. Walker and William C. Hanson, "Valuing Differences at Digital Equipment Corporation" in Susan E. Jackson and Associates, *Diversity in the Workplace: Human Resources Initiatives* (New York: Guilford Press, 1992), 119–137; Mary C. Gentile, ed., *Differences that Work: Organizational Excellence through Diversity* (Boston: Harvard Business School Press, 1994).
22. See Paul Schervish, *Care and Community in Modern Society*.
23. Carol Tresolini and others, *Health Professions Education and Relationship-Centered Care* (San Francisco: Pew Health Professions Commission, 1994), 15.
24. See Annie Dillard, *Teaching a Stone to Talk* (New York: Harper and Row, 1982), 16.
25. James Wall, "Give All You Can," *Christian Century*, 2, 1 (August 1995): 100.

Appendix

1. See Anselm Strauss and Juliet Corbin, *Basics of Qualitative Research: Grounded Theory Procedures and Technique* (Newbury Park, CA: Sage Publications, 1990), and M. Miles and M. Huberman, *Qualitative Data Analysis* (Beverly Hills, CA: Sage Publications, 1984).
2. See Jack Botwinick, *Aging and Behavior: A Comprehensive Integration of Research Findings* (New York: Springer, 1984); Y.S. Lincoln and E. G. Guba, *Naturalistic Inquiry* (Newbury Park, CA: Sage Publications, 1984), and Erik Erikson, *Gandhi's Truth* (New York: W.W. Norton, 1969), 97–101.

3. See John W. Sutherland, *A General Systems Philosophy for the Social and Behavioral Sciences* (New York: Braziller, 1973).
4. Joseph A. Maxwell, "Using Qualitative Research for Causal Explanation," *Educational Researcher* (November 1990).
5. See J.A. Maxwell and B.A. Miller, *Two Aspects of Thought and Two Components of Qualitative Data Analysis* (forthcoming), and Joseph A. Maxwell, "Understanding and Validity in Qualitative Research," *Harvard Educational Review* 62, 3 (Fall 1992): 279–300.
6. Ibid.

index

Activism, 14, 259n. 9
Adams, David, 259n. 9, 260n. 15
Adaptive challenges, 5, 214
Adolescence, 12, 37–43, 232
Adorno, T. W., 249n. 20
Adults, significant, 218; in adolescence,
38–41, 43; and "good enough" environments, 28; as healing guides,
187–88; in the neighborhood, 34–35
African American: churches, key role of,
49, 58; family lore, 138–39; health
stresses, 175; inspirational literature,
87, 146, 150; leaders, 57–58, 99;
mentoring relationships, extended
example, 80–101; racism and perfectionism, 34, 183; redeeming the soul
of America, 125; sense of history,
203; story-telling, 130
Agency: and anger, 198–99; basic construct,
26; continually enlarged, 32; and healing, 185–86; learned in the community, 37–43; learned in the home,
26–28; learned in the neighborhood,
32–37; learned in young adulthood,
44–49; and marginality, 194; and mid-
life deepening, 49–51; as "moments
of power," 129; and public policy,
231–32; and relativized role models,
128; and systemic thought, 114–16;
and taboo motivations, 177–78

Ages of study participants, 6–7, 245
Ainsworth, Mary, 27
Alinsky, Saul, 163
Altruism, 14, 178–79, 254n. 10, 255n. 17
Ambiguity: and creative process, 230;
dealing with, 94–95; and faith, 143;
and habits of mind, 108; and meaning-making, 107; and problem-solving, 115–16; within self, 189–91
Anger: and agency, 194, 198–99; consciously managed, 58–59, 61, 192;
and forgiveness, 191; as motivation,
178–80, 184; at systemic injustice,
85, 128–29, 170
Armoring, 11–13, 15, 186, 190, 226
Arts: key directions, 229–31; music as sustaining 86, 127, 130, 150; and otherness, 66; and philanthropic support,
240; as source of images, 145, 148
Asian American, 163
Astin, Helen, 255n. 14, 261n. 8
Authors, profiles of, 4–5, 16–17

Bachelard, Gaston, 133, 261n. 2
Basseches, Michael, 256n. 15
Bateson, Mary Catherine, 261n. 5
Batson, Daniel, 250n. 3
Belenky, Mary, x, 113, 253n. 33
Belief: and action, 27, 79. See also Faith;
Meaning-making

LIBRARY OF CONGRESS CATALOGING-IN-PUBLICATION DATA

Common fire : lives of commitment in a complex world / Laurent A.
   Parks Daloz . . . [et. al.].
      p. cm.
   Includes bibliographical references and index.
   ISBN 0-8070-2004-4
   1. Social participation.   2. Political participation.   3. Social change.
   4. Social problems.   I. Daloz, Laurent A.
HM131.C74276   1996
302′ . 14—dc20   95-25499